Simply
Vietnamese
cooking

Simply
Vietnamese
cooking

135 Delicious Recipes

Nancie McDermott

Robert
ROSE

For complete cataloguing information, see page 231.

Disclaimer

Design and Production: Daniella Zanchetta/PageWave Graphics Inc.
Editor: Carol Sherman
Proofreader: Karen Campbell-Sheviak
Photographer: Colin Erricson
Associate Photographer: Matt Johannsson
Prop Stylist: Charlene Erricson
Food Stylist: Michael Elliot

Cover image: Pho Noodles with Beef, Hanoi-Style (page 160)

Other photographs: GROUP 1: Gate of The Forbidden City © iStockphoto.com/YinYang; Rice farmer © iStockphoto.com/Kevin Miller; Rambutans © iStockphoto.com/Zarinmedia; Vietnamese coffee © iStockphoto.com/Offstone; Hibiscus flowers © iStockphoto.com/Tunart; Banana boat, Mekong River Delta © iStockphoto.com/Bartosz Hadyniak; Boats in mist of Halong Bay © iStockphoto.com/Anthony Brown **GROUP 2:** Scooter in Hanoi © iStockphoto.com/Nikada; Golden dragon statue © iStockphoto.com/Kyolshin; Cyclo bike © iStockphoto.com/Tunart; Dragon fruit © iStockphoto.com/Hanoded; Purple water lily © iStockphoto.com/Tunart; Harvesting rice © iStockphoto.com/Keith Molloy; Thien Mu Pagoda pillar © iStockphoto.com/Tunart **GROUP 3:** Den Ngoc Son temple doors, Hanoi © iStockphoto.com/Epixx; Terraced rice fields © iStockphoto.com/Gilsdenski; Green coconuts for sale © iStockphoto.com/Myrainjom01; Father and son © iStockphoto.com/Kerriekerr; Ho Chi Minh City view © iStockphoto.com/FabVietnam Photography; Fruit seller, floating market, Mekong River Delta © iStockphoto.com/Bartosz Hadyniak; Beach and boats © iStockphoto.com/Tunart **GROUP 4:** Ho Chi Minh City at night © iStockphoto.com/Marcus Lindstrom; Traditional Junk boat in Halong Bay © iStockphoto.com/Delpixart; Hue window © iStockphoto.com/Wysiati; Boy in Can Tho market © iStockphoto.com/BartCo; Jackfruit © iStockphoto.com/Alatom; Chiles and limes © iStockphoto.com/Wysiati; Street vendor in Hanoi © iStockphoto.com/Tony Shaw Photography

The publisher gratefully acknowledges the financial support of our publishing program by the Government of Canada through the Canada Book Fund.

Published by Robert Rose Inc.
120 Eglinton Avenue East, Suite 800,
Toronto, Ontario, Canada M4P 1E2
Tel: (416) 322-6552 Fax: (416) 322-6936
www.robertrose.ca

Printed and bound in USA

1 2 3 4 5 6 7 8 9 CKV 23 22 21 20 19 18 17 16 15

To my father, James Patrick McDermott, a magnificent, generous, brave, intelligent man, thanks to whom I love to read, travel, share, laugh and linger at the table with family and friends.

◇◇

Contents

Acknowledgments

Writing a cookbook takes me into kitchens, libraries, grocery stores, markets, cafés, bookshops, as well as on clicking expeditions all around the worldwide web. I scribble, jot, cut and paste; test, retest and test again; chase clues, theorize and revise, following trails and shuffling papers until at last I have gathered a large number of words on the page and on the screen. I have the basic ingredients for that book, but I still need enormous amounts of expert help to turn my words and recipes into the book you hold in your hand. I am so lucky to be working with the excellent team at Robert Rose Inc., in transforming my words into a book that you can pick up, take on a shopping expedition and prop up on your kitchen counter to help you cook.

I am so pleased to work on this third cookbook with Bob Dees, and I am thankful for his expertise, guidance, generosity and humor throughout the process of producing another beautiful book. I am incredibly lucky to have the brilliance, tenacity and creativity of my editor, Carol Sherman, who made this book better, clearer and more useful to readers and cooks, measurement by measurement and word by word. I love how skillfully Daniella Zanchetta at PageWave Graphics made this book look beautiful.

With every recipe I cook and with every book I write, I see more clearly how privileged I am to have the company, trust, encouragement and support of my wonderful friends and precious family. They make me happy in more ways than I can count and I am grateful for their presence, wit, understanding and love.

Introduction

From its craggy northernmost border with China to the lush paddy fields and coconut plantations of the Mekong Delta, Vietnam nurtures an extraordinary cuisine. The nation's ancient Chinese heritage has formed a deep foundation for its culinary traditions. The cuisine of Vietnam is unique, however, distinct from that of China and of all its Asian neighbors, with which Vietnam shares so much in terms of climate, geography and history.

With some 1,400 miles of seacoast, a vast network of rivers and a sultry tropical climate, Vietnam nurtures vegetables galore, fragrant herbs and luscious fruit. The Vietnamese kitchen celebrates this bounty with a fresh, delicate approach to food, bright with clear flavors and hearty with shellfish, fish, meat, noodles and wraps. Simple, unseasoned rice anchors the food of Vietnam in East Asian fashion, but the good things cooked to go with it sparkle with Southeast Asia's edible treasures: lemongrass, ginger, pineapple and papaya team with fresh cilantro, mint, basil and chiles to brighten every bite.

You won't need much in the way of new equipment to cook the Vietnamese dishes featured here in *Simply Vietnamese Cooking*. A big deep skillet will work as well as a wok in most cases; a good chef's knife will chop as well as an Asian cleaver; and a pair of V-shaped stainless-steel tongs will stand in nicely for the more traditional cooking chopsticks.

Vietnam's cooking techniques tend to be straightforward and easily translated to a Western kitchen, especially grilling, which in Vietnam is almost a national pastime. While Vietnamese cooks usually marinate meats before grilling, the time required tends to be measured in minutes rather than hours.

Contrasts prevail in Vietnamese cuisine: Sour flavors are balanced by salty ones and sweet notes are answered by a little heat from ground pepper and chiles. If the fish is fried crisp, the sauce served with it will be a smooth purée. Delicate summer rolls call for a thick and pungent sauce based on salt-preserved soybeans, an edible marriage of heaven and earth. When chicken curry appears on the table, with its velvety, spice-infused coconut sauce, so does its companion dish of lime juice, salt and pepper, balancing the richness of the curry with clear notes of citrus and heat.

In Vietnam as in most of Asia, soup is a mainstay, served right along with the rice and other dishes and enjoyed throughout the meal. Neither first course nor entrée, soup is more like a beverage within a typical Western meal. Whether it's a simple broth like Clear Soup with Catfish, Tomatoes and Fresh Dill (page 42) or the lavish, seafood-laden Sweet and Tangy Soup with Pineapple, Tamarind and Shrimp (page 44), a bowl of soup provides a little break from the variously flavored dishes on the Vietnamese table.

As in China and East Asia, the Vietnamese eat their rice in bowls with chopsticks. And like these northern neighbors, they enjoy their meals seated around a table. In the rest of Southeast Asia, the way people eat reflects their cultural connections to India.

In Thailand, Burma, Cambodia and Laos, people dine seated on woven mats, eating their rice from a plate with spoons or the fingers of the right hand.

Like all their Southeast Asian neighbors, Vietnamese cooks make brilliant use of their country's tropical bounty, from coconut milk, tamarind and limes, to chiles, green mango, lotus stems and a staggering array of fragrant and pungent fresh herbs. Vietnam's cuisine veers from the beaten path of Southeast Asian cooking in numerous ways, however. Rather than stir-frying most vegetables with a handful of meat or other protein, cooks in Vietnam tend to let meat be meat and green be green. Vegetables are cooked simply: spinach is fried with garlic, and eggplant is grilled and then topped with a tangy clear sauce. Other vegetables appear raw, cool, crisp and ready for bundling into lettuce packets or rice wrappers, along with grilled meats, fish or seafood, a tangle of rice noodles, fresh herbs and a splash of vibrant dipping sauce.

Meat often stands alone, minimally seasoned. It is briefly grilled as kebabs, meatballs or in thin strips and is served up with a pungent sauce. Meat and fish are also simmered briefly in a clay pot with fish sauce and sugar to make a *kho* dish, creating lots of delectable sauce to enjoy over rice. What in many places would be one person's serving of chicken, pork or fish can therefore satisfy many guests. In addition to stretching a little protein to feed more people, a *kho* dish requires a minimum amount of fuel and effort.

The ingredients for cooking Vietnamese food are easy to come by these days in the West. Fish sauce, rice noodles and rice papers for wraps and rolls can be found in any Asian market or through Resources (page 229). Now that soy sauce, Asian sesame oil and hoisin sauce are widely available in major supermarkets, you can often buy the condiments you will need for cooking delicious Vietnamese dishes in one trip to your local grocery store. Add some meat, fish, shellfish or a vegetarian protein source to your shopping cart, along with a big jar of dry-roasted peanuts and a small one of sesame seeds and then head for the produce section. Toss in some leaf lettuce, limes, carrots, scallions, onions and garlic. Then top it all off with a bouquet of fresh cilantro or mint and head for the checkout counter.

Vietnamese cuisine survived more than a century of French colonial presence beautifully, moving into the postcolonial world and now the new millennium with her culinary identity clear and strong. Vietnam's cuisine always remained Vietnamese, even while making room for the affectionate adoption of a few worthy French traditions, notably good strong coffee, crème caramel and baguettes freshly baked every day.

Noodles rule in Vietnam and once you get used to the simple basics of cooking them, you will be putting together fine noodle feasts: big, delicious bowls of soup noodles; tasty stir-fries; fast, fresh noodle salads; and countless noodle-centered wrap-it-up meals. These dishes start with a platter of quickly grilled or roasted chicken, pork, beef, salmon, shrimp, tofu or portobello mushrooms, cooked at home or carried in from the deli. The meat or vegetable is paired with a supply of lettuce cups or softened rice-paper triangles, aromatic herbs, a tangle of rice noodles and a bowl or two of brilliantly flavored sauces. Family and friends start picking and choosing, trying this herb and that sauce, relaxing and reviving, almost as though they were playing with their food.

The truth is playing with food is a way of life in Vietnam. So is making flavor-packed meals quickly and simply, using what you have or can find easily on any given day. Some days I create a culinary masterpiece worthy of an ovation. Most days, though, I have more on my plate than fixing dinner, but I long for something tasty and freshly made, interesting but not too complicated, something I can step away from if the phone rings or homework issues arise or the dog begs to go out. I want to make something satisfying and good enough to make my whole family start to smile. *Simply Vietnamese Cooking* is filled with that kind of food, along with a few dazzlers for the occasional tour de force. For those more complex recipes, such as spring rolls and some of the noodle soups, invite friends and family to join you in the kitchen. The feast begins early when you get cooking with lots of helping hands.

If you enjoy Vietnamese food already, look up your favorites. If you are new to Vietnamese flavors, browse through the recipes and find something that sounds good. Make a grocery list, drop by the grocery store or Asian market, and start cooking. This book aims to get you cooking Vietnamese dishes with pleasure and success. Here's to good times in your kitchen and at your table, cooking and then enjoying the vibrant, delicate feast of Vietnamese cuisine.

Appetizers and Snacks

*T**he playful nature** of Vietnamese cooking is nowhere more evident than in the skewered, bundled, wrapped or rolled foods that make up this chapter. From ethereal summer rolls to the most spectacularly delicious submarine sandwich on planet Earth, these recipes allow you to turn out lots of flavor, usually in a small amount of time.*

Lemongrass Shrimp (page 20) put Vietnam's official herbal ambassador on full display and the simple marinade is equally tasty on fish. Sugarcane Shrimp (page 14) delight the eye and come together fast because they are made with canned sugarcane. For spring roll fans, two options provide a choice between cool Summer Rolls with Shrimp and Mint (page 16), and hot, crisp Fried Spring Rolls (page 28). Both Banh Mi (page 26) and Pâté Chaud (page 32) show French inspiration within Vietnam's culinary repertoire, and each makes a hearty and tasty hand-held treat.

Many of these goodies are cooked on the grill, but don't despair if that won't work for you. Use a grill pan, countertop grilling machine, broiler, skillet or even a hot oven. However you cook them, you will find they are ready fast and disappear even faster from the plates of delighted friends and family members.

Sugarcane Shrimp

A simple, lightly seasoned shrimp mixture is pressed onto a rod of sugarcane and grilled just until firm and pink. Traditionally, the shrimp are minced, seasoned with roasted rice powder, enriched with a little pork fat and then ground to a smooth paste. This makes for a firm, chewy texture. My version is coarsely ground so that the shrimp mixture is easier to work with and it is still delicious. *Chao tom* are often steamed and then grilled, but cooking them without that initial step works fine. Grilling is the ticket to those handsome grill marks, but I've made this sensational treat in a grill pan, in a skillet on top of the stove, under a broiler and in a hot oven. However you cook them, your *chao tom* will look and taste delicious.

◇◇◇

Makes about 32 small skewers

Tips

Sugarcane is available in cans, peeled and trimmed and ready to eat, so you can easily make this signature Vietnamese presentation at home.

If the lack of sugarcane is keeping you from trying this brilliant dish, shape the shrimp mixture into small patties and fry them in a hot, well-oiled skillet.

♦ Food processor or blender

1 lb	medium shrimp, peeled, deveined and coarsely chopped	500 g
1	egg white, lightly beaten	1
2 tbsp	coarsely chopped green onion	30 mL
1 tbsp	finely chopped garlic	15 mL
1 tbsp	vegetable oil	15 mL
1 tbsp	fish sauce	15 mL
½ tsp	granulated sugar	2 mL
½ tsp	salt	2 mL
½ tsp	freshly ground black pepper	2 mL
4	peeled sugarcane stalks, each about 6 inches (15 cm) long (see Tips, left)	4
	Everyday Dipping Sauce (page 200)	
20	Boston, Bibb or other lettuce leaves, optional	20
1 cup	fresh cilantro, mint or basil leaves, or a mix, optional	250 mL

1. In a medium bowl, combine shrimp with egg white, green onion, garlic, oil, fish sauce, sugar, salt and pepper. Stir to mix everything well.

2. Transfer to a food processor and pulse briefly, 3 to 5 times, just enough to blend all ingredients together into a very rough paste, with little chunks of shrimp still visible. Or blend in a blender, stopping to scrape down the sides. Or use a knife to mince shrimp by hand. Return shrimp mixture to bowl. If you have time, cover and refrigerate for 30 minutes or so (this makes the mixture a bit easier to handle).

Variations

Instead of using a grill or the broiler, here are some other options. Preheat oven to 400°F (200°C), add shrimp to lightly oiled ovenproof skillet or grill pan and roast for 5 to 7 minutes. Or sauté over medium-high heat, turning often, until browned and cooked through.

3. Set out sugarcane stalks on a work surface and have shrimp mixture and a small bowl of water at hand. Cut each stalk of sugarcane in half crosswise, to make 8 short stalks. Then cut each short stalk lengthwise into quarters, to make a total of 32 stalks, about 3 inches (7.5 cm) long.

4. Dip your hands in water and place 1 tbsp (15 mL) of the shrimp mixture in the palm of your left hand. Press a 3-inch (7.5 cm) sugarcane skewer into shrimp mixture and then mold shrimp mixture to encircle the skewer. Press to seal shrimp to the cane, leaving both ends free to use as handles. Set aside on a plate while you prepare the remaining skewers in the same fashion.

5. Preheat gas or charcoal barbecue grill to medium or preheat broiler. Place sugarcane shrimp on the lightly oiled surface of the grill rack and cook, turning often, until shrimp are pink, nicely browned on the outside, cooked to the center and firm to the touch, 2 to 4 minutes.

6. Transfer shrimp to a serving platter and serve hot or warm, with Everyday Dipping Sauce. If using lettuce and herbs, make little packets by tucking a chunk of shrimp and a few fresh herb leaves into a lettuce leaf and rolling it up. Dip this bundle into the sauce as you eat.

Summer Rolls with Shrimp and Mint

Goi cuon are known in English as "summer rolls," "rice paper rolls," "soft spring rolls" and "salad rolls" — the latter a direct translation of their Vietnamese name. These extraordinary rice paper–wrapped bundles of shrimp, rice noodles, lettuce and fresh mint present an edible sketch of Vietnamese cuisine. Delicate and satisfying, soft and crunchy, as plain as white rice noodles and yet vibrant with the pink and green of shrimp and fresh mint, these snacks invite you to savor the contrasting pleasures of Vietnam's way with food. Get a little assembly line going with a friend or two and you will quickly wrap and roll enough *goi cuon* for your picnic or party.

◇◇◇

> **Makes
> 10 to 12 rolls**

Tip

For angel hair pasta or somen, cook in boiling water until tender, according to package directions. Drain, rinse and use as directed.

8 oz	thin dried rice noodles, angel hair pasta or somen noodles (see Tip, left)	250 g
12	round rice paper sheets, about 8 inches (20 cm) in diameter	12
10	Bibb, Boston or other tender lettuce leaves, cut crosswise into 1-inch (2.5 cm) strips (about 2 cups/500 mL) loosely packed)	10
½ cup	fresh mint leaves	125 mL
½ cup	fresh cilantro leaves	125 mL
5	green onions, trimmed, cut into 3-inch (7.5 cm) lengths and then cut lengthwise into thin strips	5
12	medium shrimp, cooked, peeled and halved lengthwise	12
	Tangy Brown Bean Dipping Sauce (page 204) or Hoisin Peanut Dipping Sauce (page 206)	

1. Bring a medium saucepan of water to a rolling boil over high heat. Drop in rice noodles and immediately remove from heat. Let stand until tender and ready to eat, 5 to 7 minutes, gently lifting and stirring noodles occasionally as they soften to keep separate and to cook evenly. Drain, rinse with cold water, drain well and set aside. You should have about 2 cups (500 mL) of noodles.

2. Arrange all ingredients in separate dishes around a large cutting board or tray set before you. Have a large platter ready to hold the finished rolls and fill a large skillet or shallow bowl with hot water.

Tip

The rice paper wrappers used in this recipe are sturdy once softened in water and wrapped around a savory filling of noodles, lettuce, herbs and shrimp, but while dry and in the package, they are fragile. A given package may contain broken disks and you may have to discard some because they tear or dry out during the rolling process. Buy extra, so that you have plenty on hand. They keep well for many months even after they are opened so they make an excellent pantry staple.

3. To make each roll, slide 1 sheet of rice paper into pan of water and press gently to submerge for about 15 seconds. Remove carefully, draining water. Place sheet before you on cutting board.

4. On bottom third of sheet, line up the following ingredients in a horizontal row: a small tangle of noodles (about $\frac{1}{4}$ cup/60 mL), some lettuce strips, some mint leaves and some cilantro leaves. Sprinkle green onion slivers on top.

5. Lift wrapper edge nearest to you and roll up and over filling, tucking it in under them about halfway along the wrapper and compressing everything gently into a cylindrical shape. When you've completely enclosed the filling in one good turn, fold in the sides tightly, as though making an envelope. Then place 2 shrimp halves, pink side down, on the rice sheet just above the cylinder. Continue rolling up wrapper and press seam to close it, wetting with a little splash of water if it has dried out too much to seal itself closed. Set roll aside on the platter to dry, seam side down. Continue to fill and roll up rice paper sheets until you have made 8 to 10 rolls. Set aside.

6. To serve, present rolls whole or cut them in half crosswise — straight or on the diagonal. Or trim away the ends and cut into bite-size lengths. Serve with dipping sauce.

◇ Vietnamese Tales

Rice paper wrappers demonstrate the culinary genius evident in Vietnamese cuisine. A sturdy and yet delicate ingredient, they are made from raw rice, ground into a powder and stirred with water to make a thick soft white dough. Traditionally, this moist pasty dough is spread thinly over woven bamboo, dried in the sun until it forms brittle, translucent disks, and then stacked up and wrapped for sale in every marketplace. Wildly popular summer rolls consist of these rice "papers" softened with water, filled with noodles, herbs and shrimp and rolled up into lovely cylinders for dipping in pungent sauces.

Shrimp Toast

Fun to make and fun to eat, this little tidbit lights up any party table. A savvy adaptation of shrimp-paste dishes like Sugarcane Shrimp (page 14), this irresistible snack is sometimes deep-fried, but you can cook it quickly and deliciously in a skillet. Stale bread works best as the vehicle for the oceanic topping, but if your bread is fresh, toast it very lightly or place it directly on the rack of a warm oven for a few minutes to dry out. Ideally served hot, these remain extremely tasty even after they cool down to room temperature.

◇◇

Serves 6 to 8 as part of a party menu

Tip

You can make this dish without a food processor. Simply chop the shrimp very finely using an Asian-style cleaver or a chef's knife. First cut each shrimp into 4 pieces and then use your knife to mince them into a soft, wet consistency. Mix in the seasonings and you're ready to make shrimp toast.

♦ Food processor or blender (see Tip, left)

1 lb	medium shrimp, peeled, deveined and coarsely chopped	500 g
1	egg white, lightly beaten	1
2 tbsp	coarsely chopped green onion	30 mL
1 tbsp	chopped cilantro leaves	15 mL
1 tbsp	finely chopped garlic	15 mL
1 tsp	vegetable oil	5 mL
2 tbsp	fish sauce	30 mL
1 tsp	granulated sugar	5 mL
½ tsp	salt	2 mL
½ tsp	freshly ground black pepper	2 mL
10	slices white bread, or 1 baguette, sliced into ovals about ½-inch (1 cm) thick	10
2 to 3 tbsp	vegetable oil	30 to 45 mL

1. In a medium bowl, combine shrimp, egg white, green onion, cilantro, garlic, 1 tsp (5 mL) oil, fish sauce, sugar, salt and pepper. Stir to mix everything well.

2. Transfer to a food processor and pulse briefly, 5 to 10 times, just enough to blend all ingredients together into a very rough paste, with little chunks of shrimp still visible. Or blend in a blender, stopping to scrape down the sides. Return shrimp mixture to the bowl. If you have time, cover and refrigerate for 30 minutes or so (this makes the mixture a bit easier to handle).

3. Set out sliced bread and shrimp mixture next to a cutting board, along with a baking sheet or platter to hold the toast once ready to cook. Slice away crusts from sliced bread. Reserve to make bread crumbs or discard.

Variation

These delightful snacks are often deep-fried into rich, super crisp golden bites. If you like deep-frying, simply drop them into the hot oil for a minute or two until the shrimp topping is done and drain well. You could also bake them in a 350°F (180°C) oven until bottoms are golden brown and crisp, and shrimp paste is pink and firm.

4. Spread each piece of bread with a rounded tablespoon (15 mL) of shrimp filling. Cover slice all the way to edges and keep filling an even thickness, about 1/4 inch (0.5 cm). Cut shrimp-covered bread into 2 triangles or rectangles. Cut each half again to make 4 pieces per slice.

5. Heat a large skillet over medium-high heat. Add 2 tbsp (30 mL) of the oil. Heat oil until a bit of shrimp paste sizzles at once. Place about 8 pieces of bread, shrimp-side down, in hot pan and cook until filling is pink, firm and lightly browned, about 1 minute. Flip each piece to cook the bread side until warm and lightly browned, about 30 seconds. Transfer to a serving platter and continue cooking all the toasts, adding more oil, if needed. Serve hot, warm or at room temperature.

◇ Vietnamese Tales

Shrimp toast is a world traveller, an illustration of how culinary traditions cross borders freely and change over time as they are adapted to please people who adopt them. Portuguese explorers introduced bread made with white wheat flour to Asian countries in the 15th century. At some point, Chinese cooks paired traditional shrimp paste with sliced white bread to make the deep fried morsel we call shrimp toast. During the centuries of Chinese influence in Vietnam, shrimp toast became a favorite Vietnamese snack, with the addition of fresh herbs, lettuce leaves, and the signature sweet-and-tangy dipping sauce that gives it an extraordinary, irresistibly bright flavor.

Lemongrass Shrimp

This inviting starter requires only a little chopping, measuring and processing for the marinade and a quick turn on the grill. The resulting dish looks and tastes delicious. If you prefer to cook the shrimp indoors, simply broil them in a very hot oven, or sear them in a pan and then stick them on skewers once they're cooked to make serving easier. You could even roast them in a 425°F (220°C) oven for 3 to 5 minutes — they may not be golden brown, but they'll be gorgeously pink and completely delicious.

Tip

Consider leaving the tails on as you peel the shrimp. The tail turns a bright red during the cooking, providing a flash of beautiful color to delight your eyes and a little handle for eating these treats.

Variations

Instead of using a grill or the broiler, here are some other options. Preheat oven to 425°F (220°C), add shrimp to lightly oiled ovenproof skillet or grill pan and roast for 3 to 5 minutes. Or sauté over medium-high heat for 2 to 4 minutes.

♦ About 30 small bamboo skewers, soaked in water for at least 30 minutes
♦ Blender or mini food processor

3 tbsp	coarsely chopped fresh lemongrass	45 mL
1 tbsp	chopped garlic	15 mL
2 tbsp	fish sauce	30 mL
2 tbsp	freshly squeezed lime juice	30 mL
1 tbsp	soy sauce	15 mL
1 tbsp	vegetable oil	15 mL
1 tbsp	Everyday Caramel Sauce (page 210), Speedy Caramel Sauce (page 211) or brown sugar	15 mL
1 tbsp	granulated sugar	15 mL
½ tsp	salt	2 mL
1 lb	medium shrimp, peeled and deveined (see Tip, left)	500 g

1. In a blender or mini food processor, combine lemongrass, garlic, fish sauce, lime juice, soy sauce, oil, Caramel Sauce, sugar and salt. Blend until fairly smooth, pulsing on and off and scraping down the sides to keep the texture uniform. Add 1 to 2 tbsp (15 to 30 mL) of water, as needed, to move the blades. Transfer marinade to a medium bowl, add shrimp and toss to coat well. Set aside for 20 to 30 minutes.

2. Preheat gas or charcoal barbecue grill to medium-high or broiler (see Variations, left, for other cooking options). Thread shrimp onto skewers, 2 or 3 per skewer, and cook on hot grill, turning once, until shrimp are pink and cooked through, 2 to 4 minutes. Serve shrimp hot, warm or at room temperature.

Chicken Wings

Perfect for parties, these sweet-and-salty wings make a fine weeknight meal as well. Marinating them increases their flavor, so give them as much time as you can manage. Three hours is dandy, but you can keep them overnight if that suits your schedule, and even 45 minutes to an hour will give you a tasty dish. If you like chile heat, stir a little Sriracha sauce or cayenne into the marinade. Grilling them gives extra flavor, but my go-to is the handy option of a hot oven right there in the kitchen.

Serves 4

Tip

Instead of a blender or food processor, you could also combine the marinade ingredients in a large bowl and use a whisk or a fork to blend them together into a sauce. Be sure to chop the ginger and garlic finely in this case, so that they season the marinade well.

♦ Blender or mini food processor (see Tip, left)
♦ Roasting pan, lined with foil and lightly greased

¼ cup	Asian fish sauce	60 mL
2 tbsp	soy sauce	30 mL
2 tbsp	dark or light brown sugar	30 mL
1 tbsp	finely chopped fresh gingerroot	15 mL
1 tbsp	finely chopped garlic	15 mL
1 tbsp	molasses, dark sweet soy sauce or Indonesian ketjap manis	15 mL
½ tsp	salt	2 mL
½ tsp	freshly ground black pepper	2 mL
1½ lbs	chicken wings	750 g
¼ cup	finely chopped green onions	60 mL

1. In blender or mini food processor, combine fish sauce, soy sauce, brown sugar, ginger, garlic, molasses, salt and pepper and blend until combined into a thick, brown sauce, pulsing the motor and stopping to scrape down the sides as you work. Transfer mixture to a large bowl. Add chicken wings and turn to coat well with marinade. Cover and refrigerate for 2 to 4 hours or overnight.

2. Preheat oven to 375°F (190°C). Remove wings from marinade and place on prepared roasting pan, making sure you leave enough room so the wings are not touching.

3. When oven is hot, place roasting pan in middle of oven and cook for 15 minutes. Remove pan and turn wings to cook the underside. Cook until wings are tender, browned and cooked through, 15 minutes more.

4. Remove from oven and transfer wings to a serving platter. Pour any pan juices over wings and sprinkle with chopped green onions. Serve hot, warm or at room temperature.

Grilled Leaf-Wrapped Beef Kebabs

Handsome and delicious, these plump little cylinders of lemongrass-infused beef are one of the dishes featured in the classic northern-style feast, *bo bay mon* or "seven-course beef." The standard wrapper is the *la lot* leaf (also known as piper leaf or pepper leaf), a lovely and delicate heart-shaped edible leaf enjoyed throughout Southeast Asia. Since *la lot* leaves are a rare find in the West, I make the kebabs with preserved grape leaves from a Middle Eastern market, which I rinse and stem. You can also use big flat spinach leaves or large leaves of fresh basil laid side by side, or the herb perilla, also known by its Japanese name, *shiso.* Roll them up as you would stuffed grape leaves, but leaving the ends exposed.

◇◇

> **Makes about 10 kebabs**

♦ Preheat oiled gas or charcoal barbecue grill to medium or preheat oven to 400°F (200°C)

♦ 10 long bamboo skewers, soaked in water for at least 30 minutes

8 oz	ground beef	250 g
2 tbsp	minced fresh lemongrass	30 mL
1 tbsp	finely chopped shallots or onion	15 mL
1 tbsp	finely chopped garlic	15 mL
1 tbsp	fish sauce	15 mL
1 tbsp	vegetable oil	15 mL
1 tsp	granulated sugar	5 mL
1 tsp	freshly ground black pepper	5 mL
½ tsp	salt	2 mL
½ tsp	ground turmeric, optional	2 mL
30 to 40	*la lot*, grape, flat spinach, large basil or red perilla leaves	30 to 40
	Everyday Dipping Sauce (page 200)	

1. In a medium bowl, combine ground beef with lemongrass, shallots, garlic, fish sauce, oil, sugar, pepper, salt and turmeric, if using, and mix well. Divide mixture into generous tbsp (15 mL) of meat and shape each portion into a plump little cylinder about 2 inches (5 cm) long. If you are using Mediterranean-style grape leaves, rinse well and trim away any stems.

Tip

You could use shorter skewers with one roll per skewer if you'd like to serve this as individual rolls on a stick. These can be served on the long skewers, right from the grill, or removed from the skewers and piled up on a platter as finger food treats.

2. Place a leaf on a cutting board with veined side down and stem end toward you and place a meat portion at the edge nearest you. Roll up in leaf and place, seam side down, on a platter. Leave the ends open, unless you are using grape leaves, which need their sides tucked in because they are wide. Continue rolling in this way until all the meat is wrapped in leaves.

3. To grill kebabs, thread 3 or 4 rolls onto each skewer, bunching them up near the pointed end and taking care to pierce each roll through the seam. Place skewers on prepared rack of hot grill and cook until nicely browned and cooked through, turning once or twice, 2 to 3 minutes per side. To bake, place rolls (without skewers), seam side down, in a 13- by-9-inch (33 by 23 cm) pan and bake in preheated oven until nicely browned and cooked through, 8 to 10 minutes. Transfer to a serving platter and serve hot, warm or at room temperature with dipping sauce.

Pork Meatballs with Fresh Herbs and Rice Noodles in Lettuce Cups

Expect cheers when you serve this street food favorite, which could be tucked into the sandwich Banh Mi (page 26) as well as tucked into delectable herb-infused packages. Invite your guests to wrap a meatball or two in a lettuce cup along with some rice noodles, scallions and fresh herbs and then dip the package into either the Hoisin-Peanut or Everyday Dipping Sauce. Or serve the meatballs with a dipping sauce as part of a barbecued feast.

◇◇

> **Makes about 12 to 15 kebabs, about 3 dozen meatballs**

♦ Preheat gas or charcoal barbecue grill to medium, optional

♦ 12 to 15 bamboo skewers, soaked in water for at least 30 minutes

♦ Large serving platter

Meatballs

1 lb	ground pork	500 g
1 tbsp	vegetable oil	15 mL
1 tbsp	finely chopped shallots or onion	15 mL
1 tbsp	finely chopped garlic	15 mL
2 tbsp	fish sauce	30 mL
1 tbsp	soy sauce	15 mL
1 tsp	granulated sugar	5 mL
½ tsp	salt	2 mL
½ tsp	freshly ground black pepper	2 mL

Accompaniments

8 oz	thin dried rice noodles	250 g
36	small, cup-shaped lettuce leaves, preferably Boston, Bibb or iceberg (approx.)	36
1½ cups	fresh cilantro, mint or basil sprigs, or a mix of all three	375 mL
1 cup	thinly sliced green onion or garlic chives, cut into 1-inch (2.5 cm) lengths	250 mL
	Hoisin-Peanut Dipping Sauce (page 206)	
	Double recipe Everyday Dipping Sauce (page 200), about 1 cup (250 mL)	

1. *Meatballs:* In a medium bowl, combine ground pork, oil, shallots, garlic, fish sauce, soy sauce, sugar, salt and pepper and mix well with your hands or a big spoon. (For a classic finely ground version, transfer meat mixture to a food processor and process for 2 to 3 minutes, stopping once or twice to scrape down the bowl, until you have a fairly smooth paste.) Cover and chill for a few minutes while you prepare the accompaniments.

2. Bring a medium saucepan of water to a rolling boil over high heat. Drop rice noodles in and immediately remove from heat. Let stand until tender and ready to eat, 5 to 7 minutes. Drain, rinse in cold water and then drain well. Pile noodles on a large serving platter and place lettuce leaves beside them. Place herbs and green onion in small bowls and arrange on the platter as well. Place bowls of Hoisin-Peanut Sauce and Everyday Dipping Sauce in the center of the platter, leaving room for the meatballs.

3. Shape meat mixture into meatballs, using about 1 tbsp (15 mL) each for large, walnut-size meatballs and about half that amount for the classic *nem nuong*. (Use a little vegetable oil on your palms or spoon if needed to help you shape the meatballs.)

4. To grill, thread 3 to 5 meatballs on each skewer and place them on a plate. Cook on preheated grill, turning occasionally, until nicely browned and no longer pink inside, 10 to 15 minutes. To pan-fry meatballs, heat 1 tbsp (15 mL) of vegetable oil in a large skillet over medium-high heat. When pan is hot, add meatballs and cook, shaking pan occasionally to brown evenly and no longer pink inside, 3 to 5 minutes. Remove from heat and thread on skewers if you like, 3 or 4 per skewer. Transfer grilled or pan-fried meatballs to prepared serving platter and serve hot or warm.

5. *To serve:* Make little packets by tucking a meatball, a small tangle of noodles and a pinch of herb leaves and green onion into a lettuce leaf and rolling it up. Dip this bundle into the sauce as you eat.

Banh Mi

Welcome to the easiest recipe in the book, your key to the inspired Vietnamese take on the submarine sandwich. Wonderful homemade *banh mi* are accessible to anyone in possession of its fairly common fixin's: good bread; a slice or two of something substantial like ham, roast pork, grilled vegetables or hard-boiled eggs; cucumber slices; mayonnaise or butter, or both; and the three "secret" ingredients elevating this pedestrian sandwich to celestial, Southeast Asian heights. Said ingredients are whole leafy sprigs of fresh cilantro; thin, diagonally sliced ovals of fresh jalapeño chiles; and a generous dose of Everyday Pickled Carrots.

Serves 4

Tips

You can use any kind of pâté, but for an old-school traditional touch, look for soft and spreadable French-style pâté, available in small cans in Asian markets and gourmet shops. Hearty country-style pâté works well, too. However, if you have that treasure, consider making it the featured ingredient of the sandwich, perhaps along with some cold cuts, and not just a schmear for background.

You can also indulge your own wishes here. Add untraditional items like lettuce and tomato, avocado or alfalfa sprouts. Or cut the sandwich into 3-inch (7.5 cm) sections and serve it on silver trays as dynamite canapés.

4	small baguettes or 2 regular baguettes, cut into four 6-inch (15 cm) sections	4
	Mayonnaise	
	Butter, softened to room temperature	
	Chicken and Pork Pâté (page 31) or prepared pâté (see Tips, left), optional	
12	slices cold cuts such as Vietnamese pâtés (*cha lua* or *cha que*), prosciutto, smoked ham or thinly sliced roast turkey	12
1	hothouse cucumber or 3 small pickling cucumbers, peeled and cut lengthwise into ¼-inch (0.5 cm) thick strips	1
1½ cups	Everyday Pickled Carrots (page 128)	375 mL
4	fresh jalapeño chiles, cut diagonally into thin ovals, or 1 tbsp (15 mL) chile-garlic sauce or any hot sauce	4
	Fresh cilantro (12 to 24 whole sprigs)	

1. Slice halfway into the side of each small baguette or section of a large one, leaving one long side attached. Set up a little assembly line, placing the 4 little loaves on a cutting board, handy to all the ingredients and condiments.

2. Generously spread both sides of each loaf with mayonnaise or butter or both. Spread a nice dollop of pâté, if using, thinly over top half of each sandwich.

Tip

The closer you can come to a warm, soft, freshly baked baguette, the better. Fabulous market versions of *banh mi* sold all over the Mekong Delta are made with bread that is fresh but no longer warm, however, and they are still divine. When I can, I use partially baked and then frozen demi-baguettes from the grocery store. Even without these, you will love *banh mi* and feel like a culinary genius every time you serve them.

Variations

For the main filling, include one of the following: Char Shiu-Style Pork (page 88) Banh Mi with Sliced Cucumber Salad (page 127); Grilled Lemongrass Beef (page 68) Banh Mi with Chopped Watercress Salad (page 122); Five-Spice Roast Chicken (page 59) Banh Mi with sliced avocado and spicy salsa; Omelet with Crabmeat (page 60) Banh Mi with sliced tomatoes and fresh dill.

3. Place 3 slices of cold cuts on bottom half of each sandwich and top with cucumber strips. Divide pickled carrots among the 4 sandwiches, spreading over meat and cucumber and adding a spoonful of the brine to each serving. Lay several jalapeño slices along each row of filling. Top with 6 cilantro sprigs.

4. Close each sandwich, pressing gently to bring the flavors together, and serve at room temperature. Or wrap each sandwich tightly in waxed paper, plastic wrap or foil, and set aside until serving time.

◇ Vietnamese Tales

Do not omit the secret ingredients, which I discovered by opening up my first *banh mi* many years ago, in search of the mysterious essence that made a simple and familiar sandwich taste so extraordinarily good. The simple source of this culinary magic? A piquant trio of Everyday Pickled Carrots (page 128), cilantro sprigs and slices of fresh jalapeño chiles. Everyday Pickled Carrots and Daikon Radish (page 129) work fine as well, and do give the chiles a chance, on the side if need be. Even chile-phobes should try the real thing because the effect is subtle rather than intense. But without the chiles, it's still wonderful.

Fried Spring Rolls

These crisp-on-the-outside, tender-on-the-inside handheld snacks make a fantastic highlight of any celebration, and earn back every bit of effort you will spend in making them at home. The filling includes ground pork, chopped shrimp and crab, all tangled up in a profusion of delightfully chewy bean thread noodles. Served with lettuce for wrapping them, a sheaf of aromatic herbs for contrast, and piquant Everyday Dipping Sauce for weaving it all together, they make a memorable part of any meal or an incredible snack.

◇◇◇

Makes about 30 to 40 spring rolls

Tips

You can use the thin pastry square spring roll wrappers found in the freezer of Asian markets instead of the rice paper rounds.

If you don't have the dried wood ear mushrooms, you could use thinly sliced fresh shiitake mushrooms caps, cut into 1-inch (2.5 cm) lengths, or omit them. They are primarily in the dish for color and a little crunch. Do buy a bag when at an Asian market, as they are beloved in Vietnamese and Asian cooking, and they keep indefinitely on the pantry shelf.

◆ Asian-style wire strainer or slotted spoon
◆ Large baking dish, lined with paper towels
◆ Candy/deep-fry thermometer

2	small bundles bean thread noodles	2
3 or 4	dried wood ear mushrooms, optional (see Tips, left)	3 or 4
⅓ cup	Egg Pancake Strips (page 215)	75 mL
¼ cup	finely chopped shallots or onion	60 mL
1 tbsp	finely chopped garlic	15 mL
2 tbsp	Asian fish sauce	30 mL
1 tsp	granulated sugar	5 mL
1 tsp	freshly ground black pepper	5 mL
½ tsp	salt	2 mL
8 oz	ground pork	250 g
8 oz	medium shrimp, peeled, deveined and finely chopped	250 g
4 oz	crabmeat	125 g
40	round dried rice paper wrappers (8 inches/20 cm in diameter) (see Tips, left)	40
	Vegetable oil for deep-frying	
	Everyday Herb and Salad Plate (page 116)	
	Everyday Dipping Sauce (page 200)	

1. Place bean thread noodles in a large bowl, add warm water to cover and soak until tender, about 30 minutes. Place dried mushrooms, if using, in another bowl, add warm water to cover and soak until softened, about 30 minutes.

2. Meanwhile, in a large bowl, combine Egg Pancake Strips, shallots, garlic, fish sauce, sugar, pepper and salt. Add ground pork, chopped shrimp and crabmeat and combine well. Set all the equipment needed for frying next to the stove. Set out strainer or heatproof slotted spoon. Place a serving platter to hold the rolls near the Everyday Herb and Salad Plate and the Everyday Dipping Sauce.

3. Drain bean thread noodles and mushrooms. Using a pair of kitchen scissors or a sharp heavy knife, cut or chop softened noodles into 1-inch (2.5 cm) lengths and transfer to pork mixture.

4. Trim wood ear mushrooms, cutting away and discarding any hard sections or lumps. Stack up and slice the dark mushroom pieces into thin shreds and add to bowl.

5. Using a large spoon or your hands, mix all ingredients together well, so pork is broken up into small bits and everything comes together evenly.

6. Place a medium bowl of warm water and dried rice paper rounds next to a cutting board. Take one round rice paper wrapper and dip into warm water. Remove quickly and place on cutting board. Let stand until it changes color a bit and wrinkles as it begins to dry. Place a small handful of filling, a little less than $\frac{1}{4}$ cup (60 mL) on bottom third of wrapper, closest to you and to edge of cutting board or counter. Use your fingers to shape into a log about 3 inches (7.5 cm) long.

7. Fold the edge closest to you up, over and around the filling. Begin to roll the wrapper and, when you've rolled halfway to the top point, fold the right and left sides in toward the middle. Then keep rolling, pressing to seal the top edge to the roll. Set roll on prepared baking sheet, seam side down.

8. Continue with remaining rice paper wrappers and filling, taking care to prevent the rolls from touching each other on the baking sheet, which would cause them to tear.

continued…

Fried Spring Rolls (continued)

9. To fry the spring rolls, pour oil into a wok or large, deep heavy skillet to a depth of $2\frac{1}{2}$ inches (6 cm). Place over medium-high heat for 5 to 10 minutes. The oil is ready when a bit of garlic or onion dropped into it sizzles and floats at once. (The oil should register 350 to 365°F/180 to 185°C on the thermometer.) Carefully add a spring roll by sliding it gently down the curved side of the wok or lowering it carefully into the skillet. Add 2 or 3 more rolls, but do not crowd the pan. Cook, turning the rolls occasionally to brown them evenly, until golden brown and pork and shrimp filling is cooked through, 5 to 10 minutes.

10. Using slotted spoon or wire strainer, remove each spring roll, holding it briefly over the pan to drain and set it on prepared baking sheet. Cook remaining rolls in the same way. When all the spring rolls are done, arrange them on serving platter and serve at once with Everyday Herb and Salad Plate and Everyday Dipping Sauce.

◈ Vietnamese Tales

Unlike Chinese-style spring rolls with a wheat-flour pastry wrapper and fillings centered on shredded cabbage, Vietnamese spring rolls are filled with an irresistible pairing of delicate bean thread noodles and pork, with handsome accents of wood ear mushrooms, shrimp or crab, and ground black pepper. Known as *cha gio* in the South and *nem ran* in the North, these classic rolls traditionally come with lettuce leaves, fresh herbs and Vietnam's signature dipping sauce. They star both as street food treats and as a special occasion favorite in restaurants or made at home. Experts can fill and wrap small triangular rice papers into tiny, bite-size crisp rolls, but beginners start with the 8-inch (20 cm) rice papers, which have become widely available in the West.

Chicken and Pork Pâté

This tasty pâté calls for poached chicken livers and ground pork seasoned simply with a little fish sauce, shallot, garlic, ginger and freshly ground pepper. This makes a rich, luxurious addition to your Vietnamese-style Banh Mi (page 26), and elevates the warm baguettes traditionally savored with Chicken Curry with Sweet Potatoes (page 54) or Beef Stew with Lemongrass (page 74).

◇◇

Serves 10

Tip

This pâté freezes well. To freeze, cover tightly and wrap well. Defrost for 10 to 12 hours in the refrigerator before serving. Timing varies, depending on the quantity you've frozen.

♦ 1½-cup (375 mL) mold or bowl, generously greased
♦ Food processor or blender

8 oz	chicken livers	250 g
8 oz	ground pork	250 g
½ cup	coarsely chopped shallots or onion	125 mL
2 tsp	chopped garlic	10 mL
2 tsp	chopped fresh gingerroot	10 mL
1 tbsp	Asian fish sauce	15 mL
1 tsp	granulated sugar	5 mL
1 tsp	salt	5 mL
½ tsp	freshly ground black pepper	2 mL
1 cup	Chicken Stock (page 216), store-bought or water	250 mL
¾ cup	butter	175 mL

1. In a deep medium skillet, combine chicken livers, ground pork, shallots, garlic, ginger, fish sauce, sugar, salt and pepper. Add chicken stock and bring to a lively boil over medium-high heat. Adjust heat to maintain a gentle simmer and cook until livers and pork are no longer pink, 12 to 15 minutes. Turn livers occasionally to help cook evenly. Gently break up pork into smaller pieces to cook evenly.

2. Meanwhile, chop butter into 1-inch (2.5 cm) chunks.

3. Remove pan from heat. Transfer mixture to food processor and process to combine everything roughly, 1 to 2 minutes. While the motor is running, add butter, dropping through the feed tube. Or stop to add a few chunks at a time. Stop often to scrape down the sides and make sure everything is coming together into a very smooth paste, 3 to 4 minutes.

4. When pâté is very smooth, transfer to prepared bowl. Smooth top. Cover and refrigerate for 1 hour. It will become firm but not hard.

5. Serve cold, cool or at room temperature.

Pâté Chaud

This irresistible savory treat dates back to the early days of French colonial presence in Vietnam, when the word "pâté" denoted flaky pastry, not a type of charcuterie, which is its modern French meaning. Chaud means that the treat is served warm, and you will find pâté chaud (pronounced pah-tay-so) all over Vietnamese communities, at snack and sandwich shops as well as in coffee shops and grocery stores. With purchased puff pastry from the freezer case, you will be able to make wonderful hand-pies to take on a picnic or eat at your desk or tuck into a lunch for someone you love.

◇◇◇

Serves 6 to 8

Tip

Remaining pastry rectangles can be refrozen. Excess pastry remaining after cutting out the circles can be refrigerated for up to 1 day. It can be rolled out into sheets and used for hand pies or tart crusts. Remaining filling can be shaped into small burgers or meatballs and cooked in a lightly oiled skillet until nicely browned and cooked through.

♦ 3-inch (7.5 cm) cookie or biscuit cutter

1	small bundle dried bean thread noodles	1
5	dried wood ear mushrooms or ⅓ cup (75 mL) chopped shiitake or button mushrooms	5
12 oz	ground pork	375 g
⅓ cup	finely chopped shallots or onion	75 mL
1 tbsp	finely chopped garlic	15 mL
2 tbsp	Asian fish sauce	30 mL
½ tsp	granulated sugar	2 mL
½ tsp	freshly ground black pepper	2 mL
1½ lbs	puff pastry, thawed	750 g
1	egg, beaten with 1 tbsp (15 mL) water	1

1. Place bean thread noodles in a large bowl, add warm water to cover and soak until tender, about 30 minutes. Place dried mushrooms, if using, in another bowl, add warm water to cover and soak until softened, about 30 minutes.

2. Meanwhile, in a medium bowl, combine ground pork, chopped fresh mushrooms, if using, shallots, garlic, fish sauce, sugar and pepper and mix to combine well.

3. Drain bean thread noodles. Using a pair of kitchen scissors or a sharp heavy knife, cut or chop softened noodles into 1-inch (2.5 cm) lengths and transfer to pork mixture.

Tip

You could cut the thawed pastry into 4-inch (10 cm) squares, add meat filling and fold diagonally into triangles. Most any shape and size will work, as long as you seal the pastry well and bake until the meat is cooked through.

4. Drain mushrooms. Trim away and discard any hard bits and bumps from wood ear mushrooms. Slice thinly into short strips and add to pork mixture.

5. Preheat oven to 350°F (180°C). Unfold one rectangle of puff pastry. Using a big round cookie or biscuit cutter, cut out 12 circles of pastry. Scoop out a 2-inch (5 cm) ball of filling and place on one circle. Continue filling pastry rounds.

6. Use remaining pastry and cut out 12 more circles. Place over meatballs. Press to seal with your finger and with a fork to close the edges tightly. Dip a pastry brush in beaten egg and generously cover surface of each pastry evenly with egg wash. Discard remaining egg wash.

7. Place on a baking sheet and bake in preheated oven until pastry is golden brown and puffed up, 15 to 20 minutes. Serve hot or warm or at room temperature.

Soups

Soup in Vietnam can be deliciously assertive or demure, a hearty centerpiece dish or a simple complement to a big, rice-centered meal. These soups range from simple to fancy, though none requires a great deal of time or work.

Start with Meatball Soup (page 36), wonderful, fast and satisfying, or the lovely and delicate Clear Soup with Catfish, Tomatoes and Fresh Dill (page 42). Either of these would work nicely served over rice or noodles as a meal in a bowl. Several soups feature winter squash, from butternut to kabocha. Two involve ground pork, while one features coconut milk and tender mushrooms, illustrating the creative and varied way Vietnamese cooks approach particular ingredients.

Pork and Cabbage Rolls in Clear Soup (page 38) is comfort food dressed up with a handsome presentation for nights when you have a little extra time. In case you hunger for it on a busy night, I also give you a shortcut. Sweet and Tangy Soup with Pineapple, Tamarind and Shrimp (page 44) is a hearty, classic Vietnamese soup open to substitutions: use salmon instead of shrimp, or make it a seafood showboat with clams, scallops, shrimp and chunks of fish. Shrimp Dumpling Soup with Watercress (page 46) takes a little time to put together, but what a reward — a green and pink creation that is peppery and good. Crab and Asparagus Soup (page 48) is elegant but still easy and a beauty with fresh asparagus turned a vivid green. Vietnamese people have soup at almost every meal and with these dishes in your repertoire, you may want to follow suit.

Meatball Soup

Make this anytime you crave the comfort of hearty homemade soup in a hurry. In the classic version of *bo vien*, cooks grind the beef to a fine paste, creating a firm meatball with the chewy texture beloved throughout Asia. My streamlined version made with ground beef puts this dish on your table in a flash. Enjoy this Vietnamese-style, along with rice and other dishes. Or savor it as we often do, ladled over noodles or rice in a big soup bowl for a one-dish supper accompanied by chile-garlic sauce or crusty bread.

◇◇

Serves 4 to 6

Tip

Add a fistful or two of tender spinach leaves to the soup.

Meatballs

1 lb	ground beef	500 g
2 tbsp	fish sauce	30 mL
2 tbsp	soy sauce	30 mL
1 tsp	Asian sesame oil	5 mL
1 tsp	cornstarch	5 mL
1 tsp	salt	5 mL
¼ tsp	freshly ground black pepper	1 mL

Soup

4 cups	Chicken Stock (page 216), store-bought or water	1 L
1 tbsp	fish sauce	15 mL
1 tbsp	soy sauce	15 mL
1 tsp	Asian sesame oil	5 mL
¼ tsp	freshly ground black pepper	1 mL
2 tbsp	thinly sliced green onion	30 mL
2 tbsp	coarsely chopped fresh cilantro	30 mL

1. *Meatballs:* In a medium bowl, combine ground beef, fish sauce, soy sauce, sesame oil, cornstarch, salt and pepper and mix to blend well. Shape into meatballs, using about 1 tbsp (15 mL) of the mixture for each one. You should have 25 to 30 meatballs.

2. *Soup:* In a medium saucepan over high heat, bring stock to a rolling boil. Drop in half the meatballs and cook, stirring occasionally, until no longer pink inside, 3 to 5 minutes. Transfer to a bowl with a slotted spoon. Cook remaining meatballs in stock and transfer to bowl.

3. Season stock in saucepan by stirring in fish sauce, soy sauce, sesame oil and pepper. Return meatballs to stock and heat through. Sprinkle with green onion and cilantro. Serve hot.

Pork Meatball Soup with Butternut Squash

This hearty soup's handsome golden hue will make you eager for a steaming bowl and a side of rice or garlic toast with which to enjoy it. Hard to believe how quickly something so satisfying can come together, but that's how it is with this dish. Traditionally this type of soup is often seasoned with rice paddy herb; use it if you can find it, or enjoy it with fresh cilantro leaves.

Serves 4

Tip

Any winter squash is delightful here: kabocha pumpkin or acorn squash work well, too.

8 oz	ground pork	250 g
1 tsp	salt	5 mL
½ tsp	freshly ground black pepper	2 mL
½ tsp	granulated sugar	2 mL
1 lb	butternut squash (see Tip, left)	500 g
4 cups	water	1 L
2 tbsp	fish sauce	30 mL
3 tbsp	thinly sliced green onion	45 mL
2 tbsp	coarsely chopped cilantro	30 mL

1. In a medium bowl, combine ground pork, salt, pepper and sugar and mix together well. Set aside.

2. Peel and halve butternut squash. Scrape out and discard seeds and fibers in center of squash. Chop peeled squash into 1-inch (2.5 cm) chunks. Measure out 3 cups (750 mL).

3. In a medium saucepan, bring water to a rolling boil. Add squash chunks and cook, stirring once or twice, for 5 minutes.

4. Add pork, pinching off or scooping up bite-size chunks and dropping into the water. Cook, stirring occasionally, until squash is tender and the meat is no longer pink, about 15 minutes.

5. Add fish sauce and green onion and stir well. Transfer to a serving bowl and sprinkle cilantro over soup. Serve hot or warm.

Pork and Cabbage Rolls in Clear Soup

These plump little cabbage bundles of savory pork look delicious in the clear broth and although they take a little time, the results are worth it. Prettily tied scallion ribbons provide adornment, but if that's too much, simply fold the leaves tightly and place them in the pot with care. However they look, you will be serving your guests a substantial and pleasing dish.

Serves 4 to 6

Tip

For a quicker version, shape the seasoned pork mixture into 16 to 18 small meatballs. Drop them into the boiling soup, simmer until they're cooked and add 2 cups (500 mL) of shredded cabbage, chopped bok choy or fresh spinach leaves. Cook for a minute or two until the cabbage or spinach leaves are vivid green and tender and serve hot. Thinly slice the green onions and sprinkle them over the finished soup along with the cilantro.

Soup

5 cups	Chicken Stock (page 216) or store-bought	1.25 L
2 tbsp	fish sauce	30 mL
½ tsp	granulated sugar	2 mL
½ tsp	salt	2 mL

Cabbage Rolls

8 to 10	large or 20 small, cabbage leaves (see Tip, right)	8 to 10
6 to 8	green onions, trimmed, white part coarsely chopped and green part left whole	6 to 8
8 oz	ground pork	250 g
1 tbsp	fish sauce	15 mL
1 tsp	Asian sesame oil	5 mL
½ tsp	granulated sugar	2 mL
½ tsp	salt	2 mL
½ tsp	freshly ground black pepper	2 mL
2 tbsp	coarsely chopped fresh cilantro	30 mL

1. *Soup:* In a medium saucepan over medium-high heat, bring stock, fish sauce, sugar and salt to a rolling boil, then adjust heat to maintain a gentle boil.

2. *Cabbage Rolls:* Make a small, V-shaped cut into base of each cabbage leaf, removing most of the thick rib. Cut larger leaves in half lengthwise and place all the leaves on a platter by the stove, along with green onion tops and a pair of tongs or 2 forks for handling the vegetables as they soften in the soup.

Tip

You could use other members of the sturdy leafy cruciferous vegetable family, such as collard leaves, savoy cabbage, napa cabbage, bok choy leaves and turnip greens, cutting them into rectangles (about 5 by 3 inches/12.5 by 7.5 cm) before blanching and rolling them up.

3. Submerge 2 cabbage leaves in hot soup just until wilted and pliable but not cooked, about 1 minute. Transfer to platter and wilt remaining leaves and then set aside. Plunge green onion tops down into soup as well, count to 10 and transfer to platter. Remove soup from heat and set aside. Rinse cabbage leaves and green onion tops in cool water, drain and blot dry. Set aside near a cutting board.

4. *To make the filling for the cabbage rolls:* In a medium bowl, combine pork, fish sauce, sesame oil, sugar, salt and pepper. Add chopped green onion (the white part) and mix well.

5. *To prepare the cabbage rolls:* Place a cabbage leaf on cutting board with stem end closest to you and veiny side down. Place a generous tbsp (15 mL) of filling near the stem and shape into a little cylinder. Fold in sides and roll up from stem to stern, enclosing meat in a little parcel. Place on the platter, seam side down, and roll up the rest of the meat in the same fashion. Tear softened green onion tops in half lengthwise and tie one strip around each bundle, making a small knot on top, to hold the cabbage wrapper in place. (You can tuck loose ends under, trim them or leave them free.)

6. When all cabbage rolls are made, return soup to a rolling boil and then adjust heat to maintain an active simmer. Carefully lower each cabbage roll into soup on a spoon. Take your time in order to keep them intact and yourself unsplashed. Cook just until meat is done, 5 to 7 minutes. Transfer rolls to a serving bowl or individual soup bowls, ladle hot soup on top and sprinkle with cilantro. Serve hot.

◇ Vietnamese Tales

This clear soup with its beautiful and substantial pork-stuffed bundles testifies to the culinary influence of China on Vietnamese cuisine. Traditionally, beverages were seldom taken during rice-centered meals, and clear soups like this one provided a palate-cleansing effect. They earn their place by being flavorful as well as useful in balancing the various components of a rice-centered meal.

Pork Rib Soup
with Kabocha Pumpkin

This soup is beautifully golden and creamy in texture, even though there is no cream in the recipe. This would traditionally be served as part of a rice meal. Be sure to serve it with rice or bread so that you can savor the luscious golden broth. Look for small pork riblets in the meat section of Asian markets.

4 to 6 servings

Variation

Instead of pork riblets, you could also use pork chops, cutting the meat into bite-size pieces, and including the meaty bone in the soup during the cooking process, then removing it before you serve the soup. Or use 8 oz (250 g) boneless pork, cut into 1-inch (2.5 cm) chunks.

12 oz	kabocha pumpkin or butternut squash	375 g
12 oz	small meaty pork riblets (1-inch/2.5 cm lengths)	375 g
4 cups	water	1 L
1 tsp	salt	5 mL
½ tsp	freshly ground black pepper	2 mL
½ tsp	granulated sugar	2 mL
1 tbsp	Asian fish sauce	15 mL
3 tbsp	thinly sliced green onion	45 mL

1. Prepare pumpkin by cutting into 3 or 4 large chunks. Scrape out and discard seeds and stem. Peel and cut into 1-inch (2.5 cm) chunks. Measure out 2½ cups (625 mL) chunks of pumpkin and set aside.

2. Place pork riblets and water in a medium saucepan. Bring to a lively boil over medium-high heat. Reduce heat to maintain a lively simmer. Cook for 15 minutes, scooping off and discarding any foam, which rises to the top in the first few minutes.

3. Add pumpkin chunks, salt, pepper and sugar and stir well. Adjust heat to maintain a lively boil and cook, stirring occasionally, until pumpkin is tender and pork is easily pulled away from the bone or cut with a fork.

4. Add fish sauce and green onion and stir well. Remove from heat and serve hot or warm.

Chicken Soup with Winter Melon

Winter melon enjoys great favor throughout Asian cuisine as a superb component of delicate soups with clear broth and subtle flavoring. Its massive size means it is often sold in large chunks, with its creamy flesh and soft seed-laced center exposed. This center is scraped clean and the lovely soft-green patterned skin is peeled away, leaving a firm-textured vegetable, which carries the meaty broth flavor well.

◇◇◇

Serves 4 to 6

Variation

Cucumber is winter melon's cousin, and makes a great substitute. Simply peel and seed cucumbers and chop them into big bite-size chunks. Reduce the cooking time by about 10 minutes because cucumber is much more tender than winter melon and mostly needs to be heated through.

12 oz	winter melon	375 g
12 oz	boneless, skinless chicken thighs or chicken breast	375 g
5 cups	Chicken Stock (page 216) or store-bought	1.25 L
½ tsp	salt	2 mL
½ tsp	freshly ground black pepper	2 mL
1 tbsp	fish sauce	15 mL
3 tbsp	thinly sliced green onion	45 mL

1. Prepare winter melon by cutting into 3 big chunks. Peel and then scrape away and discard seeds and fibers in center. Cut melon into big bite-size chunks, about 1 inch (2.5 cm) square. (You will have about 2¼ cups/550 mL.)

2. Cut chicken into big bite-size chunks, about 1-inch (2.5 cm) in diameter. Place in a medium saucepan and add chicken stock. Bring to a rolling boil over medium-high heat. Adjust heat to maintain a gentle boil and cook for 10 minutes, skimming away and discarding any foam that rises to the top.

3. Add winter melon chunks and cook until chicken juices run clear when pierced for thighs and no longer pink inside for breasts and winter melon is tender, 25 to 30 minutes. When chicken and melon are done, add salt, pepper, fish sauce and green onion and stir well. Serve hot or warm.

Clear Soup with Catfish, Tomatoes and Fresh Dill

Cooks in Vietnam and neighboring Laos often season fish dishes with fresh dill. You will love its delicate flavor in this speedy soup, which works fine with shrimp as well as fish.

Serves 4		

Tip

If fresh dill is difficult to find, use fresh cilantro or basil, or 2 tbsp (30 mL) of dried dill and add a squeeze of lime juice to the serving bowl just before you eat.

4 cups	Chicken Stock (page 216) or store-bought	1 L
12 oz	catfish fillets, tilapia, salmon or other firm-fleshed fish	375 g
5	plum tomatoes, cored	5
1 tbsp	fish sauce	15 mL
½ tsp	salt	2 mL
¼ tsp	freshly ground black pepper	1 mL
2 tbsp	thinly sliced green onion	30 mL
¼ cup	coarsely chopped fresh dill (see Tip, left)	60 mL

1. In a medium saucepan over high heat, bring stock to a rolling boil.

2. Meanwhile, cut fish into generous chunks. Cut tomatoes into chunks.

3. Add fish to saucepan, reduce heat and cook fish in gently boiling stock until opaque, 1 to 2 minutes. Stir in tomatoes, fish sauce, salt, pepper, green onion and dill and then quickly remove soup from heat. Serve hot.

Clear Soup with Shrimp and Tender Asian Greens

This pleasing little soup comes together in just a few minutes and provides a treat for the eyes as well as for the palate. Plump pink shrimp float on brilliantly green leaves of Asian vegetables or spinach. Turnip greens would be excellent here. If you have dried shrimp, they enhance the stock's flavor and give a pleasing briny note, but if not, you can omit them and still have a lovely dish to enjoy with rice and other dishes. You could also add cooked noodles, either Asian noodles or angel hair pasta and make this a speedy and beautiful one-dish lunch or supper: a meal in one bowl!

Serves 4 to 6

Tip

Look for soft, loose, leafy mustard greens, which may be curly edged or smooth in texture. You don't want mustard cabbage, which is sometimes labeled as mustard greens; its very sturdy leaves curl in to form a headed cabbage, which makes wonderful pickles. Mustard cabbage has thick, stemmy portions, which make it wrong for this type of soup. It's a wonderful vegetable, but simply not right for this dish. The greens you want are usually sold in proximity to turnip greens, chard, kale and spinach.

Variation

Instead of mustard greens, use spinach or napa cabbage.

2 tbsp	vegetable oil	30 mL
2 tbsp	chopped shallots or onion	30 mL
1 tbsp	chopped garlic	15 mL
3	large slices fresh gingerroot	3
2 tbsp	salty dried shrimp, optional	30 mL
8 oz	medium shrimp, peeled and deveined	250 g
4 cups	water	1 L
12 oz	tender leafy mustard greens, cut or torn into 2- to 3-inch (5 to 7.5 cm) lengths or pieces (see Tip, left)	375 g
2 tsp	Asian fish sauce	10 mL
1 tsp	salt	5 mL
½ tsp	granulated sugar	2 mL
½ tsp	freshly ground black pepper	2 mL
2 tbsp	thinly sliced green onion	30 mL
2 tbsp	chopped fresh cilantro leaves	30 mL

1. In a Dutch oven or large deep saucepan, heat oil over medium-high heat until hot. Add shallots and garlic and stir well. Cook, stirring often, until fragrant, about 1 minute. Add ginger and dried shrimp, if using. Toss well and continue cooking for 1 minute more.

2. Add shrimp and cook on one side, undisturbed, until they change color visibly on the sides, about 1 minute. Toss well and cook until shrimp are pink and plump, 1 minute more. They do not need to be completely done yet as they will cook on in the soup.

3. Add water and bring to a lively boil. Add greens and cook until tender, 3 to 4 minutes. Add fish sauce, salt and sugar and stir well. Remove from heat and add pepper, green onion and cilantro leaves. Serve hot or warm.

Sweet and Tangy Soup with Pineapple, Tamarind and Shrimp

Western cooks think of pineapple in terms of sweets and desserts, but Asian cooks relish the sweet-and-tangy contrast it provides to savory dishes as well as sweets. In Vietnam this celebrated soup appears on the table as one of a host of rice-centered dishes, but with its complex flavors and inclusion of shrimp, I love it as a main course, along with rice and a simple stir-fry of spinach or a crisp salad for cool contrast. The ingredient list for this soup is a bit long, but everything comes together quickly. With rice and a simple salad, you've got a wonderful meal.

Serves 6 to 8

Tip

Instead of the tamarind liquid, use 3 tbsp (45 mL) vinegar mixed with 1 tbsp (15 mL) brown sugar.

2	stalks fresh lemongrass	2
1 tbsp	vegetable oil	15 mL
1 tbsp	finely chopped garlic	15 mL
5 cups	Chicken Stock (page 216), store-bought or water	1.25 L
¼ cup	prepared tamarind liquid or Indian-style tamarind chutney (see Tip, left)	60 mL
2 tbsp	fish sauce	30 mL
2 tsp	granulated sugar	10 mL
1 tsp	chile-garlic sauce	5 mL
8 oz	medium shrimp, peeled and deveined	250 g
1 cup	pineapple chunks, canned or fresh	250 mL
4	plum tomatoes, cored and quartered	4
2 tbsp	thinly sliced green onion	30 mL
2 tbsp	chopped fresh cilantro	30 mL

Garnishes, optional

2 tbsp	chopped rice paddy herb (*rau ngo om*/page 220)	30 mL
2 tbsp	chopped fresh mint	30 mL
2 tbsp	chopped fresh Asian or any other type of basil	30 mL
1 cup	mung bean sprouts	250 mL

1. To prepare lemongrass, trim away and discard any dried root portion (to make a smooth base), the top half of stalks and any dry, tired outer leaves. Cut remaining portion of each stalk diagonally into 2-inch (5 cm) lengths.

Variation

Instead of shrimp, use 8 oz (250 g) catfish fillets, cut into 2-inch (5 cm) chunks.

2. In a large saucepan over medium-high heat, combine oil, garlic and lemongrass chunks and heat until lemongrass and garlic release their fragrance. Toss for 1 minute and add stock, tamarind liquid, fish sauce, sugar and chile-garlic sauce. Bring to a boil, reduce heat to maintain the soup at a lively simmer and cook, stirring once, for 10 minutes.

3. Increase heat to medium-high and when soup returns to a boil, add shrimp, pineapple chunks and tomatoes and stir well. Cook until shrimp are pink, 1 to 2 minutes. Stir in green onion and cilantro and remove from heat. Stir in additional herbs and bean sprouts, if using. Transfer to a serving bowl and serve at once.

◇ Vietnamese Tales

This classic soup captures Vietnam's cuisine in one delicious bowl: fresh seafood from her endless coastline; tangy tamarind from sturdy trees; luscious pineapples from the fields; garlic, tomatoes and lemongrass from the garden. This bounty comes together in a glorious soup, often savored in tandem with *ca kho to*, catfish simmered in a clay pot in a sweet and salty caramel sauce.

Shrimp Dumpling Soup with Watercress

In Vietnam, you'll find this terrific soup made with either finely ground shrimp shaped into springy little quenelles or whole shrimp marinated in seasonings. I like an in-between version, with the shrimp coarsely ground to a chunky texture so the soup is pleasing to eat and ready fast. If you want to spend a little extra time, seal the shrimp mixture into wonton wrappers and cook them in boiling water until the noodle wrapper and shrimp are cooked. Then place them in a serving bowl, add hot soup with greens and serve at once.

◇◇

Serves 4

Variation

I often use fresh spinach leaves or shredded napa cabbage in place of the watercress, which can be difficult to find.

◆ Mini food processor (see Tip, right)

Shrimp dumplings

4 oz	medium shrimp, peeled and deveined	125 g
1 tbsp	minced green onion	15 mL
1 tsp	fish sauce	5 mL
¼ tsp	salt	1 mL
¼ tsp	freshly ground black pepper	1 mL

Soup

3 cups	Chicken Stock (page 216) or store-bought	750 mL
1 cup	water	250 mL
1 tbsp	fish sauce	15 mL
¼ tsp	salt	1 mL
1½ cups	coarsely chopped watercress (see Variation, left)	375 mL

1. *Dumplings:* Coarsely chop each shrimp into 3 or 4 pieces and place in a medium bowl. Add green onion, fish sauce, salt and pepper and mix well. Transfer to mini food processor and grind to a very coarse paste, alternately pulsing and checking mixture to make sure the texture remains coarse — more lumpy than pasty. Transfer to a small bowl and let stand 10 to 15 minutes.

Tip

To prepare dumplings by hand, chop shrimp as finely as you can and add to a bowl. Or leave shrimp whole and combine with seasonings in a bowl, using your hands to blend well.

2. *Soup:* In a medium saucepan over medium-high heat, bring stock, water, fish sauce and salt to a rolling boil. Reduce heat to maintain the liquid at a gentle boil. Scoop up a tbsp (15 mL) of the shrimp mixture and drop it gently into the soup, using another spoon to coax it along as needed. Continue scooping up and adding dumplings until you've used up the shrimp mixture and then cook for about 3 minutes more. Add watercress, stir well and remove from heat. Serve at once.

◇ Vietnamese Tales

In Western cuisines, soup tends to be a humble meal in itself, a substantial meal cooked in one pot, long simmered and eaten with crusty bread on a wintry night, or as a busy day lunch with a grilled cheese sandwich or a salad on the side. Elegant versions become a first course, prelude to a special meal. In Vietnam, as in neighboring countries throughout Asia, soup is one of numerous dishes eaten with rice at almost every meal. It may be as simple as a clear broth with winter melon or tofu and green onions, or as inviting as this special soup with shrimp dumplings. Either way, it serves almost as a beverage, a palate-cleanser to mediate the numerous dishes presented with the abundance of rice that is the heart of the meal. In ordering a rice meal at a restaurant, the question wouldn't be "Shall we have a soup?" but rather, "Which soup works with these dishes?"

Crab and Asparagus Soup

This lovely soup is a French colonial creation that showcases asparagus in a standard Chinese-style egg-flower soup. The original version was made with canned asparagus, but you can enjoy the vivid green color and flavor of fresh asparagus, known in Vietnam as *mang tay* or "Western bamboo." I sometimes like to use zucchini, edamame beans, baby spinach leaves or frozen peas in place of asparagus. Canned crabmeat works nicely in this soup, making it an everyday dish.

	Serves 4	

Tip

To prepare with canned asparagus (green or white), drain, cut into 1-inch (2.5 cm) lengths and add at the end of cooking, just before the egg.

8 oz	fresh asparagus (see Tip, left)	250 g
1 tbsp	vegetable oil	15 mL
2 tbsp	finely chopped shallots or onion	30 mL
1 tbsp	finely chopped garlic	15 mL
½ tsp	salt	2 mL
¼ tsp	freshly ground black pepper	1 mL
4 cups	Chicken Stock (page 216) or store-bought	1 L
2 tsp	cornstarch	10 mL
2 tbsp	water	30 mL
1	egg, well beaten	1
4 oz	cooked lump crabmeat, or one 6-oz (175 g) can, drained (about ¾ cup/175 mL)	125 g
2 tbsp	thinly sliced green onion	30 mL

1. Trim asparagus, breaking off and discarding the base of each stalk about where the bright green color fades. Cut each stalk crosswise diagonally into 1-inch (2.5 cm) pieces, but leave the beautiful tips intact. (You should have about 2 cups/500 mL.)

2. Heat oil in a medium saucepan over medium-high heat for 1 minute. Add asparagus, shallots, garlic, salt and pepper. Cook until shallots and garlic are fragrant and asparagus is shiny and bright green, 1 to 2 minutes. Add stock and bring to a boil.

3. In a small bowl, combine cornstarch and water, stirring to make a thin, smooth paste. Add to soup. Stir soup well and drizzle in the beaten egg, letting it swirl to form lacy shreds in the hot stock. Add crabmeat and stir well. Sprinkle in green onion. Remove soup from heat and serve hot or warm.

Butternut Squash with Zucchini and Mushrooms in Coconut Soup

This vegetarian dish warms you up on a cold day, even before you taste its simple goodness. Reddish-golden cubes of butternut squash or any other hardy winter squash or pumpkin team up with bright green zucchini and plump mushrooms in a creamy coconut sauce. Traditionally this dish often includes raw peanuts cooked until they soften to a beany texture, and wood ear mushrooms, softened and cut into handsome threads. I've used fresh shiitake instead of wood ears. Serve this with rice and sautéed spinach for a simple, satisfying meal.

Serves 4	2½ cups	bite-size chunks butternut squash or another winter squash such as acorn squash or kabocha pumpkin	625 mL
	1 cup	sliced shiitake mushroom caps, or small button mushrooms, sliced lengthwise	250 mL
	1 cup	bite-size chunks zucchini or seeded cucumber	250 mL
	1	can (14 oz/400 mL) unsweetened coconut milk (about 1½ cups/375 mL)	1
	½ cup	water	125 mL
	1½ tsp	salt	7 mL
	1 tsp	granulated sugar	5 mL

1. In a medium saucepan, combine pumpkin, shiitake mushroom caps and zucchini. Add coconut milk, water, salt and sugar and bring to a gentle boil over medium-high heat.

2. Adjust heat to maintain a gentle but visible simmer, and cook, stirring gently occasionally, until pumpkin is tender and easily speared with a fork, but not mushy. Remove from heat and serve hot or warm.

Chicken and Eggs

*C*hicken is beloved* in Vietnamese kitchens and this chapter gives you lots of ways to enjoy it, from luxurious curry in coconut sauce to poached chicken Hainan-style, served with a vibrant lime sauce and rice cooked in the chicken's ginger-infused broth. I especially like the first dish in this chapter, Lemongrass Chicken or ga xao xa ot (page 52). Like many Vietnamese stir-fried dishes, it showcases the chicken on its own merits rather than using it as one element in a vegetable-and-meat combination. In Chicken Stir-Fried with Fresh Ginger (page 53), the chicken provides a similarly strong flavor note. It is perfect with rice, couscous, polenta or bread for soaking up every bit of gingery sauce.*

You will also find four omelets, which are enjoyed in Vietnam morning, noon and night. Serve any of these with rice and Everyday Dipping Sauce (page 200) as one of many dishes composing a meal, or accompanied with a warm baguette. The pork omelets are hearty, while those with crabmeat are elegantly divine. I don't know whether the chicken came before the egg, but I do know you will enjoy making and eating these Vietnamese classics while you sort it out.

Lemongrass Chicken

This simple dish packs a trio of Vietnamese flavors into a quick stir-fry: a bouquet of lemongrass, a salty bass note of fish sauce and garlic and a sassy little chile kick. Serve this dish with rice or noodles so you can savor the delicious sauce.

◇◇

Serves 4

Tip

To prepare lemongrass, trim to about 4 inches (10 cm) from the rounded base and discard the grassy tops and any very dry and brown outer portions. Slice the lemongrass crosswise into thin rounds and then mince them. Or check the freezer at your Asian market for wonderful finely ground and then frozen lemongrass imported from Vietnam.

♦ Mini food processor or a blender

12 oz	boneless, skinless chicken thighs, cut into generous bite-size chunks, or boneless, skinless chicken breasts, cut into strips	375 g
2 tsp	finely chopped garlic	10 mL
2 tbsp	fish sauce, divided	30 mL
1 tbsp	soy sauce	15 mL
2 tsp	granulated sugar	10 mL
1 tsp	cornstarch	5 mL
¼ cup	chopped onion	60 mL
2	stalks fresh lemongrass, trimmed and chopped (see Tip, left)	2
½ cup	Chicken Stock (page 216), store-bought or water	125 mL
2 tbsp	vegetable oil	30 mL
½ tsp	salt	2 mL
¼ to ½ tsp	hot pepper flakes	1 to 2 mL

1. In a medium bowl, combine chicken with garlic, 1 tbsp (15 mL) of the fish sauce, soy sauce, sugar and cornstarch. Mix well and set aside for 15 to 20 minutes. Or cover and refrigerate for up to 1 day.

2. In mini food processor or blender, combine onion, lemongrass and stock and process until fairly smooth.

3. Heat oil in a medium skillet over medium heat until very hot. Add marinated chicken and toss well. Add lemongrass mixture and cook, tossing often, until chicken is light golden. Add salt and hot pepper flakes and remaining 1 tbsp (15 mL) of fish sauce and cook, tossing occasionally, until chicken is no longer pink inside for breasts or juices run clear when pierced for thighs, 3 to 4 minutes. Transfer to a serving dish and serve hot or warm.

Chicken Stir-Fried with Fresh Ginger

Toss a few ingredients with strips of chicken, give them a few turns in a hot pan and you have a flavor-filled dish to serve with rice or toss with noodles. If you have any left, tuck it into a small baguette the next day, along with a tangle of pickled carrots and a sprinkling of fresh herbs and you'll have Banh Mi (page 26), a fabulous sub sandwich for lunch.

Serves 4		

2 tbsp	fish sauce	30 mL
1 tbsp	soy sauce	15 mL
1 tbsp	liquid honey or brown sugar	15 mL
½ tsp	salt	2 mL
¼ tsp	freshly ground black pepper	1 mL
12 oz	boneless, skinless chicken thighs, cut into long thin strips, or boneless, skinless chicken breasts, cut into big bite-size chunks	375 g
2 tbsp	vegetable oil	30 mL
2 tbsp	finely chopped fresh gingerroot	30 mL
2 tbsp	finely chopped green onion	30 mL

1. In a medium bowl, combine fish sauce, soy sauce, honey, salt and pepper and stir to mix everything well. Add chicken and toss to coat with seasonings. Set aside for 15 to 20 minutes. Or cover and refrigerate for up to 1 day.

2. Heat oil in a medium skillet over high heat until a bit of ginger sizzles at once. Add chicken and marinade and cook until chicken is golden brown on one side, 1 to 2 minutes. Toss well, add ginger and toss again. Cook, tossing occasionally, until chicken is nicely browned and no longer pink inside for breasts or juices run clear when pierced for thighs, 5 to 7 minutes. Transfer to a serving dish, sprinkle with green onion and serve hot or warm.

Chicken Curry with Sweet Potatoes and Lime Pepper–Salt Dipping Sauce

Make this curry and enjoy it in traditional Vietnamese style, accompanied by a warm, crusty baguette, perfect for dipping in the luscious and fragrant sauce. It's also wonderful with rice and other dishes, as well as over cooked rice noodles in a big bowl. Vietnamese cooks make it with potatoes, taro root and carrots, as well as sweet potatoes. I love it with chunks of butternut squash or kabocha, a small pumpkin with a bumpy greenish orange skin.

◇◇

Serves 6 to 8

Tip

If you want to prepare *ca ri ga* in advance, omit the sweet potatoes and add them when you reheat the curry, cooking them until they are tender. You'll find the curry flavors blossom wonderfully when the sauce has the chance to sit overnight in the refrigerator.

2 tbsp	vegetable oil	30 mL
1 tbsp	coarsely chopped garlic	15 mL
1 cup	sliced onion or shallots	250 mL
2	stalks fresh lemongrass, trimmed and cut into 2-inch (5 cm) lengths (see Tip, right)	2
5	slices fresh gingerroot	5
3 tbsp	curry powder	45 mL
1½ lbs	whole bone-in chicken thighs or legs, or 1 lb (500 g) boneless, skinless chicken breasts or thighs, cut into big bite-size chunks	750 g
2 tbsp	fish sauce	30 mL
1 tsp	granulated sugar	5 mL
½ tsp	salt	2 mL
1 tsp	hot pepper flakes or chile-garlic sauce	5 mL
2¾ cups	Chicken Stock (page 216), store-bought or water	675 mL
1	can (14 oz/400 mL) unsweetened coconut milk (about 1½ cups/375 mL)	1
2½ cups	chunks peeled sweet potatoes or carrots	625 mL
	Lime Pepper–Salt Dipping Sauce (page 203) or 2 tbsp (30 mL) freshly squeezed lime juice	

1. In a large, deep saucepan or Dutch oven, heat oil over medium-high heat for 1 minute. Add garlic, onion, lemongrass and ginger and toss well. Add curry powder and cook, tossing often, until herbs are fragrant and onion is translucent, 1 to 2 minutes.

Tip

To prepare lemongrass, trim to about 4 inches (10 cm) from the rounded base and discard the grassy tops and any very dry and brown outer portions. Slice the lemongrass crosswise into thin rounds and then mince them. Or check the freezer at your Asian market for wonderful finely ground and then frozen lemongrass imported from Vietnam.

2. Add chicken, spreading out in one layer if you can and cook for 1 minute. Toss well and cook until chicken changes color and begins to brown. Add fish sauce, sugar, salt and hot pepper flakes and toss again. Add stock and bring to a boil. Reduce heat to maintain a lively simmer and cook, stirring occasionally, for 10 minutes.

3. Add coconut milk and sweet potatoes and simmer until sweet potatoes are tender and chicken is no longer pink inside, 10 to 15 minutes. Remove lemongrass chunks and discard. Transfer chicken and sauce to a serving bowl and serve hot or warm. Provide a tiny dish of Lime Pepper–Salt Dipping Sauce for each guest. (Or stir the lime juice into the curry right after removing the lemongrass chunks.)

◇ Vietnamese Tales

Like all Asian nations, Vietnam's cuisine centers on rice, with a varied and imaginative array of highly seasoned dishes to accompany the beloved grain. Served in rice bowls and eaten with chopsticks, milled white rice cooked without seasonings anchors traditional meals at breakfast, lunch and dinner. Rice cultivation centers in the Red River Delta in the North and the Mekong Delta in the South. Northern cooking includes hearty and robust dishes, such as the signature beef noodle dish, *pho*, and grilled pork patties known as *bun cha ha noi*. Southern cuisine reflects the warmer climate and extended growing season with an emphasis on an abundance of fresh vegetables and fragrant herbs, and a taste for bright, sweet and tangy flavors. Central Vietnam includes the ancient capital city of Hue, where the tradition of serving numerous small specialty dishes at one meal reflects a royal cuisine of centuries past. With Vietnam's long and curving coastline and major rivers, it's no wonder that fish, shellfish and seafood, fresh and preserved, are central and cherished features of the country's cuisine.

Hainan Chicken and Rice with Ginger-Lime Dipping Sauce

This popular one-dish meal consists of chunks of perfectly poached chicken, rice cooked in the stock created by cooking the chicken and a bowl of the same broth to savor on the side. In Vietnam it's easy to find Hainan chicken and rice in specialty restaurants as well as in homes. In either place, it's traditionally served with a ginger dipping sauce and crispy shallots, as well as cucumbers and fresh herbs. Each accompaniment works beautifully to brighten and balance the rich, mild flavors of the dish. You can make this at home with minimal effort and wonderful results.

◇◇◇

Serves 4 to 6

Variation

Instead of Ginger-Lime Dipping Sauce, you could serve the chicken with Everyday Dipping Sauce (page 200), Hoisin-Peanut Dipping Sauce (page 206) or Lime Pepper–Salt Dipping Sauce (page 203).

♦ Large saucepan with tight-fitting lid

Chicken

3 lbs	boneless, skinless chicken breasts	1.5 kg
6 cups	Chicken Stock (page 216) or store-bought	1.5 L
10	slices fresh gingerroot	10
2 tsp	salt	10 mL
	Handful cilantro leaves	
	Handful *rau ram* leaves, optional	
	Crispy Shallots (page 213)	
	Ginger-Lime Dipping Sauce (page 202)	

Rice

3 tbsp	vegetable oil or rendered chicken fat	45 mL
1 tbsp	chopped garlic	15 mL
5	thin slices or 2 tbsp (30 mL) finely chopped fresh gingerroot	5
2 cups	long-grain rice, such as jasmine	500 mL
1 tsp	salt	5 mL

1. In large saucepan with tight-fitting lid, combine chicken with stock, ginger and salt. Bring to a boil over medium heat and then adjust the heat to maintain a gentle simmer. Cook, skimming the stock occasionally to remove any foam that rises to the surface, until chicken is cooked through and no longer pink inside but still tender, about 25 minutes. While chicken cooks, prepare Ginger-Lime Dipping Sauce and set aside until serving time.

2. When chicken is cooked and no longer pink inside, transfer to a bowl or platter to cool. Measure out 2¼ cups (550 mL) of the chicken stock and set aside for cooking the rice. (You can serve any remaining stock alongside the rice, in small bowls, garnished with sliced green onions, or save for another meal.)

3. *Rice:* Heat oil in a medium saucepan over medium-high heat for 1 minute. Add garlic and ginger and cook, tossing once or twice, for 1 minute. Add rice and salt and cook, stirring often, until rice is shiny and white, 2 to 3 minutes. Add reserved chicken stock, stir well and bring to a lively boil. Reduce heat to maintain a gentle simmer, cover and cook, stirring occasionally, until rice is tender, 20 to 25 minutes. Remove from heat and let stand for 10 minutes or so. Meanwhile, chop chicken into big chunks.

4. To serve, place chicken and small bowl of Ginger-Lime Sauce on one side of a serving platter and mound rice on the other side. Garnish the rice with cilantro leaves, *rau ram* leaves, if using, and Crispy Shallots. Serve hot, warm or at room temperature.

◇ Vietnamese Tales

The chunk of southern China known as Hainan Island sits in the center of the Gulf of Tonkin, across the hauntingly beautiful Ha Long Bay from northern Vietnam. Hainan Island's namesake dish is enjoyed all over Southeast Asia. In Vietnam it's easy to find Hainan chicken and rice in restaurants, served with the refreshing herb *rau ram* and a vibrant ginger sauce, *nuoc mam gung*. Vietnamese cooks often prepare this for special occasions, using the freshest, most flavorful chicken they can find, and taking care to create a clear, fragrant broth. Vietnam's neighbors adore this dish, preparing it in the same way, but accompanying it with different sauces: a pungent fermented soybean-ginger sauce in Thailand, and a trio of chile sauce, fresh ginger sauce and dark sweet soy sauce coming on the side with Hainan Chicken Rice in Singapore. Each works beautifully to brighten and balance the rich, mild flavors of the dish.

Chicken Simmered in Caramel Sauce

After you've made this lovely dish, you'll understand why the clay pot cooking method called *kho* holds such a beloved place on the Vietnamese table. Pork, chicken, fish steaks and even shrimp are all cooked in this manner: simmered until tender and permeated with a luxurious, reddish brown essence of caramelized sugar and salty fish sauce, spiked with black pepper or chiles. By simmering substantial ingredients such as meat or fish in a clay pot, Vietnamese cooks create enormous flavor for a hungry family while economizing on food and fuel. You will adore this dish, whether you make it as I do in a small sturdy saucepan or a deep skillet on a conventional stove, or in a traditional clay pot on a charcoal stove.

Serves 4 to 6

Tips

The sauce will thicken a bit once the dish cools, so add a bit of water or stock to correct its texture if you are reheating this dish.

Look for clay pots or sand pots in Asian markets in a wide variety of sizes. You can use them on top of the stove, but take care to use medium-low to medium heat, and to avoid adding cold liquid to the clay pot when it is hot to prevent cracking.

1½ lbs	boneless, skinless chicken thighs	750 g
2 tbsp	vegetable oil	30 mL
3 tbsp	finely chopped fresh gingerroot	45 mL
2 tbsp	chopped shallots or onion	30 mL
1 tbsp	chopped garlic	15 mL
2 tbsp	fish sauce	30 mL
2 tbsp	brown sugar or palm sugar	30 mL
1 tbsp	granulated sugar	15 mL
½ tsp	salt	2 mL
½ tsp	freshly ground black pepper	2 mL
1 tsp	hot pepper flakes	5 mL
¼ cup	water	60 mL
3	green onions, trimmed and cut into 2-inch (5 cm) lengths	3

1. Chop chicken into big chunks by halving each thigh and then cutting each half into quarters. In a large, deep skillet or a large saucepan, heat oil over medium-high heat until a bit of garlic sizzles at once. Add chicken and cook, tossing once or twice, about 2 minutes.

2. Push meat to sides of pan and add ginger, shallots and garlic to middle of pan. Cook for about 1 minute and then toss well. Add fish sauce, brown and granulated sugars, salt, pepper and hot pepper flakes and toss to mix everything well. Let sauce come to a strong boil and begin to thicken and then add water. Adjust heat to maintain a lively simmer and then cook chicken, tossing occasionally, until sauce is a handsome reddish brown syrup and chicken juices run clear when pierced, 10 to 15 minutes. Add green onions and toss well. Transfer to a serving dish and serve hot or warm.

Five-Spice Roast Chicken

The rich, handsome color of Five-Spice Roast Chicken promises a deep, inviting flavor. One bite and I think you will agree that it delivers on that promise. You can roast a whole chicken or small Cornish hens in this way, but I love to cook this with chicken legs and thighs. If you like, serve this hot from the oven along with Sticky Rice (page 144) and Chopped Watercress Salad with Peanuts (page 122) or Spinach Sautéed with Garlic and Pepper (page 134).

Serves 4 to 6

Tip

Use any leftovers in Summer Rolls (page 16) or in Banh Mi (page 26).

¼ cup	soy sauce	60 mL
2 tbsp	fish sauce	30 mL
1 tbsp	Asian sesame oil	15 mL
1 tbsp	brown sugar or granulated sugar	15 mL
2 tsp	five-spice powder	10 mL
½ tsp	salt	2 mL
1 tbsp	finely chopped garlic	15 mL
2 tsp	finely chopped gingerroot	10 mL
3½ lbs	bone-in chicken legs and thighs, or chicken wings	1.75 kg

1. In a large bowl, combine soy sauce, fish sauce, sesame oil, sugar, five-spice powder and salt and stir to mix well. Stir in garlic and ginger and then add chicken pieces, turning to coat all sides with marinade. Cover and refrigerate for at least 1 hour or overnight. Turn the pieces occasionally so that the marinade coats them evenly.

2. Preheat oven to 375°F (190°C). Place chicken in a roasting pan and roast until richly browned and juices run clear when pierced, 30 to 45 minutes. Transfer to a serving platter and serve hot, warm or at room temperature.

Omelet with Crabmeat and Green Onions

Eggs aren't just for breakfast in Vietnam and that means more chances to enjoy speedy, satisfying inspirations like this little omelet. It's worthy of center stage at lunchtime, or a costarring role at supper with rice and other dishes. The omelet is fabulous with Everyday Dipping Sauce (page 200) and a warm baguette. For brunch, accompany it with fresh pineapple, biscuits and honey and steaming cups of sweet, strong coffee, Vietnamese-style (page 192).

◇◇◇

Serves 2 to 4

Tip

You could prepare this in advance, beating the eggs with fish sauce in a medium bowl, and combining the crabmeat, green onion, salt and pepper in another bowl. Cover both and refrigerate until you are ready to cook.

4	eggs	4
1 tbsp	fish sauce	15 mL
2 tbsp	vegetable oil, divided	30 mL
4 oz	cooked lump crabmeat, or one 6-oz (170 g) can, drained (about ¾ cup/175 mL)	125 g
1 tbsp	thinly sliced green onion	15 mL
¼ tsp	salt	1 mL
	Generous pinch of freshly ground black pepper	

1. In a medium bowl, combine eggs and fish sauce, beat well and set aside.

2. Heat 1 tbsp (15 mL) of the oil in a medium skillet over medium-high heat for 1 minute. Add crabmeat, green onion, salt and pepper and cook, tossing gently, until heated and fragrant, 1 to 2 minutes. Transfer to a small bowl and place by the stove.

3. Add remaining 1 tbsp (15 mL) of oil to the pan and heat until a bit of egg sizzles and blooms at once. Add eggs and cook, gently pulling cooked egg toward center of pan so that most of the uncooked egg spreads out in the hot pan. When the omelet is lightly browned on the bottom and fairly set on top, spread crabmeat mixture over half. Gently fold other half over crab-covered side and transfer to a plate. Serve hot or warm.

Egg Pancake with Crabmeat and Cilantro

Bright and sunny on the serving plate, this swiftly prepped and cooked dish is simply satisfying and equally worthy as a simple main course or a pleasing part of a menu created to go with rice. Fresh crabmeat? Lovely! But you can use canned or frozen crabmeat here, too. Serve as is, or accompany this dish with Sriracha sauce or another hot chile sauce, or Everyday Dipping Sauce (page 200).

◇◇

Serves 4

4	large eggs	4
½ cup	crabmeat	125 mL
2 tsp	fish sauce	10 mL
⅓ cup	coarsely chopped cilantro leaves	75 mL
¼ cup	finely chopped green onions	60 mL
½ tsp	salt	2 mL
2 tbsp	vegetable oil	30 mL

1. In a medium bowl, beat eggs well with a fork or whisk. Add crabmeat, fish sauce, cilantro leaves, green onion and salt and stir gently, just enough to mix everything well.

2. In a large skillet or wok, heat oil over medium-high heat until very hot and a bit of green onion sizzles at once. Add egg and crab mixture and spread to cover surface of pan. Cook, undisturbed, for 1 minute. As omelet begins to set, use a spoon to work your way around pan, pulling cooked edges toward the center so that some of the uncooked egg spreads out in the hot pan, 2 to 3 minutes.

3. When almost all the omelet is set and cooked, gently lift on one side with a large spatula and flip over so uncooked side can finish cooking, about 1 minute. When this side has set and turned a nice delicate brown, gently slide out onto a serving plate. Serve hot or warm.

Egg Pancake with Ground Pork

Eggs for breakfast? Sure, but why not morning, noon and night as well? Vietnamese cooks follow the Asian wisdom that eggs are too wonderful to be restricted to one meal. This delicious omelet can be a main course with a steamed or stir-fried vegetable and rice, or one of an array of dishes for a rice-centered feast. I love it with a little Sriracha sauce or a bowl of Everyday Dipping Sauce (page 200) to make its satisfying flavors dazzling and memorable.

Serves 4

Tip

Use your imagination to enhance this simple, speedy dish with chopped fresh herbs or vegetables that cook quickly. Stir in a few tablespoons (30 mL) of fresh dill or basil, finely diced red bell pepper or minced ham for a pleasing variation.

4	large eggs	4
4 oz	ground pork	125 g
2 tsp	Asian fish sauce	10 mL
½ tsp	salt	2 mL
¼ tsp	freshly ground black pepper	1 mL
2 tbsp	vegetable oil	30 mL
2 tbsp	thinly sliced green onions	30 mL

1. In a medium bowl, beat eggs well with a fork or a whisk. Add pork, fish sauce, salt and pepper and stir well until pork breaks up into small bits evenly distributed throughout the egg mixture.

2. In a large skillet or a wok, heat oil over medium-high heat until a bit of egg blooms and sizzles at once. Pour in egg mixture and tilt pan to spread out evenly over hot surface. Let cook, undisturbed, until edges set, beginning to brown and puffing up a bit. Gently pull on section toward the middle, using your spatula to lift it and allowing the liquid egg mixture to flow under the cooked portion and onto the hot pan. As omelet begins to set, use a spoon to work your way around pan, pulling cooked edges toward the center so that some of the uncooked egg spreads out in the hot pan, 2 to 3 minutes.

Tip

If you have leftovers, cover and refrigerate for up to 1 day. Then slice into thin strips and toss them into Fried Rice with Sweet Chinese Sausage, Cilantro and Peas (page 148), or a simplified version of fried rice, made without meat.

3. When omelet is set and firm with only a little liquid remaining on the surface, gently turn over to cook other side on the hot pan's surface. If difficult to turn, set a dinner plate over skillet and placing a hand on the dinner plate, flip pan over so omelet drops onto the plate. Slide back into pan, so cooked surface is visible and bottom surface has chance to cook. Cook just until bottom side has browned and set, less than 1 minute. Slide omelet onto a serving platter and serve hot or warm.

◇ Vietnamese Tales

Like all savory dishes within Vietnamese cuisine, this omelet benefits from a generous splash of fish sauce, known in Vietnamese as *nuoc mam*. Made by salting anchovies or other small saltwater fish, this ubiquitous condiment adds complexity and salty depth to soups, stews, curries, salads, sandwiches and snacks. In addition to its use in flavoring dishes like this everyday omelet, it shines as the central ingredient in *nuoc cham* (see Everyday Dipping Sauce, page 200), the dipping sauce that delivers a sparkling sweet-sour-salty flavor to many Vietnamese dishes. Asian markets carry a variety of brands of fish sauce, most of which are imported from Thailand, though increasing numbers now come from Vietnam. Many brands feature a map of Vietnam and the name Phu Quoc on the label. Phu Quoc is an island off the Vietnamese mainland, which is legendary for the high quality of fish sauce produced there. A particular bottle may have that name without being an actual product of the island. As a general rule, choose a more expensive brand sold in a glass bottle. Check supermarkets for fish sauce in smaller-size glass bottles, and keep it on the counter as it needs no refrigeration and you will have it handy for cooking great Vietnamese food.

Hearty Egg Pancake with Ground Pork, Bean Thread Noodles and Cloud Ear Mushrooms

Order *com tam bi* in a Vietnamese café serving rice dishes and you'll get a fabulous feast of rice along with shredded pork, peppery pork chops and a chunk of this tasty omelet, which is called *cha trung* when served by itself. It's meaty and hearty, great with rice and other dishes, Vietnamese-style. Traditionally this dish is steamed, but baking in the oven works well, too. For the classic Vietnamese plate lunch, see Plate Lunch, Vietnamese-Style (page 153), which includes this tasty pork meat loaf along with rice and Everyday Dipping Sauce.

◇◇◇

Serves 6 to 8

Tips

You could also bake this in a 9-inch (23 cm) square or round cake pan and then cut into squares or wedges after it has cooled.

I love this tucked into a Banh Mi (page 26) or served with Everyday Dipping Sauce (page 200) or Ginger-Lime Dipping Sauce (page 202) and fried rice.

♦ 9- by 5-inch (23 by 12.5 cm) loaf pan, generously greased (see Tips, left)

2 oz	dried bean thread noodles (approx.)	60 g
1/3 cup	dried cloud ear mushrooms or 5 dried Chinese mushrooms (approx.), optional	75 mL
5	eggs	5
4 oz	ground pork	125 g
1 tbsp	fish sauce	15 mL
1/2 tsp	salt	2 mL
1/2 tsp	freshly ground black pepper	2 mL
3 tbsp	finely chopped green onion	45 mL
2 tbsp	vegetable oil	30 mL

1. Place bean thread noodles and dried mushrooms, if using, in a medium bowl and cover with warm water. Set aside to soften for 10 to 20 minutes. Preheat oven to 350°F (180°C).

2. Meanwhile, beat eggs in a medium bowl. Add pork and stir well with a fork to break up into small pieces. Stir in fish sauce, salt, pepper and green onion and set aside.

3. When noodles are soft and clear, drain and rinse well with cool water. Transfer to a cutting board and chop into 2-inch (5 cm) lengths. Drain softened mushrooms, cut away and discard any hard lumps or stems and cut into thin strips. Add noodles and mushrooms to eggs and pork and mix everything together well.

Recipe continues on page 65...

Summer Rolls with Shrimp and Mint (page 16)
and Tangy Brown Bean Dipping Sauce (page 204)

Banh Mi (page 26)

Sweet and Tangy Soup with Pineapple,
Tamarind and Shrimp (page 44)

Chicken Curry with Sweet Potatoes (page 54)
and Lime Pepper–Salt Dipping Sauce (page 203)

Shaking Beef with Purple Onions
and Watercress (page 72)

Grilled Lemongrass Pork with Rice Noodles and
Peanuts (page 86) and Everyday Dipping Sauce (page 200)

4. Pour egg mixture into prepared loaf pan and smooth out into an even layer. Bake in preheated oven until puffed up, golden and firm, 20 to 30 minutes. Let cool to room temperature. Using a butter knife and a spatula, carefully loosen baked egg loaf from pan on all sides and on bottom. Gently turn out onto a plate and set top side up. Serve at room temperature. Cut into 1-inch (2.5 cm) slices.

5. To keep on hand, wrap well and refrigerate for up to 2 days. Warm gently in a covered skillet over low heat, or let come to room temperature before serving.

◈ Vietnamese Tales

This hearty dish, somewhere between a meat loaf, a hearty custard and a omelet, is a cherished accompaniment to broken rice, a form of rice that grew from a frugal use of rice grains damaged in the milling process into a beloved variation on everyday rice. Known as *com tam*, broken rice is cooked in the same manner as whole rice, but its texture is soft, and over time it came to be viewed as a pleasing alternative rather than an inferior form of intact grade-A rice. Look for it in Asian markets catering to Vietnamese clientele, and on menus in Vietnamese cafés, served with this dish and other components of a classic plate lunch, Vietnamese-style.

Beef and Pork

Beef is such a big deal in Vietnam that it has its own ritual: the special occasion restaurant meal known as bo bay mon. It's translated as "seven-course beef" or "beef seven ways," and if you see it featured at a Vietnamese dining establishment, I recommend you treat yourself. This chapter doesn't quite have seven courses of beef, but it comes close. And Vietnam's pork dishes are so beloved, they are not to be left in the shadow for lack of their own restaurant legend.

Delicious Lemongrass Burgers (page 70) are fabulous with either pork or beef. Pork in Caramel Sauce (page 83) is a classic southern braise that seems impossibly good for something so easy to prepare. If you can call in some helpers, put on a little grill fest featuring Grilled Pork Patties with Lettuce, Noodles and Fresh Herbs, Hanoi-Style (page 80). It's my version of the street-food standout, bun cha ha noi. Once you have the grill going, why not put together a few skewers of Lemongrass Beef (page 68), so that you have lots of smoke-kissed flavors to share with friends.

If you have access to a Chinese-style barbecue shop, you can buy sweet, red-tinged barbecued pork to enjoy with rice or noodle soups. If you don't or if you enjoy a most rewarding DIY project, cook up a batch of Char Shiu-Style Pork (page 88) to keep on hand for noodle dishes, Banh Mi (page 26) and fried rice.

Lemongrass Beef, Grilled or Sautéed

Lemongrass beef is definitely on the short list of almost-irresistible Vietnamese dishes. You can grill the beef on skewers, restaurant-style, or quickly sauté it in a hot pan and get it on the table fast. I enjoy using lemongrass beef in place of the roast chicken for Big Cool Noodle Bowl (page 178), transforming it into the Vietnamese noodle classic *bun bo xa*.

Serves 4 to 6

Tip

You will need 2 to 3 stalks of fresh lemongrass, trimmed (see Tip, page 55) and chopped. Finely ground lemongrass is now available frozen in small and large containers imported from Vietnam. Convenient and of high quality, it's perfect for busy days or anytime fresh lemongrass is difficult to find.

♦ 15 to 20 bamboo skewers, soaked in water for at least 30 minutes
♦ Mini food processor or blender

1 lb	boneless beef, such as tri-tip or sirloin tip	500 g
3 tbsp	finely chopped fresh lemongrass	45 mL
1 tbsp	chopped garlic	15 mL
1 tbsp	chopped shallots or onion	15 mL
2 tbsp	fish sauce	30 mL
1 tbsp	granulated sugar	15 mL
1 tsp	soy sauce	5 mL
1 tsp	Asian sesame oil	5 mL

1. Slice beef thinly into strips about 2 inches (5 cm) long and place in a medium bowl.

2. In mini food processor or blender, combine lemongrass, garlic, shallots, fish sauce, sugar, soy sauce and sesame oil and blend until fairly smooth. (Add a little water if needed to move the blades.) Transfer marinade to bowl, toss beef to coat evenly and set aside for 30 minutes to 1 hour or cover and refrigerate for up to 1 day.

3. Thread beef onto bamboo skewers, pushing pieces together to fill most of the skewer and leaving about 2 inches (5 cm) at each end. Preheat gas or charcoal barbecue grill to medium heat or preheat broiler. To grill, place skewers on hot grill and cook for 1 to 2 minutes on each side, moving skewers off the grill as soon as they are done. To broil, place skewers in a roasting pan and slide under broiler until cooked, 1 to 2 minutes per side. You could also sauté marinated beef quickly in a hot pan with 2 tbsp (30 mL) of oil, turning once. Transfer beef to a serving platter and serve hot or warm.

Beef Stir-Fried with Asparagus

Although Vietnamese cooks usually prepare meat and vegetables separately, they sometimes stir-fry them together, just as people do in China and throughout Southeast Asia. Beef is often paired with cauliflower or broccoli florets, thin slices of bamboo or celery, or asparagus. This dish cooks in a flash, each component complementing the other and inviting you to cook a pot of rice and pull up a chair. There is not much sauce, but the flavors are simple and clear. At my house we add a bowl of Everyday Dipping Sauce (page 200) for a fast, satisfying meal, but in Vietnam this would be one of many dishes served at a rice-centered meal.

◇◇

Serves 4

Variation

Instead of asparagus, use 8 oz (250 g) broccoli florets or 3 to 4 stalks celery. Cut broccoli florets into bite-size pieces. Or trim both ends of celery stalks and pull off stringy outer layer with a paring knife or a vegetable peeler, then cut diagonally into thin pieces.

4 oz	boneless beef, such as flank steak, tri-tip or sirloin, thinly sliced	125 g
2 tbsp	fish sauce, divided	30 mL
1 tbsp	soy sauce	15 mL
½ tsp	freshly ground black pepper	2 mL
½ tsp	granulated sugar	2 mL
8 oz	asparagus	250 g
2 tbsp	vegetable oil	30 mL
1 tbsp	chopped garlic	15 mL
2 tbsp	water	30 mL
2 tbsp	thinly sliced green onion	30 mL

1. In a medium bowl, combine beef with 1 tbsp (15 mL) of the fish sauce, soy sauce, black pepper and sugar and toss to mix well. Set aside for 15 to 20 minutes.

2. Meanwhile, trim asparagus, breaking off grayish base of each stalk and cutting green upper portion diagonally into 2-inch (5 cm) lengths. You should have about 2 cups (500 mL) of sliced vegetables. Set aside.

3. In a large skillet or a wok, heat oil over high heat for 30 seconds. Add garlic and toss well. Scatter beef in pan and cook briefly on one side, then toss once to sear other side. Add asparagus and toss well. Add remaining fish sauce, water and green onion. Cook, tossing once or twice, until asparagus is shiny and tender, but not soft, about 1 minute. Transfer to a serving dish and serve hot or warm.

Delicious Lemongrass Burgers with Beef or Pork

A handful of inspired Vietnamese seasonings can make your same old burger extraordinary. Make this with beef and you have one of the parade of beef dishes composing *bo bay mon*, a special-occasion feast originating in northern Vietnam. Use ground pork and you have *cha heo*, a lemongrass-infused patty enjoyed as a street-food snack throughout the Mekong Delta.

Serves 4 to 6

Makes 12 small patties

Tip

This recipe makes a dozen snack-size burgers, great for wrapping in lettuce-and-herb packets for dipping, or simply for nibbling along with other starters. If you prefer, you can make 24 meatballs, or double the recipe to make 4 standard-size burgers.

8 oz	ground beef or pork	250 g
2 tbsp	finely chopped fresh lemongrass	30 mL
2 tbsp	finely chopped green onion	30 mL
2 tbsp	finely chopped fresh cilantro	30 mL
1 tbsp	finely chopped garlic	15 mL
1 tbsp	vegetable oil	15 mL
1 tbsp	fish sauce	15 mL
2 tsp	soy sauce	10 mL
½ tsp	granulated sugar	2 mL
½ tsp	salt	2 mL
¼ tsp	freshly ground black pepper	1 mL

Accompaniments

Everyday Dipping Sauce (page 200)

Everyday Herb and Salad Plate (page 116), made with lettuce cups, cilantro and mint

1. In a medium bowl, combine ground beef or pork with lemongrass, green onion, cilantro, garlic, oil, fish sauce, soy sauce, sugar, salt and pepper and mix well. Set aside to season for at least 15 minutes or refrigerate for as long as 1 day.

2. Preheat gas or charcoal barbecue grill to medium heat or preheat broiler. Divide meat mixture into 12 chunks and shape each into a small patty about 2 inches (5 cm) in diameter. Cook on hot grill until nicely browned and no longer pink, 3 to 4 minutes on each side. To broil, place in a roasting pan and slide under broiler until cooked, 3 to 4 minutes per side. You could also cook the patties quickly in a hot pan with 1 or 2 tbsp (15 to 30 mL) of oil, turning once. Serve hot, warm or at room temperature with Everyday Dipping Sauce and Everyday Herb and Salad Plate, so guests can make small bundles for dipping into the sauce.

Beef Stir-Fried with Bamboo Shoots and Sesame Seeds

You'll want to keep bamboo shoots on hand once you've enjoyed this robust and tasty dish. Beloved in Asian cuisines for their heft, smooth crunchiness and gift for receiving and amplifying flavors, they make a great addition to many stir-fries, curries and soups. This classic combination pairs bamboo shoots with toasted sesame seeds for a double delight of texture and flavor.

Serves 4

3 tbsp	white sesame seeds	45 mL
1 tbsp	Asian fish sauce	15 mL
1 tsp	granulated sugar	5 mL
½ tsp	salt	2 mL
¼ tsp	freshly ground black pepper	1 mL
2 tbsp	vegetable oil	30 mL
12 oz	thinly sliced beef, such as sirloin, rib-eye or flank steak	375 g
1 tbsp	chopped garlic	15 mL
1 cup	bamboo slices, rinsed and drained	250 mL
⅓ cup	thinly sliced green onions	75 mL

1. Heat a medium saucepan over medium-high heat until hot. Add sesame seeds and reduce heat to medium. Toast sesame seeds, stirring and tossing often to help brown gently and evenly without burning, 1 to 2 minutes. When just golden and fragrant, transfer to a saucer and set aside and let cool.

2. In a small bowl, combine fish sauce, sugar, salt and pepper. Stir well and leave spoon in bowl. Set bowl by stove.

3. Heat a wok or a large deep skillet over medium-high heat. Add oil and swirl to coat pan. When a bit of garlic sizzles at once, scatter in beef and spread out in a single layer. Cook, undisturbed, until edges change color and are done to your liking, 1 to 2 minutes. Toss well. Add garlic and cook for 1 minute more.

4. Add bamboo slices and toss well. Stir fish sauce mixture well and add to pan and toss well. Add green onions and cook for 1 minute more. Add sesame seeds and toss well. Transfer mixture to a serving plate. Serve hot or warm.

Shaking Beef with Purple Onions and Watercress

A few easy steps and you'll have a hearty centerpiece for a quick meal with rice, or a spectacular starter. Use any kind of vinegar you like and try serving Shaking Beef with little saucers of Lime Pepper–Salt Dipping Sauce (203) for an extra burst of flavor. This popular dish is traditionally served with Red Rice (page 143), a simple fried rice with a generous dollop of tomato paste which transforms everyday white rice into a handsomely colored accompaniment for this special-occasion dish. I love a dish of sliced, chilled spears of cucumber served alongside.

Serves 4

Variation

You can use fresh spinach instead of watercress, tearing any large leaves into bite-size pieces. Or try arugula or one of the packaged lettuce mixtures in the produce section.

Beef

12 oz	thickly cut steak, such as New York strip or rib-eye	375 g
1 tbsp	fish sauce	15 mL
2 tsp	soy sauce	10 mL
½ tsp	granulated sugar	2 mL
½ tsp	freshly ground black pepper	2 mL

Watercress Salad

2 tbsp	vinegar	30 mL
1 tsp	vegetable oil	5 mL
1 tsp	granulated sugar	5 mL
½ tsp	salt	2 mL
½ tsp	freshly ground black pepper	2 mL
½ cup	very thin onion slices, preferably purple onion	125 mL
2 cups	bite-size or torn pieces of watercress	500 mL
2 tbsp	vegetable oil	30 mL
2 tbsp	finely chopped garlic	30 mL

1. *Beef:* Cut beef into big, bite-size chunks, about 1 inch (2.5 cm) square. In a medium bowl, combine fish sauce, soy sauce, sugar and pepper and stir well. Add beef, toss to coat evenly and set aside for 20 to 30 minutes while you make the salad. Or cover and refrigerate for up to 1 day.

2. *Watercress Salad:* In a medium bowl, combine vinegar, oil, sugar, salt and pepper and stir well. Add thinly sliced onion and toss with dressing to wilt and soften. Add watercress to the bowl but don't toss yet.

3. Heat oil in a large, heavy skillet over high heat until a bit of garlic sizzles at once. Add beef and let cook on one side, undisturbed, until nicely browned, 1 to 2 minutes. Shake pan to turn meat and cook other surface same way. Add garlic and continue cooking, shaking and searing meat, until evenly browned and done to your liking. Remove pan from heat and set aside while you prepare the serving platter.

4. Toss watercress to coat with dressing and mix with the wilted onions. Arrange the salad on a small serving platter. Scoop up steak, pile in center of watercress salad and serve hot or warm.

◇ Vietnamese Tales

Part of the traditional meat-centric banquet menu known as seven-course beef or *bo bay mon*, this dish calls for a juicy steak, cut into generous chunks and speedily seared in a very hot wok or skillet. The name "shaking beef" provides a recipe instruction for the cook, as this hearty dish gets shaken and tossed about by the cook, who shakes the pan deftly, tossing and turning throughout its fairly brief cooking time. Its simple sugar-and-soy sauce seasoning receives a Vietnamese flourish from the flavorful trio of lime juice, freshly ground pepper and salt traditionally served on the side.

Beef Stew with Lemongrass, Star Anise and Cinnamon

Vietnamese cooks enlivened this French original with herbs and spices, embracing it as a hearty breakfast served over noodles, with rice or with a crisp baguette.

◇◇◇

Serves 4 to 6

Tip

Look for star anise in Asian markets as well as in the spice section of well-appointed supermarkets. These gorgeously shaped and marvelously aromatic spices keep extremely well, so buy a package and transfer the whole star-shaped pods and pieces to a sealed glass jar, and store at room temperature for up to 1 year. If you can't find star anise, you could get by with 1 tsp (5 mL) five-spice powder in its place.

2 lbs	boneless beef, cut into 1½-inch (4 cm) chunks	1 kg
2 tbsp	chopped fresh gingerroot	30 mL
1 tbsp	chopped garlic	15 mL
2 tbsp	Asian fish sauce	30 mL
3	whole star anise (see Tip, left)	3
2	pieces (each about 2 inches/5 cm) cinnamon sticks or 1 tsp (5 mL) ground cinnamon	2
1 tsp	paprika	5 mL
1 tsp	granulated sugar	5 mL
1 tsp	salt	5 mL
½ tsp	ground cloves	2 mL
½ tsp	freshly ground black pepper	2 mL
¼ tsp	hot pepper flakes	1 mL
2	stalks fresh lemongrass	2
3 tbsp	vegetable oil, divided	45 mL
1½ cups	chopped onion	375 mL
5 cups	Chicken Stock (page 216) or store-bought	1.25 L
3	medium carrots, peeled and chopped into 1-inch (2.5 cm) chunks	3

1. In a large bowl, combine beef, ginger, garlic and fish sauce. Stir and mix beef to season meat evenly. Set aside for 20 to 30 minutes.

2. Meanwhile, in a small bowl, combine star anise, cinnamon sticks, paprika, sugar, salt, cloves, pepper and hot pepper flakes and stir to mix well.

3. Trim lemongrass stalks, halving crosswise and discarding top portions. Cut bulbous bottom sections in half lengthwise and press down with side of a chef's knife or cleaver to bruise a bit.

Tip

Like most stews, this cherished Vietnamese one-dish meal develops an even deeper, richer flavor if prepared in advance. If you want to make it ahead, omit the carrots, cool to room temperature, and chill the stew for up to 1 day. To serve, gently reheat the stew, stirring occasionally, until hot. Then bring to a boil, add the carrots, adjust heat to maintain a lively simmer, and cook until carrots are tender. Taste and add a little salt, if needed.

4. Heat 2 tbsp (30 mL) of the oil in a large heavy pot such as a Dutch oven over medium-high heat until a bit of garlic sizzles at once. Add about half the beef and scatter over hot pan's surface, allowing room between pieces. Don't crowd the pan. Let cook, undisturbed, until nicely brown, 1 to 2 minutes. Stir well. Turn and brown other side for 1 to 2 minutes. Remove lightly browned beef from pot and place on a platter by the stove. Repeat with remaining beef.

5. Add remaining oil to pot and heat until a bit of onion sizzles at once. Add onions and toss well. Cook, tossing occasionally, until onions are fragrant and shiny but not browned, 3 to 4 minutes.

6. Add spice mixture and stir to mix with onions. Cook, stirring often, until fragrant, 1 to 2 minutes. Add lemongrass and beef, including any juices on the plate and stir well.

7. Add chicken stock and bring to a lively boil over high heat. Reduce heat to maintain an active simmer, cover and cook, stirring occasionally, until meat is tender and almost done, about 1 hour. Add carrots and cook, covered, until softened and beef is very tender and done to your liking. Remove from heat and let stand, covered, for 10 minutes. Serve hot or warm.

Stir-Fried Beef over Rice Noodles with Fresh Herbs and Crispy Shallots

A small bowl of noodle goodness, this dish is a version of *bun*, the big cool noodle bowls that make a one-dish meal. This Southern street food version draws guests to small one-dish food shops where hot woks cook batch after batch of sizzling beef for each guest's bowl. It's a quick pick-me-up bowl, fueling locals and travellers for a return to the demands of the day. Toss it up and dig in for a super snack or quick lunch.

Serves 4

Tip

Remember the magic words for stir-fry cooking: Prep is key. Since the action happens fast once you heat up the pan, all the chopping, measuring out and serving pieces need to be in place by the stove. Mix up the simple marinade, toss it with the meat and then take care of all the other small tasks while it rests. By the time you've cooked the rice noodles and arranged the accompaniments, you'll be ready to cook and serve in a few minutes flat.

Marinade

1 tbsp	soy sauce	15 mL
1 tbsp	oyster sauce	15 mL
1 tbsp	finely chopped onion	15 mL
1 tsp	finely chopped garlic	5 mL
1 tsp	granulated sugar	5 mL
1 tsp	salt	5 mL
1/2 tsp	freshly ground pepper	2 mL
8 oz	boneless beef, thinly sliced into bite-size pieces	250 g
8 oz	thin dried rice noodles	250 g
2 tbsp	vegetable oil	30 mL

Accompaniments

2 cups	shredded soft lettuce, such as Boston, Bibb or oak leaf	500 mL
1 1/2 cups	coarsely chopped fresh herbs, such as cilantro, basil and mint	375 mL
1 1/2 cups	Everyday Dipping Sauce (page 200)	375 mL
2 cups	bean sprouts	500 mL
1 1/2 cups	sliced peeled cucumbers	375 mL
1 cup	coarsely chopped salted dry-roasted peanuts	250 mL
1 cup	Crispy Shallots (page 213)	250 mL

1. Bring a large covered saucepan of water to a rolling boil over high heat.

Tip

While this traditional beef-over-noodles dish is prepared to order, bowl-by-bowl, you could make one big, generous bowl and then serve out portions to each guest after tossing everything together. A large, shallow bowl would be ideal. Fill the bottom with lettuce and herbs, and season with dipping sauce. Add noodles, bean sprouts and cucumbers, and then stir-fry the beef. Scoop it onto the noodles and herbs, add peanuts and shallots, and serve, tossing everything together well with tongs before portioning it out into big individual serving bowls for each guest.

2. *Marinade:* Meanwhile, in a medium bowl, combine soy sauce, oyster sauce, onion, garlic, sugar, salt and pepper and stir to mix well. Add thinly sliced beef and toss to season evenly with marinade. Set aside for 10 to 15 minutes or cover and refrigerate for up to 1 day.

3. When water is boiling, drop in rice noodles and immediately remove from heat. Let stand until tender and ready to eat, 5 to 7 minutes. Drain, rinse in cold water and then drain well. Return to the saucepan and set aside.

4. Prepare remaining ingredients and set up a preparation spot with everything in easy reach: Serving bowls, noodles and accompaniments.

5. Heat a large deep skillet or a wok over high heat until very hot. Add oil and swirl to coat pan. When a bit of garlic sizzles at once, scatter in meat and spread out into a single layer. Let cook, undisturbed, until edges change color, about 1 minute. Toss well and let meat cook again, undisturbed, for about 30 seconds. Cook, tossing occasionally, until meat is done to your liking, about 2 minutes. Remove from pan and set aside on stove.

6. Divide shredded lettuce and fresh herbs among four bowls. Pour about $1/4$ cup (60 mL) of Everyday Dipping Sauce on lettuce in each bowl. Divide cooked noodles among bowls, covering lettuce and sauce. Scatter a layer of bean sprouts, cucumbers and freshly cooked beef over each bowl. Finish by sprinkling one-quarter of the peanuts and Crispy Shallots over each bowl. Serve at once, inviting guests to toss their noodles well first and offering additional sauce on the side.

Vietnamese Meat Loaf

Make this satisfying dish over the weekend and you can enjoy it in quick hearty meals during the week. Vietnamese-style meat loaf makes a fine addition to Banh Mi (page 26) or a Big Cool Noodle Bowl (page 178). In Vietnamese kitchens, *cha dum* takes many forms, every one of them delicious. It's often steamed in a small bowl, rather than baked. Then it's inverted onto a plate, sliced and served with an array of side dishes and rice. You could also shape the mixture into big meatballs for steaming or pan-frying. Look for *cha dum* as part of the popular Vietnamese celebration meal *bo bay mon* or "seven-course beef."

◇◇

Serves 6

Tip

The dried mushrooms and bean thread noodles add texture and amplify the flavors, but you'll have a tasty dish even if you leave them out.

5	dried Chinese mushrooms, optional	5
1 to 2 oz	dried bean thread noodles, optional	30 to 60 g
1 lb	ground beef or pork, or a mixture of both	500 g
2 tbsp	finely chopped onion or shallots	30 mL
1 tbsp	finely chopped garlic	15 mL
2 tbsp	fish sauce	30 mL
½ tsp	salt	2 mL
½ tsp	freshly ground black pepper	2 mL
1	egg, well beaten	1

1. Place Chinese mushrooms and bean thread noodles, if using, in separate bowls and cover each with warm water. Set aside for 10 to 20 minutes or until flexible enough to cut. Drain both ingredients and transfer to a cutting board. Cut away any hard lumps or stems and chop mushroom caps into small pieces. Pile up noodles and coarsely chop.

2. Preheat oven to 375°F (190°C). In a medium bowl, combine meat with onion, garlic, fish sauce, salt, pepper, egg and chopped mushrooms and noodles. Mix with your hands or two large spoons to combine everything well. Transfer to a small loaf pan, pie pan or heatproof bowl.

3. Bake meat loaf in preheated oven until firm, fragrant and no longer pink, 30 to 40 minutes. Or place pan on tray of a steamer and steam for 30 to 40 minutes. Set meat loaf aside and let cool for 10 minutes or so and then transfer to a serving platter and serve hot, warm or at room temperature. (Or cool to room temperature, cover and refrigerate for up to 2 days.)

Pork and Hard-Boiled Eggs Simmered in Coconut Juice

This classic dish has roots in Chinese clay pot cooking, but the tropical note of green coconut juice used to braise the meat is pure Vietnamese. If your coconut tree is bare, don't fret. Asian markets often carry fresh, clear coconut juice in cans, both as a refreshing drink and as a cooking ingredient. Although this dish takes a while to cook, the prep work is easily and quickly done and then it's a simple matter of letting the pork simmer until your comfort-food stew is ready for savoring, ideally with lots of rice or a wonderful bread. Vietnamese families often include this dish in a feast during Tet, a celebration of the lunar New Year.

◇◇

Serves 6 to 8

Tips

Marbled pork with some fat included makes for a particularly rich version, but even lean pork will give you a wonderful, substantial dish.

Look for *nuoc dua tuoi* on the label of the coconut juice and don't worry if it includes some pulp — traditional cooks include a little young coconut meat in the dish when working from a plump, green coconut fresh off the tree. If you don't have coconut juice, just use Chicken Stock (page 216) or store-bought or water instead.

1½ lbs	boneless pork, cut into 3-inch (7.5 cm) chunks (see Tips, left)	750 g
3½ cups	coconut juice (see Tips, left)	875 mL
3 tbsp	fish sauce	45 mL
2 tbsp	Everyday Caramel Sauce (page 210), Speedy Caramel Sauce (page 211) or brown sugar	30 mL
1 tbsp	finely chopped shallots or onion	15 mL
1 tsp	salt	5 mL
½ tsp	freshly ground black pepper	2 mL
3	hard-boiled eggs	3
3	green onions, cut into 2-inch (5 cm) lengths	3

1. In a large, heavy saucepan, combine pork, coconut juice, fish sauce, Caramel Sauce, shallots, salt and pepper. Bring to a rolling boil over medium-high heat and then reduce heat to maintain an active simmer. Cover and cook until pork is tender and surrounded by a handsome brown sauce, 45 to 50 minutes.

2. Add eggs and green onions to pan and simmer, turning eggs gently occasionally until a handsome brown, about 15 minutes. Remove from heat, remove eggs and halve lengthwise. Carefully return eggs to sauce, transfer everything to a serving bowl and serve hot or warm.

Grilled Pork Patties with Lettuce, Noodles and Fresh Herbs, Hanoi-Style

Incredibly delicious and easy, this brilliant dish is a street-food classic originating in northern Vietnam. The real thing can be had from sidewalk vendors and open-air shops specializing in *bun cha ha noi*, where customers flock as soon as the day's first batch fills the air with its signature grill-fired aroma, an irresistible olfactory invitation. While this home version can't deliver the atmosphere, it makes for a memorable feast and takes only a few minutes to prepare.

◇◇◇

Serves 4 to 6

Tip

Look for fresh bacon or belly pork at the butcher counter in large Asian markets or specialty supermarkets.

Pork

2 tbsp	fish sauce	30 mL
2 tbsp	Everyday Caramel Sauce (page 210), Speedy Caramel Sauce (page 211) or brown sugar	30 mL
2 tsp	vegetable oil	10 mL
1 tsp	salt	5 mL
1 tsp	freshly ground black pepper	5 mL
8 oz	fresh bacon or any boneless pork, sliced ¼ inch (0.5 cm) thick and cut into 3-inch (7.5 cm) pieces (see Tip, left)	250 g
8 oz	ground pork	250 g
¼ cup	finely chopped green onion	60 mL

Accompaniments

4 oz	thin dried rice noodles	125 g
	Triple recipe Everyday Dipping Sauce (page 200), about 1½ cups (375 mL)	
	Everyday Pickled Carrots (page 128)	
3 cups	shredded lettuce leaves	750 mL
½ cup	fresh mint leaves	125 mL
½ cup	fresh cilantro leaves	125 mL
½ cup	chopped dry-roasted salted peanuts	125 mL

Tip

For a classic presentation, immerse the grilled patties and pork strips in a bowl of Everyday Dipping Sauce (page 200) for a few minutes. Then provide each guest with chopsticks or a fork and a small bowl in which to combine the pork with the accompaniments. Or serve the meat hot off the grill with hot sauce or barbecue sauce or with bowls of Everyday Dipping Sauce, a plate of cucumber slices and Sticky Rice (page 144).

1. *Pork:* In a small bowl or cup, combine fish sauce, Caramel Sauce, oil, salt and pepper and stir to mix everything well. Place sliced bacon in one medium bowl and ground pork in another and divide marinade evenly between the two. Turn sliced bacon to coat evenly and set aside. Add green onion to ground pork and mix well. Set both bowls aside for 20 to 30 minutes while you prepare the accompaniments, or cover and refrigerate for up to 1 day.

2. *Accompaniments:* Bring a medium saucepan of water to a rolling boil over high heat. Drop in rice noodles and immediately remove from heat. Let stand until tender and ready to eat, 5 to 7 minutes. Drain, rinse in cold water and then drain well. Return to the saucepan and set aside. Prepare remaining accompaniments and arrange on serving platters.

3. When you are ready to serve *bun cha ha noi*, preheat gas or charcoal barbecue grill to medium heat. Shape ground pork into small patties, using about 2 tbsp (30 mL) for each one. Set aside on a platter and drain marinated sliced pork and place alongside them. Cook sliced pork and patties on the hot grill, turning once or twice, until pleasingly browned and no longer pink. (You could also cook the pork in 2 tbsp/30 mL of vegetable oil in a very hot skillet, or roast in a hot oven until the meat is nicely browned and cooked through.)

4. Transfer meat to a serving platter. Provide each guest with two bowls: a small one for Everyday Dipping Sauce and a medium soup-size bowl for their servings of meat and noodles. Present guests with plates and platters of the meat and accompaniments. Serve each guest $1/4$ cup (60 mL) of Everyday Dipping Sauce in the small bowl, and invite them to combine rice noodles with all other ingredients in the medium bowl and eat with chopsticks or a fork.

Grilled Garlic-Pepper Pork Chops

Sweet and salty, these pork chops fit any menu and can be grilled or roasted in the oven. You could also use them on *com tam*, the classic rice dish popular in Vietnamese restaurants. A sort of blue plate special created to provide a hearty and varied rice meal for people dining alone, *com tam* consists of rice topped with thin strips of sweet-and-salty pork chops like these, a portion of Hearty Egg Pancake with Ground Pork, Bean Thread Noodles and Cloud Ear Mushrooms (page 64) and a sunny-side-up egg. Everyday Dipping Sauce and a garnish of lettuce, cucumber and tomato round out the offerings.

Serves 4 to 6

Tip

If you have leftover Grilled Garlic-Pepper Pork Chops, slice the meat thinly and use it in the Vietnamese submarine sandwich, Banh Mi (page 26).

♦ Mini food processor or blender

2 tbsp	fish sauce	30 mL
1 tbsp	soy sauce	15 mL
2 tbsp	granulated sugar	30 mL
1 tbsp	Everyday Caramel Sauce (page 210), Speedy Caramel Sauce (page 211) or brown sugar	15 mL
1 tbsp	vegetable oil	15 mL
1 tbsp	garlic	15 mL
½ tsp	salt	2 mL
½ tsp	freshly ground black pepper	2 mL
4 to 6	bone-in pork chops (about 2 lbs/1 kg)	4 to 6
	Everyday Dipping Sauce (page 200)	

1. In mini food processor or blender, combine fish sauce, soy sauce, sugar, Caramel Sauce, oil, garlic, salt and pepper and process until fairly smooth.

2. In a medium bowl, combine marinade with pork chops and turn chops to coat them evenly. Set aside for 30 minutes to 1 hour or cover and chill for up to 1 day.

3. Preheat gas or charcoal barbecue grill to medium heat or preheat the oven to 400°F (200°C). Place chops on hot grill and cook, turning once or twice, until nicely browned and just a hint of pink remains in pork. Or roast in preheated oven until just a hint of pink remains in pork. Transfer pork chops to a serving platter and serve whole or let stand on a cutting board for 10 to 15 minutes and then cut into strips. Serve hot, warm or at room temperature with Everyday Dipping Sauce.

Pork in Caramel Sauce

Kho dishes made economic sense in hard times and they make gastronomic sense any time because they taste so good. Marbled pork with some fat is traditional, but lean pork is delicious as well. Clay pots, which are traditionally used for this dish in Vietnam, are lovely, but you can make an outstanding kho dish in a small, sturdy saucepan. Caramel Sauce is perfect here, but even if you use sugar, you'll still have a wonderful dish.

Serves 4 to 6

Tips

To slice the meat thinly, put it in the freezer for up to an hour before you cut it.

Vietnamese cooks often serve this with pickled bean sprouts for a sour counterpoint to the intense sweet-and-salty flavor of the pork and its sauce.

8 oz	boneless pork, thinly sliced (see Tips, left)	250 g
3 tbsp	fish sauce	45 mL
3 tbsp	water	45 mL
2 tbsp	granulated sugar	30 mL
1 tbsp	Everyday Caramel Sauce (page 210), Speedy Caramel Sauce (page 211) or brown sugar	15 mL
½ tsp	freshly ground black pepper	2 mL

1. In a small saucepan or a clay pot, combine pork, fish sauce, water, sugar and Caramel Sauce, stir well and bring to a gentle boil over medium-high heat. Adjust heat to maintain a lively simmer and cook, stirring often, for 8 to 10 minutes. The sauce should be filled with voluptuous, caramel-colored bubbles blooming among the pork pieces and the pork should take on a gorgeous, shiny, caramel hue as it cooks through.

2. Continue cooking until just a hint of pink remains in pork and sauce is satiny, 2 to 3 minutes more. Remove from heat and stir in pepper. Transfer to a small serving dish and serve hot, warm or at room temperature, ideally with lots of rice.

"Cotton" Pork

This dish allows cooks to prepare a generous amount of high quality pork in such a way that it can be kept for a few days and enjoyed in flavor-packed bursts, as a way to season rice, Everyday Rice Porridge (page 150) or buns and sandwiches. This preparation comes from a time when refrigeration was unknown or a luxury. Preserving meat in a tasty and appealing way inspired cooks to invent solutions like this one. Even with the convenience of refrigeration, this dish is still worth making because it is so tasty and pleasing. It gives you something special to draw on when inspiration is lacking and hunger is great.

◇◇

**Makes about
8 oz (250 g)**

Tip

Pork loin makes a good choice for this dish because it's easy to see the grain when it's time to tease and tear the cooked meat into shreds.

1 lb	pork tenderloin (see Tip, left)	500 g
5 tbsp	Asian fish sauce	75 mL

1. Cut pork into large, thick strips, each about 3 inches (7.5 cm) wide and 2 inches (5 cm) thick. Place pieces in a single layer in a saucepan just large enough to hold the meat. You want a snug fit. Add fish sauce and turn to coat meat well. Cover and let stand for 10 minutes. Turn pork pieces over and let stand for 10 minutes more.

2. To cook pork, place pot over medium heat and let fish sauce come to a gentle boil. Adjust heat to maintain a simmer without boiling or burning and cover pot. Cook for 20 minutes, turning occasionally, so meat cooks evenly. When meat is cooked through, remove from heat and transfer to a platter and let cool.

Tip

Also known as pork floss, this preserved meat is popular all over Asia and is sometimes made with sugar for a sweet-and-salty flavor. Store it at room temperature in a covered container. If it hardens beyond a pleasantly chewy state, simmer it in a little water to soften it and then add it to a simple omelet, fried rice or clear soup.

3. When meat is cool enough to touch, place a large skillet on the stove. Pick up a piece of cooked meat and carefully pull apart into the thinnest possible shreds. Press and work to separate into threads and fluff. When you have turned all the chunks of meat into shreds and long bits, transfer some of the pork to the skillet. Heat over medium heat until hot. Spread out meat to cover bottom of skillet. Leave it to release its moisture and become dry and fluffy, turning over and over to encourage that process to happen. You will hear sizzling sounds at first, but as the meat dries out, these will subside. When you hear no more sizzling and feel and see the dryness of the fluffy pork, it is done, 20 to 30 minutes. Remove from heat and continue with any remaining pork. Let cool to room temperature and then cover and refrigerate for up to 1 month.

Grilled Lemongrass Pork with Rice Noodles and Peanuts

This robust and delicious street-food favorite needs only a little time to marinate and a swift session on the grill to produce a memorable, fun-to-eat dish. It's an ideal starter for a summertime grill-centered gathering. Even if you're cooking it indoors on a grill pan or in a hot oven, you'll be thrilled with the luscious flavors and contrasting textures and temperatures these little bundles offer in every bite.

◇◇◇

Serves 4 to 6

Tip

Vietnamese cooks use lightweight wire grill baskets, which flip open for arranging the meat and then flip back over to enclose it while you flip back and forth to cook quickly. Look for these in Asian markets.

♦ Grill basket
♦ Bamboo skewers, soaked in water for 1 hour or metal skewers, optional

Marinade

2	stalks fresh lemongrass	2
3 tbsp	finely chopped shallots or onion	45 mL
1 tbsp	finely chopped garlic	15 mL
2 tbsp	granulated sugar	30 mL
2 tbsp	soy sauce	30 mL
1 tbsp	freshly squeezed lime juice or white vinegar	15 mL
1 tsp	salt	5 mL
1/2 tsp	freshly ground black pepper	2 mL
1 lb	boneless pork, such as pork butt or shoulder	500 g

Accompaniments

8 oz	thin dried rice noodles	250 g
	Scallion Oil (page 214)	
1	head soft lettuce, such as Boston, Bibb, butter or iceberg, separated into cups (see Tips, right)	1
1 cup	sliced peeled cucumbers, cut into matchsticks	250 mL
1 1/2 cups	bean sprouts	375 mL
1 1/2 cups	fresh herb leaves and sprigs of cilantro, basil or mint	375 mL
	Everyday Dipping Sauce (page 200)	
1 1/2 cups	coarsely chopped dry-roasted salted peanuts	375 mL

1. Trim lemongrass, cutting away leafy top half and chopping each stalk in half lengthwise. Cut away and discard hard root portions, leaving only purple-tinged bulb portions. Slice very thinly and chop finely.

Tips

You could also thread the pork on skewers for quick turns as these cook in a flash.

Instead of lettuce cups, you could use soft lettuce, such as oak leaf, separated into leaves for folding into packets.

2. *Marinade:* In a large bowl, combine lemongrass, shallots, garlic, sugar, soy sauce, lime juice, salt and pepper. Using a whisk or a large spoon, stir to mix well.

3. Slice pork against the grain into very thin strips, about 6 inches (15 cm) long. Place in marinade and stir and toss to coat evenly and well. Set aside to marinate for 30 minutes to 1 hour.

4. Meanwhile, bring a large saucepan to a rolling boil over high heat. Drop in rice noodles and immediately remove from heat. Let stand until tender and ready to eat, 5 to 7 minutes. Drain, rinse in cold water and then drain well. Transfer to a shallow bowl or a deep plate and place next to the lettuce cups among accompaniments. Pour about $\frac{1}{4}$ cup (60 mL) of the Scallion Oil over the noodles.

5. Arrange a platter or a tray with small plates and bowls to hold the components of the lettuce cups.

6. Preheat grill or indoor grill to medium. Arrange pork in a grill basket or indoor grill and grill pork just until done but still moist and a little charred, 2 to 4 minutes. Transfer to serving platter with accompaniments and serve hot or warm.

7. *To serve:* Invite guests to make small bundles in each lettuce cup or lettuce leaf (see Tips, left). Each cup would include a small handful of noodles, some lemongrass pork, cucumbers, bean sprouts and herbs, a drizzle of Scallion Oil and a good splash of Everyday Dipping Sauce. Sprinkle with chopped peanuts and enjoy. Or prepare bundles for your guests and serve the ready-to-eat bundles from a tray or platter.

Char Shiu-Style Pork

This luscious, sweet and salty roast pork is a Cantonese classic that has found a home on Asian menus around the world. Buy a supply and keep it in the refrigerator or freezer, or make this streamlined version in your kitchen. Classic *char shiu* pork has brilliant red thanks to edible food coloring. For me, the handsome bronze hue this recipe produces works just fine.

Makes about 1 lb (500 g) barbecued pork

Tip

For an extra boost of color and flavor, reserve the marinade and use a pastry brush or a spoon to baste the pork occasionally during the roasting process.

♦ Roasting pan with ovenproof rack

2 tbsp	soy sauce	30 mL
2 tbsp	hoisin sauce	30 mL
2 tbsp	oyster sauce	30 mL
2 tbsp	ketchup	30 mL
2 tbsp	dry sherry or Shaoxing rice wine	30 mL
2 tbsp	dark brown or light brown sugar	30 mL
1 tbsp	finely minced garlic	15 mL
1 tbsp	molasses or dark soy sauce	15 mL
1 tbsp	paprika	15 mL
2 lbs	boneless pork, preferably fatty pork shoulder, pork butt or country-style pork ribs	1 kg

1. In a medium bowl, combine soy sauce, hoisin sauce, oyster sauce, ketchup, sherry, brown sugar, garlic, molasses and paprika. Stir with a whisk or a fork to combine everything evenly and well.

2. Cut pork with the grain into long plump strips, about 2 inches (5 cm) in diameter. (Boneless country-style ribs are just the right size already.) Immerse pork strips in soy sauce mixture and turn to coat evenly. Cover and refrigerate for at least 1 hour or for as long as 8 hours.

3. Preheat oven to 375°F (190°C). Rub vegetable oil on an ovenproof rack and set it in a roasting pan. Add water to a depth of ½ inch (1 cm). Remove pork from soy sauce mixture and place on rack 2 inches (5 cm) apart. Roast in preheated oven for 30 minutes.

4. Reduce heat to 350°F (180°C). Turn pork pieces over to cook evenly and cook until pork is cooked through but not dry, 15 to 20 minutes more.

Tip

Once you've made this, you'll find ways to enjoy it as a rich accent to an array of dishes. It stars in Wonton Soup with Noodles and Barbecued Pork (page 168), but it makes a delicious alternative to Chinese sausage in Fried Rice with Sweet Chinese Sausage, Cilantro and Peas (page 148) and an excellent main ingredient in Banh Mi (variation, page 27).

5. When pork is cooked through, remove pan from oven and transfer pork to platter and let cool to room temperature.

6. Thinly slice pork across the grain. Or transfer pork to a container, cover and refrigerate for up to 5 days. Tightly wrapped, pork pieces can be frozen for up to 1 month.

◇ *Vietnamese Tales*

Vietnamese cooks chop up roast pork and use it to fill puffy steamed buns, slice it thinly and float it atop soup noodle bowls, dice it up and toss it into fried rice, or simply stir it briefly in a hot wok and serve it over rice paired with cucumber slices. You will find it in Asian supermarkets and Chinese-style barbecue specialty shops, hanging in the display window alongside salt-crusted pork belly and crispy-skinned duck.

Sizzling Savory Pancake with Shrimp and Pork

Though this filled and folded pancake resembles an omelet, there's no egg involved. A spoonful of ground turmeric tints the coconut milk-and-rice flour batter a lovely golden hue, and the dish's delights come from its chewy-crunchy texture and robust, rich filling of shrimp and pork. The standard accompaniments, a vivid green pile of lettuce and leafy herbs for wrapping up mouthwatering bites, make it a visual feast as well. This is a hands-on eating experience with many small tasks: tearing off a big bite of the filled pancake, bundling it up with herbs in a leaf of lettuce and dipping the little package into sweet-sour-salty sauce for each fantastic bite.

Serves 4

Tip

Skilled cooks make a good living preparing and selling this dish, and the more you do it, the more confident and successful you will become. Enjoy the process and the results, and ask for lots of help as you prepare, cook and clean up. Even broken uneven crêpes can be folded into packets to make a memorable treat.

Batter

1¼ cups	rice flour	300 mL
1 tsp	salt	5 mL
½ tsp	ground turmeric	2 mL
1½ cups	water	375 mL
¾ cup	coconut milk	175 mL
⅓ cup	thinly sliced green onion	75 mL

Filling

6 tbsp	vegetable oil, divided	90 mL
1 cup	long strips of onion, sliced lengthwise	250 mL
8 oz	boneless pork, thinly sliced into 2-inch (5 cm) strips	250 g
8 oz	shrimp, peeled, deveined and halved lengthwise	250 g
2 tsp	fish sauce	10 mL
½ tsp	granulated sugar	2 mL
½ tsp	salt	2 mL
3 cups	bean sprouts	750 mL

Accompaniments

Everyday Herb and Salad Plate (page 116)

Soft lettuce

Array of herbs, ideally including red perilla (see Tip, right)

Everyday Pickled Carrots (page 128)

Double batch of Everyday Dipping Sauce (page 200)

Tip

Like the big rice noodle salad bowls known as *bun*, these tasty pancakes are traditionally served with red perilla, the ruffled edged heart-shaped herb beloved in Japan, Korea and Laos as well as in Vietnam. Perilla is known as shiso in Japanese and beefsteak plant in English. Its bubbly surfaced leaves have a gorgeous purple underside and add beauty as well as bright aroma and flavor to Vietnamese dishes. Mint and basil leaves make a good alternative or companion to red perilla.

1. *Batter:* In a medium bowl, combine rice flour, salt and turmeric and stir with a fork to mix well. Add water and coconut milk and stir with a fork or whisk to combine evenly. Add green onions and stir to mix in. The batter should be smooth and thin. Set aside.

2. *Filling:* Heat 2 tbsp (30 mL) of the oil in a large frying pan or wok over medium-high heat until hot. When a bit of onion sizzles at once, add onion and toss well. Add pork and cook, undisturbed, for 1 minute. Toss well and cook, tossing often, until no longer pink inside, 1 minute more. Add shrimp and toss well. Add fish sauce, sugar and salt and continue cooking, tossing often, until shrimp and pork are done and evenly seasoned. Transfer to a bowl, along with all the juices and sauce. Set aside.

3. Arrange all the accompaniments along with small serving plates and utensils, so that you can serve each pancake as soon as it is done. Guests use lettuce leaves to fill with herbs and carrot pickles and a big chunk of pancake, creating a big bite to dip in the Everyday Dipping Sauce. Provide each guest with a personal bowl of Dipping Sauce for best results.

4. Heat a small heavy skillet or wok over high heat until hot. Reduce heat to medium-high and add 1 tbsp (15 mL) of the oil to pan. Swirl to coat it well.

5. Stir batter well, as it tends to settle as it stands. Scoop out about $1/2$ cup (125 mL) and pour into hot pan. Swirl to spread out into a large thin pancake. Cook, lifting edges gently as they set, curl and begin to brown, for 1 to 2 minutes.

6. When crêpe is nearly set and curling away from the edges, scatter filling over crêpe, leaving center free for folding. Make sure you have a little shrimp and a little pork and some onions, scooped up without the sauce. Add a handful of bean sprouts to one side. Drizzle a tiny bit of oil around the curling edges of the pancake.

continued…

Sizzling Savory Pancake
with Shrimp and Pork (continued)

7. When nicely browned and firm enough to lift and cooked inside, fold crêpe over gently. Lift pan and turn folded pancake out onto a plate and serve at once. Guests should cut or break into chunks, enfold in lettuce with herbs and pickled carrots, dip in sauce and devour.

8. Continue in this way, cooking and serving, adding oil as needed, until all the pancake batter and filling are gone.

◈ Vietnamese Tales

This signature Vietnamese street food dish draws eager customers to vendors all over Vietnam and to cafés and food courts around the world, wherever there's a Vietnamese culinary presence. Watching a pro cook it is fascinating. They can keep several pancakes cooking at once, timing it all for a sizzling, hot scrumptious result. The finished dish is gorgeous, and it's a unique and active pleasure to eat. Each crispy-crunchy sunny yellow griddlecake is fried with shrimp, pork and bean sprouts and served up with a bouquet of lettuce and aromatic herbs lettuce for wrapping and dipping.

Everyday Sweet and Salty Ground Pork

This hearty dish comes together quickly and provides a meaty sweet-and-salty boost to simple rice meals. Serve it along with a quick stir-fry of greens or broccoli, or enjoy it with scrambled eggs, sliced cucumbers and tomatoes, and hot sauce over rice. Dollop it over bowls of comforting Everyday Rice Porridge (page 150) or use it on the rice noodle bowls known as *bun* (page 178).

Serves 4

Tip

The ground pork keeps for 2 days in the refrigerator or in the freezer for 1 month.

2 tbsp	vegetable oil	30 mL
12 oz	ground pork	375 g
¼ cup	chopped onion	60 mL
1 tbsp	chopped garlic	15 mL
2 tbsp	dark or light brown sugar	30 mL
1 tbsp	Asian fish sauce	15 mL
½ tsp	salt	2 mL
½ tsp	freshly ground black pepper	2 mL
⅓ cup	chopped green onions	75 mL

1. Heat oil in a wok or a large, deep skillet over medium-high heat until a bit of garlic sizzles at once. Add ground pork and use a metal spatula to break up chunks into smaller and smaller bits. Toss well and cook, turning often, until most of the meat is no longer pink, 1 to 2 minutes.

2. Add onion and garlic and cook, tossing often, until fragrant and onion has begun to wilt, about 1 minute more.

3. Add brown sugar, fish sauce, salt and pepper and toss well.

4. Cook, tossing often, until meat is no longer pink and has formed a small amount of thin, dark brown sauce, 1 to 2 minutes more. Add green onions, toss well, and remove from heat. Transfer to a small serving platter or bowl and serve hot or warm.

Pork-Stuffed Tomatoes with Garlicky Tomato Sauce

This French-inspired party dish tastes as fine as it looks. Pretty enough for special occasions, it's simple enough for a weeknight rice-centered meal, and makes good use of sturdy plum tomatoes available year-round. The pork-and-bean thread noodle mixture filling is enjoyed throughout Vietnam. The tomatoes turn tender and their juices create a luscious sauce to flavor rice or season the last of a warm baguette.

1	small bundle dried bean thread noodles	1
5	dried wood ear mushrooms, optional	5
4	medium tomatoes or 8 small plum (Roma) tomatoes	4
8 oz	ground pork	250 g
1 tbsp	Asian fish sauce	15 mL
1 tsp	granulated sugar	5 mL
½ tsp	salt	2 mL
½ tsp	freshly ground black pepper	2 mL
2 tbsp	finely chopped green onion	30 mL
3 tbsp	vegetable oil, divided	45 mL
1 tbsp	finely chopped shallot or onion	15 mL
1 tbsp	finely chopped garlic	15 mL
1 tbsp	water	15 mL
2 tsp	fish sauce	10 mL
2 tbsp	coarsely chopped cilantro	30 mL

1. Place dried bean thread noodles, and dried wood ear mushrooms, if using, in separate bowls and add very warm water to cover by 1 inch (2.5 cm). Set aside to soften.

2. Meanwhile, cut tomatoes in half crosswise. Carefully scoop out seeds and liquid from each tomato half and place in a small bowl for a pan sauce. Place each tomato shell cut side up on a plate for filling.

3. In a medium bowl, combine pork, fish sauce, sugar, salt, pepper and green onion and stir to mix well.

4. To prepare wood ear mushrooms, remove from soaking water, trim away any hard, knotty portions and stack smooth portions. Slice thinly into short strips and add to pork mixture.

Tip

If you're in a hurry but long for the delightful color and flavor of this dish, make a deconstructed version. Shape the meat mixture into 1-inch (2.5 cm) meatballs and place in a hot skillet to brown, turning and shaking the pan. Slice a pint of cherry tomatoes in half crosswise, and add to the pan once the meatballs are cooked through. Cook, tossing and shaking the pan, until the cherry tomatoes are just shiny and tender but still intact. Serve over or tossed with pasta or include in a rice-centered meal.

5. To prepare bean thread noodles, remove from soaking water, mound on a cutting board and shape into a log about 8 inches (20 cm) long. Cut crosswise into 1-inch (2.5 cm) lengths. (You could use kitchen shears to snip them over a bowl to make small noodle sections.) Add chopped noodles to meat mixture and use a wooden spoon or your hands to mix evenly.

6. Using a spoon, scoop up enough meat mixture to fill each tomato completely, rounding off the top just a bit. Set on a plate meat side up and place by the stove.

7. Heat a large, heavy frying pan over medium high heat and add 2 tbsp (30 mL) of the vegetable oil. Heat until a bit of meat mixture sizzles at once. Carefully place half the tomatoes meat side down in the hot pan. Cook, undisturbed, until meat has browned nicely and tomato has begun to soften, 3 to 5 minutes. Carefully turn and place each tomato on its base. Cook until meat is no longer pink and tomatoes are tender, 3 to 5 minutes more. Transfer tomatoes to a serving platter and cook remaining tomatoes.

8. When all the tomatoes are done, add remaining oil to pan over high heat. Add shallots and garlic and cook until fragrant and softened but not browned, about 2 minutes. Add reserved tomato seeds and juices, water and fish sauce, and cook just until a little gravy forms, 1 to 2 minutes more. Pour tomato gravy around tomatoes, sprinkle with cilantro leaves and serve hot or warm.

Fish and Shellfish

In Vietnam, water seems to flow through every aspect of life. Veined with streams and rivers and flanked by the ocean along its curving southern and eastern borders, the Vietnamese landscape places its people in relation to the water. No wonder fish and seafood show up so often, and with such inspiration, on the Vietnamese table.

Despite Vietnam's proximity to the ocean, freshwater fish are more common fare than saltwater fish and shellfish. This reflects both economics and preference. Harvesting the ocean's bounty takes long hours, big boats and many hands, while catfish, snakehead and mullet can be had for a stroll to the riverbank and a brief fishing session. The Vietnamese preference for freshness is reflected here as well. If they don't catch the fish themselves, they buy it at the daily market from a local vendor who did.

These recipes offer an array of dishes illustrating the Vietnamese approach to cooking fish and shellfish. Freshwater fish stars in Cha Ca Fish with Fresh Dill, Hanoi-Style (page 104), the signature dish of the venerable restaurant Cha Ca La Vong. My version offers a delicious taste of this grilled tour de force, streamlined for cooking at home. Salmon takes wonderfully to Vietnamese-inspired preparations as in Grilled Salmon with Chile-Lime Sauce (page 100) and Salmon Steaks in Caramel Fish Sauce (page 102). Both show off salmon's color and flavor, but either could be made with almost any firm-fleshed fish.

Shrimp, crab and squid complete this chapter centered on aquatic treasures. Dive in! The water's fine and filled with an array of ways to create bright and varied dishes inspired by experts, the accomplished cooks of fish-and-seafood-loving Vietnam.

Grilled Tuna Steaks with Pineapple-Chile Sauce

Don't settle for good fast food when you can have great food fast. The tuna is simple and tasty and the sauce is fantastic. It's a simplified version of *mam nem*, a pungent dipping sauce made with anchovies and pineapple that Vietnamese cooks pair with grilled and fried foods, particularly fish. Serve your tuna steaks with Everyday Dipping Sauce (page 200), the inspired Vietnamese go-with-everything table sauce known as *nuoc cham*.

◇◇◇

Serves 4

Tip

I suggest anchovy paste here, but you could substitute fish sauce or chopped anchovies and still have a terrific sauce.

♦ Mini food processor blender

Fish

2 tbsp	fish sauce	30 mL
1 tbsp	soy sauce	15 mL
1 tbsp	vegetable oil	15 mL
1 tsp	granulated sugar	5 mL
¼ tsp	freshly ground black pepper	1 mL
1¼ lbs	tuna steaks, or salmon, mackerel or bluefish fillets or steaks	625 g

Pineapple-Chile Sauce

⅓ cup	fresh or canned pineapple chunks or drained crushed pineapple	75 mL
3 tbsp	freshly squeezed lime juice	45 mL
2 tbsp	chopped green onion	30 mL
2 tbsp	chopped fresh cilantro	30 mL
2 tbsp	granulated sugar	30 mL
1 tbsp	anchovy paste, chopped anchovies or fish sauce (see Tip, left)	15 mL
2 tsp	minced garlic	10 mL
½ tsp	chile-garlic sauce or chopped fresh hot chiles	2 mL

1. *Fish:* In a medium bowl, combine fish sauce, soy sauce, oil, sugar and pepper and stir to dissolve sugar. Add fish steaks and turn to coat well. Let marinate, turning once, for 20 to 30 minutes. Cover and refrigerate for up to 1 day if you won't be cooking the fish right away.

Tip

The Pineapple-Chile Sauce pairs wonderfully with grilled or sautéed salmon, and makes a lovely companion to shrimp or chicken wings.

2. *Pineapple-Chile Sauce:* In mini food processor or blender, combine pineapple, lime juice, green onion, cilantro, sugar, anchovy paste, garlic and chile-garlic sauce and blend until fairly smooth. Transfer to a small bowl and set aside until serving time.

3. Preheat a gas or charcoal barbecue grill to medium heat or preheat oven to 375°F (190°C). Place fish steaks carefully on grill and cook until firm and opaque, about 5 minutes on each side. Or bake for about 15 minutes. Transfer to a serving platter, add bowl of Pineapple-Chile Sauce and serve hot or warm.

◈ Vietnamese Tales

This bright-flavored dipping sauce uses fish sauce rather than the pungent, thick and chunky sauce called *mam nem*. Made from salted and fermented anchovies, it adds intense saltiness and depth to Vietnamese dishes. *Mam nem* can be found in Asian markets and keeps well. It's essential in the dipping sauces accompanying the beloved surf-and-turf hot pot known as *bo nhung dam*, in which thinly sliced beef with shrimp and other seafood are cooked at the table in a tangy broth and then tucked with herbs into rice paper hand rolls.

Grilled Salmon with Chile-Lime Sauce

Fine enough for company and fast enough for a weeknight supper, this briefly marinated salmon sparkles with the sharp, sweet and hot notes of its simple dipping sauce. The same marinade works nicely with other meaty fish or with shrimp and the sauce is grand even with plain rice. Toss together a crisp green salad and you can ring the dinner bell in short order. Or serve it Vietnamese-style, with Spinach Sautéed with Garlic and Pepper (page 134), Crab and Asparagus Soup (page 48) and a steaming bowl of rice.

◇◇

Serves 3 to 4

Tip

I make this dish in a grill pan on top of the stove or in my cast-iron skillet with great results.

Salmon

2 tbsp	vegetable oil	30 mL
2 tbsp	coarsely chopped fresh gingerroot	30 mL
1 tbsp	chopped garlic	15 mL
1 tbsp	chopped shallots or onion	15 mL
2 tbsp	fish sauce	30 mL
1 tbsp	soy sauce	15 mL
1 tbsp	granulated sugar	15 mL
1¼ lbs	thick salmon fillets, tuna, halibut or other meaty fish	625 g

Chile-Lime Sauce

¼ cup	fish sauce	60 mL
3 tbsp	freshly squeezed lime juice or white vinegar	45 mL
2 tbsp	water	30 mL
2 tbsp	granulated sugar	30 mL
¼ tsp	chile-garlic sauce or other hot sauce	1 mL
1 tbsp	thinly sliced green onion	15 mL

1. *Salmon:* In a medium bowl, combine oil, ginger, garlic, shallots, fish sauce, soy sauce and sugar. Stir to dissolve sugar and mix everything well. Add salmon fillets and turn to coat with marinade. Cover and set aside for 20 to 30 minutes, or cover and refrigerate for up to 1 day.

Variation

Pineapple-Chile Sauce (page 207) makes a fine alternative to Chile-Lime Sauce, though it is a bit more effort to prepare. For a speedy side sauce, this one really shines with any grilled dish or even with an omelet or fried rice.

2. *Chile-Lime Sauce:* In a small bowl, combine fish sauce, lime juice, water, sugar, chile-garlic sauce and green onion. Stir to dissolve sugar and mix everything well. Place on the serving platter you will use for the fish.

3. Preheat a gas or charcoal barbecue grill to medium heat or preheat oven to 375°F (190°C). Place fish steaks carefully on grill and grill for about 5 minutes on each side, or until cooked to your liking. Or bake in preheated oven for about 15 minutes. Transfer to the serving platter alongside Chile-Lime Sauce and serve hot or warm.

◈ Vietnamese Tales

If you love grilled food and cooking over a charcoal or wood fire, you will find an abundance of dishes to love within Vietnamese cuisine. Cooking over fire and coals is at the heart of traditional cooking in Vietnam, and massive gas-powered grills are not part of the original picture. Whether you have a small, hibachi-type grill, a rounded kettle-type grill or a gas grill of any kind, you can expand and enhance your grilling repertoire with Vietnamese dishes. From grilled fish such as salmon or branzino to pork chops, stuffed squid and *bun cha ha noi* (page 80), you will find endless ways to please yourself and your guests. With vibrant dipping sauces and the signature Vietnamese way with lettuce and herb wraps, you can make a hands-on meal from start to finish. Cooks in Vietnam use a wood or charcoal fire for stir-frying, cooking rice and making clay-pot braises, so consider taking the wok out into the open air for an entire menu outside.

Salmon Steaks in Caramel Fish Sauce

This exceptional dish is a type of *kho*, a traditional clay pot cooking method for braising meat or fish in a sweet-and-salty sauce. You can find clay pots in Asian markets, or simmer your delicious *kho* dish in a small saucepan or small deep, heavy skillet on your kitchen stove. Like all *kho* dishes, this richly sauced salmon goes wonderfully with a rice-centered meal. Try it with Green Papaya Salad (page 118) or a simple plate of sliced cucumbers and tomatoes for cool contrast. Or serve it with Sweet and Tangy Soup with Pineapple, Tamarind and Shrimp (page 44). If you use catfish in both this dish and that soup and serve them with rice, you'll have the classic combination of *com canh chua ca kho to*.

Serves 4 to 6

Variation

Any hearty fish steaks will do here. Instead of the salmon, use catfish, mackerel or bluefish, for example, as long as the steaks fit tightly into the pan so that they are surrounded by the sauce.

1 tbsp	vegetable oil	15 mL
1 tbsp	coarsely chopped shallots or onion	15 mL
1 tbsp	coarsely chopped garlic	15 mL
¼ cup	fish sauce	60 mL
⅓ cup	water	75 mL
2 tbsp	granulated sugar	30 mL
1 tbsp	Everyday Caramel Sauce (page 210), Speedy Caramel Sauce (page 211) or brown sugar	15 mL
½ tsp	freshly ground black pepper	2 mL
1¼ lbs	salmon steaks or other meaty fish, about 1 inch (2.5 cm) thick	625 g
3	green onions, trimmed, white part chopped and green part cut into 2-inch (5 cm) lengths	3

1. In a small, deep skillet or a small saucepan over medium-high heat, combine oil, shallots and garlic and warm until garlic sizzles.

2. Add fish sauce, water, sugar, Caramel Sauce and pepper and bring to a boil. Cook, stirring occasionally, until sugar dissolves and sauce thickens a bit, 2 to 3 minutes.

3. Add salmon steaks and let sauce return to a gentle boil. Cover and cook for 10 minutes. Carefully turn steaks over, add green onions and cook for 5 minutes more. Transfer fish steaks to a shallow serving bowl, sauce and all. Serve hot or warm.

Catfish Simmered in Caramel Sauce

Among the many irresistible Vietnamese braised in a clay pot, this one featuring peppery sweet-and-salty catfish stands out. Made with 1-inch (2.5 cm) thick bone-in steaks and a caramelized fish sauce braising liquid, it shines over rice and is worth a trip to an Asian market where skilled fishmongers can cut a fresh fish to just the right size. While the fish tastes fantastic, it's the sauce in the bottom of the pot that can bring out the competitive spirit in aficionados.

Serves 4

Tip

Though this dish is traditionally cooked in a clay pot over a charcoal fire, you can make a wonderful version in a small Dutch oven on your stove.

♦ Small Dutch oven with a tight-fitting lid

¼ cup	Asian fish sauce	60 mL
2 tbsp	granulated sugar	30 mL
1 tsp	freshly ground pepper	5 mL
1½ lbs	bone-in catfish steaks, about 1-inch (2.5 cm) thick	750 g
1 tbsp	vegetable oil	15 mL
1 tbsp	chopped garlic	15 mL
1 tbsp	chopped shallots	15 mL
3 tbsp	Everyday Caramel Sauce (page 210)	45 mL
3	green onions, trimmed and cut into 2-inch (5 cm) lengths	3
½ cup	water	125 mL
2 tbsp	chopped cilantro	30 mL

1. In a medium bowl, combine fish sauce, sugar, and pepper, and stir to mix them well. Add catfish steaks and turn to coat them evenly with the sauce. Set aside to marinate for 10 to 15 minutes while you prepare the remaining ingredients.

2. In a medium Dutch oven, heat oil over medium-high heat until a bit of garlic sizzles at once. Add garlic and shallots and toss well. Cook just until they release their fragrance, and then push them to the side. Place catfish steaks in the pan, and then scrape all the marinade over them. Cook for 1 minute, and then carefully turn to sear the other side.

3. Add caramel sauce, green onions, and ½ cup (125 mL) water. Let sauce come to a lively boil, and then reduce heat to maintain a lively simmer. Cover and cook until fish is opaque and has formed a handsome brown sauce, 10 to 12 minutes.

4. Remove the lid and turn fish steaks carefully to the other side. Cook 2 minutes more and remove from heat. Serve hot or warm.

Cha Ca Fish with Fresh Dill, Hanoi-Style

Vivid color and flavor come to mind when I think of this lovely classic dish. Gold and green — the gold from turmeric and the green from fronds of fresh aromatic dill. Cooked at the table in Vietnamese restaurants, it's a show-stopping treat. My streamlined version of *cha ca* gives you a delicious, aromatic and gorgeous dish so appealing you will want to make it often and so easy that you can do just that. If time is an issue, you can omit accompaniments, sprinkle with the chopped peanuts and serve this as a main dish.

◇◇◇

Serves 4

Tip

Fresh dill is essential in this traditional dish, but it can be difficult to find, especially during winter. If you can't find it, use a bouquet of fresh cilantro or basil in its place. It won't be a proper *cha ca ha noi*, but it will still be a most tasty and pleasing dish.

Marinade

2 tbsp	fish sauce	30 mL
1 tbsp	vegetable oil	15 mL
1 tbsp	finely minced fresh gingerroot or fresh or frozen galanga	15 mL
1 tsp	ground turmeric	5 mL
¼ tsp	salt	1 mL
1 lb	firm-fleshed fish fillets, such as catfish, monkfish or tilapia	500 g

Accompaniments

8 oz	thin dried rice noodles	250 g
3 cups	shredded lettuce leaves, such as Boston, Bibb or oak leaf	750 mL
1 cup	fresh mint, cilantro or Asian basil leaves	250 mL
½ cup	chopped dry-roasted salted peanuts	125 mL
	Double recipe Everyday Dipping Sauce (page 200) or Pineapple-Chile Sauce (page 207)	
2 tbsp	vegetable oil	30 mL
2 cups	coarsely chopped fresh dill (see Tip, left)	500 mL
5	green onions, trimmed, white part chopped and green part cut into 2-inch (5 cm) lengths	5

1. *Marinade:* In a medium bowl, combine fish sauce, oil, ginger, turmeric and salt and stir to mix well. Cut fish into big bite-size chunks (2 to 3 inches/5 to 7.5 cm square) and add to bowl, tossing to coat well. Set aside while you prepare noodles and other accompaniments, or cover and chill to marinate for up to 1 day.

2. Bring a medium saucepan of water to a rolling boil over high heat. Drop in rice noodles and immediately remove from heat. Let stand until tender and ready to eat, 5 to 7 minutes. Drain, rinse in cold water and then drain well. Transfer to a shallow bowl or a deep plate. Prepare and arrange the remaining accompaniments next to a serving platter for the cooked fish.

3. To cook the fish, place oil, dill and green onions by the stove. Heat oil in a large, heavy skillet over medium-high heat until a bit of dill sizzles at once. Add fish to pan and cook on one side, about 2 minutes. Gently turn and let fish cook for another minute. Add dill and green onions to pan and cook, tossing gently to wilt herbs, for 1 minute. Transfer to a serving platter.

4. To serve this dish the classic small-bowl way, start each guest off with a small bowl holding a portion of each accompaniment: noodles, lettuce and a few leaves of mint, cilantro or Asian basil. Top with a piece or two of fish with dill and green onions, sprinkle with chopped peanuts and drizzle with a spoonful of Everyday Dipping Sauce. Invite your guests to continue serving themselves in this way.

5. To serve the big-noodle-bowl way, divide the accompaniments, fish, dill and green onions among 4 big noodle bowls or pasta plates. Season each bowl with Everyday Dipping Sauce and invite each guest to toss with chopsticks or a fork and spoon and enjoy.

Grilled Shrimp with Tamarind Sauce

I love the flavor of tamarind, an intense sweet-and-sour essence that makes a fabulous partner for shrimp. Tamarind liquid is made by soaking, mashing and straining the ripe bean-shaped pods of the tamarind tree. Years ago tamarind concentrate was sticky, hard and lacking the complex flavor I adore but modern versions suit me fine.

◇◇

Serves 4

Makes about 1/2 cup (125 mL) of sauce

Tip

You can find tamarind pulp in soft blocks at Asian markets and make tamarind liquid as you need it or check out the thick, luscious, ready-to-use tamarind liquid widely available among the seasonings in Asian markets. It offers a welcome shortcut to the pleasures of using tamarind in your kitchen. Look for the Vietnamese words for tamarind liquid, *nuoc me chua*, displayed on the label and store it in the refrigerator after opening. It's handy but it won't keep forever, so make this yummy sauce a lot. I also use Indian-style tamarind chutney, often available in well-stocked supermarkets as well as South Asian grocery stores, when I need good tamarind flavor fast.

◆ 12 to 15 bamboo skewers, soaked in water for at least 30 minutes

Tamarind Sauce

1 tsp	vegetable oil	5 mL
1 tsp	minced garlic	5 mL
1/3 cup	prepared tamarind liquid, Indian-style tamarind chutney or freshly made Tamarind Liquid (page 209)	75 mL
2 tbsp	fish sauce or 1 tsp (5 mL) salt	30 mL
2 tbsp	water	30 mL
2 tbsp	granulated sugar	30 mL
1 tbsp	brown sugar	15 mL
1/2 tsp	freshly ground black pepper	2 mL
1/4 tsp	hot pepper flakes or chile-garlic sauce	1 mL

Shrimp

8 oz	medium shrimp, peeled and deveined	250 g
1 tbsp	vegetable oil	15 mL
1/2 tsp	salt	2 mL
1/4 tsp	freshly ground black pepper	1 mL

1. *Tamarind Sauce:* In a small saucepan or skillet, heat oil and garlic over medium heat until garlic is fragrant and sizzles, about 1 minute. Add tamarind liquid, fish sauce, water, granulated sugar, brown sugar, pepper and hot pepper flakes and stir well. Cook, stirring often, until sugars dissolve and sauce is smooth and thickened a bit, 3 to 5 minutes. Set aside while you cook shrimp. Serve warm or at room temperature, or transfer to a sealed jar, close tightly and refrigerate for up to 2 days.

Variation

Start with shrimp, but don't stay there. You can pair this dark, sweet-and-tangy sauce with garlicky chicken wings, grilled salmon or tuna, or skewers of sweet peppers, onion and summer squash.

2. *Shrimp:* Preheat a gas or charcoal barbecue grill to medium heat or preheat broiler or oven to 425°F (220°C). Or lightly oil a skillet or grill pan and heat until very hot. In a medium bowl, combine shrimp, oil, salt and pepper and toss to coat well. Set aside for 10 to 15 minutes. Thread shrimp onto skewers, 2 or 3 per skewer, place on hot grill and cook, turning once, until shrimp are pink, firm and opaque, 2 to 4 minutes. Or place in a lightly greased pan and broil, turning once or twice, for 2 to 4 minutes, or roast in oven for 3 to 5 minutes. Or sauté quickly in skillet or grill pan for 2 to 4 minutes. Serve shrimp hot, warm or at room temperature with small bowls of Tamarind Sauce on the side.

Speedy Shrimp in Caramel-Chile Sauce

This beautiful, delicious dish is perfect for lighting up a weeknight supper. Accompany with Spinach Sautéed with Garlic and Pepper (page 134) or Everyday Herb and Salad Plate (page 116) and a bowl of rice. You could also toss these shrimp with rice noodles and edamame beans, or with spaghetti and peas, for a pretty and tasty noodle bowl.

Serves 4

Tip

Keeping frozen shrimp on hand makes this a spur-of-the-moment supper that seems like a specially planned meal. Look for bargains and buy shrimp in quantity for future meals. Divide into 8-oz (250 g) or 1-lb (500 g) portions and freeze in airtight containers. Leave peeling and deveining until cooking time because shrimp maintain their flavor best in the shell.

2 tbsp	vegetable oil	30 mL
1 tbsp	finely chopped garlic	15 mL
¼ cup	finely chopped onion	60 mL
8 oz	medium shrimp, peeled and deveined	250 g
2 tbsp	fish sauce	30 mL
1 tbsp	granulated sugar	15 mL
¼ tsp	hot pepper flakes	1 mL
¼ cup	water	60 mL
2 tbsp	thinly sliced green onion	30 mL
2 tbsp	finely chopped fresh cilantro	30 mL

1. In a medium skillet over medium heat, heat oil until hot. Add garlic and onion and toss well. Add shrimp and cook, tossing once, until they turn pink. Stir in fish sauce, sugar and hot pepper flakes and then add water. Cook, tossing once or twice, until shrimp are cooked through and other ingredients combine to make a thin sauce, 2 to 3 minutes. Sprinkle with green onion and cilantro and toss well. Transfer to a serving dish and serve hot or warm.

Shrimp and Rice Porridge with Cilantro and Tomatoes

Don't wait for a sick day to make this satisfying and beautiful dish. Rice porridge simmers away all over Asia. Each cuisine makes its own particular improvements to the genre, but each version possesses the defining qualities of hot, thick, salty, soothing and welcome anytime, day or night. In Vietnam, the shrimp go in early and cook along with the rice, but I like the delicate texture I get by adding them just before serving.

◇◇

Serves 4 to 6

Tip

If you have *chao tom* left over, expect it to thicken a lot once it cools down. Reheat it gently, adding a little chicken stock, salt as needed and a handful of green onions and cilantro to restore its freshly made qualities.

8 oz	medium shrimp, peeled, deveined and coarsely chopped	250 g
1 tbsp	finely chopped shallots	15 mL
1 tbsp	finely chopped garlic	15 mL
2 tbsp	fish sauce	30 mL
½ tsp	freshly ground black pepper	2 mL
¼ tsp	salt	1 mL
6 cups	Chicken Stock (page 216) or store-bought	1.5 L
¾ cup	long-grain rice, rinsed and drained	175 mL
2 tbsp	vegetable oil	30 mL
1 cup	coarsely chopped plum tomatoes, optional	250 mL
2 tbsp	thinly sliced green onion	30 mL
2 tbsp	coarsely chopped fresh cilantro	30 mL

1. In a medium bowl, combine shrimp with shallots, garlic, fish sauce, pepper and salt. Toss to mix well and set aside while the rice cooks.

2. Bring stock to a rolling boil in a medium saucepan over medium-high heat. Stir in rice. Return to a boil and then reduce heat to maintain a gentle simmer. Cook until rice is very soft, about 15 minutes. Remove from heat and cover to keep warm.

3. In a medium skillet over medium-high heat, heat oil until hot. Add shrimp mixture and cook, tossing well, until garlic is fragrant and shrimp are turning pink, 1 to 2 minutes. Transfer shrimp mixture to rice, scraping pan to get out every bit of flavor. Return porridge to a gentle boil and cook, 2 to 3 minutes. Stir in tomatoes, if using, green onion and cilantro. Remove from heat and serve hot or warm.

Hearty Crab Cakes with Pork, Shiitakes and Bean Thread Noodles

At seaside cafés along the coastline of Vietnam and at Vietnamese seafood cafés around the world, crab shells stuffed with a hearty filling of crab, ground pork and bean thread noodles are an ever popular dish. Crab shells can be difficult to find, but that needn't keep you from the pleasures of this dish. Simply form the mixture into crab cakes, drizzle them with Scallion Oil (page 214), and enjoy them with Pineapple-Chile Sauce or Everyday Dipping Sauce. Paired with Chopped Watercress Salad (page 122) and rice or a warm baguette, this makes a delightful al fresco lunch or cozy supper.

Serves 4 to 6

Variation

Hearty Crab Cake Sliders: Lightly toast small slider buns and spread with mayonnaise, butter or olive oil and toast lightly. Set out cool crisp leaves of butter lettuce and thinly sliced tomatoes, along with Scallion Oil (page 214) and Pineapple-Chile Sauce (page 207). When buns are ready, divide crab-pork mixture into small burger-size portions and cook in a mixture of butter and olive oil until done and handsomely browned. Place each crab cake on a bun, season with Scallion Oil and Pineapple-Chile sauce, add lettuce and tomato and enjoy right away.

1	small bundle dried bean thread noodles	1
5	dried wood ear mushrooms, optional	5
8 oz	ground pork	250 g
4 oz	crabmeat	125 g
¼ cup	finely chopped shallots or onion	60 mL
2 tsp	finely chopped garlic	10 mL
1 tbsp	Asian fish sauce	15 mL
1 tsp	granulated sugar	5 mL
1	egg	1
½ tsp	salt	2 mL
½ tsp	freshly ground black pepper	2 mL
2 tbsp	butter or vegetable oil	30 mL
2 tbsp	coarsely chopped cilantro	30 mL
	Pineapple-Chile Sauce (page 207) or Everyday Dipping Sauce (page 200)	
	Lettuce leaves	
	Sliced cucumbers	

1. Place dried bean thread noodles, and dried wood ear mushrooms, if using, in separate bowls and add very warm water to cover by 1 inch (2.5 cm). Set aside to soften.

2. Meanwhile, in a medium bowl, combine pork, crabmeat, shallots, garlic, fish sauce, sugar, egg, salt and pepper and stir to mix well.

3. To prepare bean thread noodles, remove from soaking water, mound on a cutting board and shape into a log about 8 inches (20 cm) long. Cut crosswise into 1-inch (2.5 cm) lengths. (You could use kitchen shears to snip them over a bowl to make small noodle sections.) Add chopped noodles to crab and pork mixture and use a wooden spoon or your hands to mix evenly.

4. To prepare wood ear mushrooms, remove from soaking water, trim away any hard, knotty portions and stack smooth portions. Slice thinly into short strips and add to crab and pork mixture.

5. Wet your hands and form crab and pork mixture into little cakes, the size of small burgers, about 2 inches (5 cm) in diameter and $\frac{1}{2}$-inch (1 cm) thickness. (Shape them to suit yourself, keeping in mind that thicker cakes mean longer cooking time, so pork will be done. You can cover pan and keep turning if you need more heat or more time for them to cook. Cut into a very thick one when you think they are done, as a test.)

6. When you are ready to cook crab cakes, set out a serving platter and garnish with bowls of either Pineapple-Chile Sauce or Everyday Dipping Sauce, along with lettuce leaves and sliced cucumbers to accompany the feast.

7. Heat a large, heavy frying pan over medium-high heat and add butter. When sizzling hot, add 3 or 4 crab cakes to pan and let cook, undisturbed, until bottom is nicely golden brown and sides show a little color at the edge, about 2 minutes. Carefully turn over and cook on other side in the same way. When second side is brown, check to see if cakes are cooked through. If not, cook 1 or 2 minutes more or cover pan and increase heat a bit, watching carefully to avoid burning crab cakes while making sure they cook through.

8. Continue cooking, transferring crab cakes to a serving platter as they are done. When all are done, serve at once, hot or warm, with dipping sauce, lettuce and cucumbers.

Pork-Stuffed Squid in Sweet and Tangy Tamarind Sauce

With its extraordinarily long, curving coastline, Vietnam is home to endless creative and tasty ways to feast on the treasures of the sea. This delightful dish takes squid to new heights, stuffing them with seasoned ground pork, browning in a hot skillet and then serving them up sliced as snacks or whole as one of many dishes at a rice meal. Sometimes paired with a rich tomato sauce, pork-stuffed squid in this sweet and tangy tamarind sauce makes a spectacular dish.

◇◇◇

Serves 4 to 6

Tip

Though some squid are sold with only the cleaned tubes, other types include their curling tentacles. If you have tentacles, you could chop them very finely and add them to the pork mixture or cook them in the hot oil with a little garlic, salt, pepper, sugar and fish sauce. Add them to the platter along with the stuffed squid and sauce.

◆ Wooden toothpicks

Sweet and Tangy Tamarind Sauce (page 208)

1	small bundle dried bean thread noodles	1
5	dried wood ear mushrooms, optional	5
8 oz	ground pork	250 g
¼ cup	finely chopped onions	60 mL
1 tbsp	fish sauce	15 mL
1 tsp	finely chopped garlic	5 mL
½ tsp	salt	2 mL
½ tsp	freshly ground black pepper	2 mL
½ tsp	granulated sugar	2 mL
1½ lbs	cleaned and prepared squid, with hollow tubes for stuffing	750 g
3 tbsp	vegetable oil	45 mL
⅓ cup	finely chopped green onions	75 mL
¼ cup	chopped cilantro	60 mL

1. Prepare Sweet and Tangy Tamarind Sauce and set aside.

2. Place bean thread noodles, and wood ear mushrooms, if using, in separate bowls and add very warm water to cover by 1 inch (2.5 cm).

3. In another medium bowl, combine ground pork, onions, fish sauce, garlic, salt, pepper and sugar and stir together well. Place squid on a baking sheet or a platter.

4. To prepare wood ear mushrooms, remove from soaking water, trim away any hard, knotty portions and stack smooth portions. Slice thinly into short strips about 1 inch (2.5 cm) and add to pork mixture.

Tip

Squid vary greatly in size, so you may be stuffing lots of filling into fewer big squid, or smaller bits of filling into lots of petite squid. The thing to remember is to fill them well, avoiding air pockets, but leaving space at the top (about 1/4 inch/0.5 cm) to press the top portion together and seal it with a toothpick to keep filling inside during cooking. If you have filling left over, make little meatballs or patties to enjoy with any of the book's dipping sauces.

5. To prepare bean thread noodles, remove from soaking water, mound on a cutting board and shape into a log about 6 inches (15 cm) long. Cut crosswise into 1-inch (2.5 cm) lengths. (You could use kitchen shears to snip them over a bowl to make small noodle sections.) You'll have about 1/2 cup (125 mL) of short flexible clear noodles. Add chopped noodles to pork mixture and use a wooden spoon or your hands to mix evenly.

6. To stuff squid, pick up one tube and use your fingers to insert 2 tbsp (30 mL) of meat mixture. Gently push to very end of the squid body. Continue, pushing gently to fill the tube about three-quarters full. Use a sharp toothpick to close tube and keep filling inside for cooking, threading through both sides and out again. Continue until all the squid are filled. Using a sharp toothpick, poke 4 holes in each stuffed squid to help cook evenly.

7. Before you begin to cook the stuffed squid, warm up Sweet and Tangy Tamarind Sauce and have it nice and hot on the stove for serving. Set out a serving platter to hold the cooked squid and have the chopped green onions and cilantro handy.

8. Heat a large heavy skillet over medium-high heat. Add vegetable oil and swirl to coat pan. When oil is hot enough for a bit of meat mixture to sizzle at once, gently place 3 squid and cook, undisturbed, until lightly browned, about 3 minutes. Turn and continue cooking top side of squid, then each side, until squid are puffed and firm and meat has cooked through, 6 to 8 minutes. To be sure meat is cooked, cut largest one in two to check the thickest part to confirm that the meat is no longer pink. Transfer cooked squid to serving platter and continue cooking remaining squid, adding as many as pan will hold without crowding.

9. When squid are all cooked and arranged on serving platter, pour warm Sweet and Tangy Tamarind Sauce over squid. Sprinkle with green onion and cilantro leaves. Serve hot or warm.

Salads, Pickles and Vegetables

*T*his chapter opens *with an everyday pattern for a salad platter, called* dia rau song *in Vietnamese. A base of leaf lettuce is built up with cucumbers, green onions, bean sprouts, chile slices and a sheaf of aromatic and pungent fresh herb sprigs. Dia rau song can be tailored to suit a particular dish or to feature seasonal goodies along with the basic components. You can pare it down to lettuce cups and cilantro or mint or build it up with slices of avocado or sweet peppers, chunks of ripe tomato, baby carrots or sugar snap peas.*

The salads included in this chapter range from simple ones such as Sliced Cucumber Salad (page 127) to fancy or substantial ones such as Green Mango Salad with Shrimp and Mint (page 119) and Chicken and Cabbage Salad with Mint (page 124). Simple or elaborate, pure vegetable or hearty with meat or seafood, this Vietnamese way with the concept of salad works beautifully either as elements of a traditional Vietnamese meal with rice, or as inviting dishes on a buffet. Served up with your famous barbecued chicken, baked ziti or steaks on the grill, they can add bright and unexpected pleasure to any menu.

Easy-to-prepare pickles light up Vietnamese dishes, whether they're tucked into Banh Mi (page 26) or tossed with rice noodles in a Big Cool Noodle Bowl (page 178). Everyday Pickled Carrots (page 128) and Pickled Bean Sprouts (page 130) are make-ahead condiments you can enjoy with the dia rau song or as accompaniments to anything grilled or saucy. They provide a bright note against the velvety richness of heartier food.

Simple stir-fried dishes complete this vibrant chapter. Delicious hot, warm or at room temperature, these dishes illustrate the Vietnamese habit of appreciating a given vegetable on its own terms. The principle is to do as little as possible, making it easy to appreciate each vegetable's particular gifts, and to cook it often.

Everyday Herb and Salad Plate

Vietnamese people devour *dia rau song* because they love the bright, crisp, fresh essence and aromatic boost provided by the bouquet of herbs and greens. Many dishes, from *pho* noodles (pages 160 and 162) to Sizzling Savory Pancakes (page 90) presume such a salad plate as an accompaniment. Don't let the number of ingredients overwhelm you. Use what you can find in terms of herbs: A simple collection of lettuce leaves, cucumbers and cilantro (or mint or basil) will suffice as a version of this Vietnamese herbal extravaganza.

Serves 4

Tip

The herbs beloved by Vietnamese cooks grow easily and can be found at specialty food shops and farmer's markets throughout the warmer months. Buy a few pots to enjoy, both for dining purposes and for their beauty. Asian markets carry a wide range of Vietnamese herbs throughout the year, so check there for a cold weather supply.

12 cups	tender shaped lettuce leaves, such as Bibb or Boston	3 L
1	lime, cut into 6 wedges	1
2 cups	strips or slices peeled cucumber	500 mL
2 cups	mung bean sprouts	500 mL
2	green onions, trimmed, cut crosswise into thirds and then cut lengthwise into shreds	2
2	fresh jalapeño chiles, cut diagonally into thin ovals	2
1½ cups	fresh cilantro, trimmed to 3-inch (7.5 cm) sprigs (approx.)	375 mL
1½ cups	fresh mint, trimmed to 3-inch (7.5 cm) sprigs (approx.)	375 mL
1½ cups	fresh basil, trimmed to 3-inch (7.5 cm) sprigs (approx.)	375 mL
	Everyday Dipping Sauce (page 200)	

1. Assemble components of your salad on a big platter, placing lettuce leaves and lime wedges on one end, small piles of cucumber, bean sprouts, green onions and jalapeño chiles at the other and herb sprigs in the center. Divide the Everyday Dipping Sauce into several small bowls so that each guest can easily reach one.

2. Invite your guests to make small packets for dipping into the sauce. This is done by placing a piece or two of meat or seafood on a lettuce leaf, adding a sprig of herbs, some cucumber, a few bean sprouts, a pinch of green onions and a slice of chile and rolling it into a little bundle. The lime wedges are squeezed over soup, noodles, fried rice or grilled food for a bright, tangy note, while the cucumbers and bean sprouts are enjoyed as a crudité throughout the meal.

Farmer's markets often have an array of Asian herbs on offer, both as cut herbs and as small pots for your kitchen window, deck or summer garden. Look for Asian basil with purple stems and pointed leaves and a familiar yet unique basil aroma. The long, smooth, feather-shaped leaves known as saw-leaf herb or *culantro* may be waiting for you in Latin grocery stores, and the distinctive, stemmy herb known as *rau ram* is increasingly available and especially simple to grow.

3. To prepare the salad in advance, cover salad platter loosely with foil, plastic wrap or a damp kitchen towel and refrigerate for 8 to 12 hours. Set out 30 minutes or so before you plan to serve the accompanying food.

◇ *Vietnamese Tales*

In Vietnam and everywhere else around the world that Vietnamese people sit down to eat, you will see small plates stacked high with cool green things: leaves of lettuce, bouquets of fresh herbs, slabs of cucumber, stacks of bean sprouts, ovals of fresh hot green chile and glistening hunks of lime. Watch them disappear as diners pinch, tear, wrap, munch and dip, eating their way through this petite garden. No stern nutritional guidelines lie behind this tradition, unique on the planet, of enjoying the dance of flavors and textures provided by an abundance of greens and herbs.

Green Papaya Salad

Think of this as coleslaw made easier. The hardest part could well be finding a source of green, unripe papaya. Asian markets often carry it. Look for a small one and expect the green peel to ooze thick, white goo when you cut into it. This is papain, a powerful enzyme used in Southeast Asia as a natural meat tenderizer.

Serves 4 to 6

Tip

To shred papaya for this salad, halve a papaya, peel and rinse well, seed and then grate the sturdy, greenish white flesh on a box grater or in a food processor fitted with the shredding disk. Or look for freshly shredded papaya, ready to use, in the nearest Asian market.

Variation

I also make this salad with finely shredded cabbage, blanched in boiling water for 1 minute and then refreshed in cold water; or cucumber, thinly sliced and cut in long thin strips; or cooked spaghetti squash; or a mixture of diced green apples and jicama with shredded carrots.

3 tbsp	fish sauce	45 mL
2 tbsp	freshly squeezed lime juice	30 mL
2 tbsp	water	30 mL
2 tbsp	granulated sugar	30 mL
½ tsp	chile-garlic sauce	2 mL
2½ cups	shredded green papaya (see Tip, left)	625 mL
½ cup	shredded carrots	125 mL
2 tbsp	coarsely chopped fresh mint	30 mL
2 tbsp	coarsely chopped *rau ram* (page 220), optional	30 mL
3 tbsp	coarsely chopped dry-roasted salted peanuts	45 mL
2 tbsp	coarsely chopped fresh cilantro	30 mL

1. In a medium bowl, combine fish sauce, lime juice, water, sugar and chile-garlic sauce and stir well to make a smooth sauce. Add green papaya, carrots, mint and *rau ram*, if using, and toss well. Let stand for 15 minutes. Transfer salad to a serving platter and top with chopped peanuts and cilantro. Serve at room temperature.

Green Mango Salad with Shrimp and Mint

Make this when you spy unripe, green mangos in the market. Firm and a little tangy in flavor, they stand up nicely to the piquant flavors of Everyday Dipping Sauce and pair wonderfully with plump pink grilled shrimp, in color, texture and flavor.

◇◇◇

Serves 4			
8 oz	shrimp, peeled and deveined	250 g
2 tsp	Asian fish sauce	10 mL
1 tsp	salt	5 mL
½ tsp	freshly ground black pepper	2 mL
2 cups	shredded (peeled) green, unripe mango	500 mL
¼ cup	finely chopped green onions	60 mL
¼ cup	coarsely chopped fresh mint or *rau ram* (page 220)	60 mL
¼ cup	coarsely chopped fresh cilantro	60 mL
2 tbsp	vegetable oil	30 mL
⅓ cup	Everyday Dipping Sauce (page 200)	75 mL
¼ cup	Crispy Shallots (page 213)	60 mL

1. In a medium bowl, combine shrimp, fish sauce, salt and pepper and toss well. Set aside to marinate.

2. In a large bowl, combine shredded green mango, green onions, mint and cilantro and toss to mix well.

3. Heat a medium skillet over high heat until very hot. Add vegetable oil and swirl to cover bottom of the pan. Scatter in shrimp and cook, undisturbed, on one side for 1 minute. Toss well and cook for 30 seconds more. Cook, tossing often, until shrimp are pink, firm and opaque, 1 to 2 minutes. Scoop out into the bowl with mango mixture and let cool briefly.

4. Add Everyday Dipping Sauce and toss well. Mound salad on a serving platter and sprinkle with fried shallots. Serve at once.

Pomelo Salad with Shrimp and Cilantro

Pomelo belongs in the same sunny-colored citrus family as oranges, lemons and grapefruit, the latter being its closest cousin. But pomelo, an Asian variety with more sweetness and a drier texture, makes a wonderful addition to your tropical treasures repertoire. Its super-thick soft white pith encloses generous lobes of jewel-like droplets, filled with juice, which stays inside until you take a bite. This makes pomelo a superb salad component, and Southeast Asian cooks love accenting both its sweetness and tang. The Vietnamese way with pomelo salad highlights the plump citrus fruit's sweet, sharp and bright flavors with a piquant fish sauce dressing and a crunchy peanut finish.

◇◇

Serves 4 to 6

Tips

If you want to prepare this a little in advance, omit the dressing and peanuts, and assemble the salad shortly before serving.

Consider this dish a blank canvas, one in which you can turn up the chile heat, sweetness or sharpness by flavoring the dressing accordingly. You could use chopped pistachios for peanuts, add edamame beans to the mix or use whole freshly grilled shrimp or chunks of crabmeat to liven it up.

1	pomelo	1
¾ cup	finely shredded carrot	175 mL
12	cooked shrimp, peeled, deveined and halved lengthwise	12
3 tbsp	coarsely chopped fresh mint	45 mL
3 tbsp	coarsely chopped fresh cilantro	45 mL
½ cup	Everyday Dipping Sauce (page 200) (approx.)	125 mL
¼ cup	chopped dry-roasted salted peanuts	60 mL

1. Cut pomelo in half lengthwise, exposing the juicy, fruit center and thick white pith between skin and fruit. Place one half cut side down and slice away top and bottom portions, leaving the juicy fruity interior exposed. Repeat with other half.

2. Using your fingers, pull away and discard pomelo's thick skin and pith, leaving lobes of citrus fruit enclosed in soft sacs. Using your fingers or a paring knife, separate each section, gently pull out fruit and leave seeds and enclosing sacs behind. Seek to keep the pomelo in large chunks, but do not worry if it disintegrates into individual teardrop-shaped juicy bits. Discard pile of peel, pith and sacs. Place fruit in a large bowl.

Variations

You could use crab instead of shrimp, or omit the seafood and let the fruit shine.

You can use grapefruit instead of pomelo, keeping in mind that it will be juicier and more sour.

3. Add shredded carrot, halved shrimp, mint, cilantro and about half the Everyday Dipping Sauce. Toss gently to mix everything together well. Taste and see if you need more dressing. Mound salad on a small platter and sprinkle with peanuts. Serve at once.

◇ Vietnamese Tales

This refreshing and lively tumble of pomelo, shrimp, peanuts and fresh herbs illustrates the distinctive nature of salads within Vietnamese cuisine. The category of dishes known as *goi* share many qualities with salads in the West. They are served at room temperature rather than hot or warm. They showcase vegetables such as cucumber, carrot, watercress and cabbage, as well as green papaya, green mango and bean sprouts. In contrast, they often feature fruit, such as pomelo, pineapple and jicama. It's also common to see seafood or meat included in these hearty, bright-flavored dishes, from thinly sliced shrimp and chewy preserved jellyfish to beef jerky and shredded chicken.

Chopped Watercress Salad with Peanuts

Brilliant green and slightly bitter in a most appealing way, fresh watercress makes a fine, vibrant accompaniment to robust grilled dishes like Grilled Salmon with Chile-Lime Sauce (page 100). This dish can be stirred together 30 minutes or so in advance to wilt a little, or right before serving to deliver maximum crunchiness.

◇◇

Serves 4 to 6

Variation

You can use baby spinach leaves, a mix of spinach and arugula or thinly sliced celery or cucumber sliced or chopped, for this refreshing salad.

2	bunches watercress	2
¼ cup	white vinegar or apple cider vinegar	60 mL
2 tbsp	water	30 mL
2 tbsp	granulated sugar	30 mL
1 tbsp	vegetable oil	15 mL
½ tsp	salt	2 mL
¼ tsp	freshly ground black pepper	1 mL
3 tbsp	coarsely chopped dry-roasted salted peanuts	45 mL

1. Separate watercress, trim away coarse ends, rinse in cold water and drain well. Chop into 2-inch (5 cm) lengths. Measure out 3 cups (750 mL) watercress, reserving remaining greens for another use.

2. In a small bowl combine vinegar, water, sugar, oil, salt and pepper and stir well to dissolve sugar and salt. Pour over watercress and toss well. Transfer seasoned watercress to a small platter, sprinkle with chopped peanuts and serve.

Roasted Eggplant Salad with Mint

This humble-looking dish delivers incredibly bright flavor for very little effort. Fancier versions involve topping the salad with sautéed ground pork or chunks of crabmeat. But I prefer this rendition — less work and more reason to appreciate the simple, rustic deliciousness of this dish.

◇◇

Serves 4

Tip

Look for Asian eggplants in supermarket produce sections as well as in Asian markets and at farmer's markets. They are exceptionally easy to grow, prolific and beautiful, with tiny purple flowers. Colors range from pale lavender to deepest purple; even some variegated ones. Any of these slender vegetables work well in this recipe.

3	slender purple Asian eggplants (about 1½ lbs/750 g total) (see Tip, left)	3
3 tbsp	fish sauce	45 mL
3 tbsp	freshly squeezed lime juice	45 mL
2 tbsp	water	30 mL
2 tbsp	granulated sugar	30 mL
1 tsp	minced garlic	5 mL
1 tsp	minced fresh hot chiles	5 mL
1 tbsp	thinly sliced green onion	15 mL
1 tbsp	coarsely chopped fresh mint	15 mL

1. Prick each eggplant all around with a fork or tip of a sharp knife to discourage it from bursting as it roasts. Then place eggplants on a hot grill. Or place eggplant right on the burner of a gas or electric stove, over low to medium-low heat. Turn eggplant as it browns and puffs, roasting as evenly as possible, until fairly soft and blistery brown, 3 to 5 minutes. Transfer to a plate and let cool.

2. When eggplants are cool enough to touch, peel gently, holding under cool running water, when necessary, to get the job done. You can leave them whole with the stem attached or discard the stem and chop the eggplants into big pieces. Place eggplants in a small, shallow serving bowl and set aside.

3. In a medium bowl, combine fish sauce, lime juice, water and sugar and stir well to dissolve sugar. Stir in garlic and chiles and then pour sauce over eggplant. Scatter green onion and mint over dressed eggplant and serve at room temperature.

Chicken and Cabbage Salad with Mint

This simple assembly of everyday ingredients produces a marvelously refreshing dish. The signature Vietnamese herb called *rau ram* is a perfect complement for the chicken and other seasonings, but fresh mint is lovely if you don't have *rau ram*. In Vietnam this salad, *goi ga*, is traditionally served with *mien ga*, a nourishing chicken dish made with the broth created by poaching chicken for this salad. *Mien* means "noodles," referring to the clear tangle of bean thread noodles that fortify the soup. The *goi ga/mien ga* combination is inspired — a cool, brightly flavored salad paired with a warm, satisfying soupy dish, putting the broth from one to deliciously good use in the other.

◇◇

Serves 4 to 6

Tip

You can also use 2 cups (500 mL) cooked, shredded chicken in place of the boneless chicken breasts.

1 lb	boneless, skinless chicken breasts (see Tip, left)	500 g
3 tbsp	freshly squeezed lime juice	45 mL
2 tbsp	fish sauce	30 mL
1 tbsp	white or cider vinegar or freshly squeezed lime juice	15 mL
1 tbsp	granulated sugar	15 mL
½ tsp	freshly ground black pepper	2 mL
¾ cup	very thinly sliced onion	175 mL
½ cup	fresh mint, cilantro or basil leaves	125 mL
½ cup	*rau ram* leaves (page 220), optional	125 mL
2 cups	finely shredded green, savoy or napa cabbage	500 mL
¾ cup	shredded carrots	175 mL
3 tbsp	coarsely chopped dry-roasted salted peanuts, optional	45 mL

1. Place chicken in a medium saucepan and add 2 to 3 cups (500 to 750 mL) of water, enough to cover chicken by about ½ inch (1 cm). Bring to a rolling boil over medium-high heat, reduce heat to maintain a lively simmer and cook until chicken is no longer pink inside, 10 to 15 minutes.

2. Meanwhile, in a medium bowl, combine lime juice, fish sauce, vinegar, sugar and pepper and stir to dissolve sugar and mix everything well. Add onion and toss to coat. Set aside for 20 to 30 minutes, until you are ready to complete the dish.

Tip

If you'd like to prepare this wonderful salad in advance, it is ideal to keep the vegetables and herbs separate from the dressing. For maximum brightness and crunch, combine the dressing and vegetables about 15 minutes prior to serving so that the flavors can develop without wilting the cabbage. You can also toss it all together and keep chilled for up to 1 day.

3. Transfer meat to a plate to cool, reserving broth for another use, such as making soup or cooking rice. When chicken is cool, tear into long, thin shreds. Coarsely chop mint and *rau ram*, if using. Add shredded chicken, cabbage, carrots, mint and *rau ram* to bowl of onions and seasonings and toss to coat everything well. Mound salad on a serving plate and top with chopped peanuts, if using. Serve at room temperature or chilled.

◇ Vietnamese Tales

Enormous platters of salad, crudités and herbs adorn the table at mealtime. Although they create beautiful, glistening green islands on the table, they are neither garnishes nor a still life. Lettuce and herbs allow for folding tidbits of meat or omelet into packets for dipping in a sauce. Cucumbers and bean sprouts refresh the palate between bites of rich, sour, spicy or salty dishes. They also provide crunch and coolness that contrasts with the soft texture of sustaining rice.

Cool Shredded Cucumber Relish

Quick as a flash, you can have this essential refreshing sidekick to any savory grilled, fried or sautéed dish on the table as a visually cool and bright accompaniment. Ideal components are short, chubby summertime cucumbers such as Kirby, but you can make a great version with hothouse cucumbers/English cucumbers. Even big waxy cukes will work as long as you peel them well and scoop out the seedy centers before you grate them.

◇◇

**Makes about
1½ cups (375 mL)**

Tip
This relish does not keep well, so enjoy it fresh, or cover and refrigerate for a few hours.

2 lbs	cucumbers, such as Kirby or hothouse cucumbers	1 kg
1 tbsp	salt	15 mL
2 tsp	granulated sugar	10 mL
1 tsp	freshly ground black pepper	5 mL
2 tbsp	chopped cilantro	30 mL
¼ cup	chopped dry-roasted salted peanuts	60 mL

1. Trim cucumbers, removing ends and peeling each one.

2. Using a box grater placed in a large bowl, shred whole cucumbers into a small mountain of tiny cucumber ribbons.

3. Sprinkle salt over cucumbers and toss well. Set aside for about 20 minutes or for up to 1 hour.

4. Rinse and drain cucumbers well. Add sugar, pepper and cilantro and toss well. Transfer to a small serving plate or shallow bowl and sprinkle with peanuts. Serve at room temperature or chill and serve cold.

Sliced Cucumber Salad

Stir this up while the rice steams or as the grill heats up. Look forward to this salad's bright refreshing contrast to salty intense flavors from whatever you've got cooking on the grill or the stove. It's best the day it's made, but if you have extra, it will keep a day or two, with a bit less crunch but still maintaining the pleasing flavors.

◇◇

**Makes about
1½ cups (375 mL)**

Tips

Small pickling cucumbers and hothouse cucumbers are the most delicious ones, but the big waxy cucumbers are available year-round in the supermarket and will work in this recipe, too, since you peel them completely and scoop out the seeds.

This simple salad makes a pleasing accompaniment to any curry. A plate of rice with a bowl of spicy curry and a generous spoonful of this cucumber salad makes a great plate lunch or quick supper.

1 lb	cucumbers, such as Kirby or hothouse cucumbers	500 g
3 tbsp	finely chopped shallots or purple onion	45 mL
¼ cup	vinegar	60 mL
2 tbsp	granulated sugar	30 mL
2 tbsp	water	30 mL
1 tbsp	fish sauce	15 mL
½ tsp	salt	2 mL
½ tsp	freshly ground black pepper	2 mL

1. Peel cucumbers and cut in half lengthwise. Scoop out seeds in center and slice crosswise into thin crescent-shaped pieces. Place in a medium bowl along with shallots.

2. In a small saucepan, combine vinegar, sugar and water and stir well. Bring to a gentle boil over medium-high heat until sugar and salt dissolve. Stir in fish sauce, salt and pepper. Set aside and let cool to room temperature.

3. Pour cooled brine over pickles and shallots and stir well. Let stand for 15 minutes or cover and chill for up to 2 days. Serve chilled or at room temperature.

Everyday Pickled Carrots

This tasty carrot relish should live in your refrigerator, along with two bunches of fresh cilantro and a handful of fresh jalapeño chiles, so that you are never more than a baguette's length away from enjoying Vietnam's signature sub sandwich, Banh Mi (page 26). The carrots are wonderful in Everyday Dipping Sauce (page 200) as an edible garnish and they make a tasty addition to noodle soups and Big Cool Noodle Bowl (page 178).

Makes about 3 cups (750 mL)

Tip

I shred carrots on a box grater or in the food processor if I have time and I use already shredded carrots from the produce section if I'm in a rush.

1½ cups	water	375 mL
¾ cup	white vinegar	175 mL
¾ cup	granulated sugar	175 mL
1 tsp	salt	5 mL
3 cups	shredded carrots (about 12 oz/375 g)	750 mL

1. In a small saucepan over medium heat, combine water, vinegar, sugar and salt. Cook, swirling once or twice, until sugar and salt dissolve and brine is clear and smooth, 3 to 4 minutes. Transfer to a bowl and let cool to room temperature. (Pour brine into a cake pan, pie pan or a metal bowl and place it in the freezer briefly if you're in a hurry.)

2. Add shredded carrots to cooled brine, toss well and set aside for 20 to 30 minutes. Serve at room temperature or transfer to a jar, cover and refrigerate until serving time. Scoop out carrots from the brine as you need them and store the remainder in the refrigerator for up to 5 days.

Everyday Pickled Carrots and Daikon Radish

This mixture of pungent daikon radish and carrots typically fills out the Vietnamese submarine sandwich Banh Mi (page 26), and makes a dandy tart-sweet accompaniment to grilled meats, fried dishes and omelets. You can keep it on hand for spur-of-the-moment additions to sandwiches and rice meals.

Makes about 3 cups (750 mL)

Tip

Daikon radish is a firm, plump, ivory-colored root vegetable that is beloved throughout Asia. Found in clear soups and some stews, it becomes delicate when simmered. When placed in a brine, it softens in texture while adding its assertive tangy flavor and aroma to various types of pickles.

1½ cups	water	375 mL
¾ cup	white vinegar	175 mL
¾ cup	granulated sugar	175 mL
2 tsp	salt	10 mL
2 cups	shredded carrots	500 mL
1 cup	shredded daikon radish (see Tip, left)	250 mL

1. In a small saucepan over medium heat, combine water, vinegar, sugar and salt. Cook, swirling once or twice, until sugar and salt dissolve and brine is clear and smooth, 3 to 4 minutes. Transfer to a bowl and let cool to room temperature. (Pour brine into a cake pan, pie pan or a metal bowl and place in the freezer briefly if you're in a hurry.)

2. Add shredded carrots and daikon radish to cooled brine and toss well. Set aside for 20 to 30 minutes. Serve at room temperature or transfer to a jar, cover, and refrigerate until serving time. Scoop out carrot-daikon relish from brine as you need and store remainder in the refrigerator for up to 5 days.

Pickled Bean Sprouts

These simple preserved bean sprouts serve as a tangy and salty counterpoint to rich, sweet dishes, such as fish, shrimp or pork simmered in a clay pot and Pork and Hard-Boiled Eggs Simmered in Coconut Juice (page 79).

Makes about 3 cups (750 mL)

Tip

Sprouted from mung beans, these sprouts are widely available in supermarkets in the West, but often neglected and allowed to wilt in the produce bin. Look for crisp, firm sprouts with little scent.

3 cups	water	750 mL
¼ cup	white or cider vinegar	60 mL
1 tbsp	salt	15 mL
1 tsp	granulated sugar	5 mL
3 cups	mung bean sprouts (see Tip, left)	750 mL

1. In a medium saucepan over medium-high heat, bring water, vinegar, salt and sugar to a boil and stir to dissolve salt and sugar. Set aside and let cool to room temperature.

2. Meanwhile, place sprouts in a medium bowl and add water to cover. Discard any green mung bean hulls and tired sprouts you find, drain well and set aside.

3. When brine is cool, pour over bean sprouts and set aside for at least 1 hour. Serve at room temperature or cover and refrigerate for up to 3 days.

4. To serve, scoop sprouts out of brine and transfer to a small serving bowl or plate.

Pickled Mustard Greens

With mustard greens curvy, curly and sturdy shape, and their intense, peppery flavor, these members of the cruciferous vegetable family make a powerful impression whether they are raw, cooked or preserved. They thrive even in imperfect soil and unfriendly climates, making them a favorite throughout Asia. Pickling enables you to keep them handy for enjoying with such rich and luscious dishes as caramelized clay pot pork belly or chicken, as well as in stir-fries and soups.

<<<<<<<<<<<<<<<<<<<<<<<<<<<<<<<<<<<<<<<<<<<<<<<<<<<<<<<<<<<<<<<<

Makes 3 to 4 cups (750 mL to 1 L)

Tip

This recipe is traditionally made with mustard cabbage, which is a sturdy, rounded, stemmy cabbage with leaves curling into a head. English language translations typically call these "mustard greens," a term used in the West to denote softer textured loose-leaved greens, which resemble turnip greens, kale, collards, chard and spinach. Either would work and produce a tasty pickle, but the ideal for this recipe is mustard cabbage, which you will most likely find in Asian markets. Loose leafy mustard greens are available widely in supermarkets as well as farmer's markets.

♦ 1-quart (1 L) jar with tight-fitting lid
♦ Long-handled heatproof tongs or Asian-style strainer
♦ Large roasting pan or baking sheet with sides

2¼ lbs	fresh mustard cabbage or mustard greens (see Tip, left)	1.125 kg
2 tbsp	salt	30 mL
2 tsp	granulated sugar	10 mL

1. In a large stockpot, bring 2 quarts (2 L) water to a rolling boil over high heat. Meanwhile, trim mustard greens, trimming away and discarding base and the bottom 2 inches (5 cm), along with any woody, leafless portions at the base. Sliced trimmed leaves crosswise into 2-inch (5 cm) lengths. Measure out 5 cups (1.25 L) loosely packed leaves and set aside, reserving remaining leaves for another use.

2. Drop trimmed mustard greens into boiling water and stir well. Let blanch for about 30 seconds. Then using tongs or a strainer, remove quickly from pot. Place on roasting pan or baking sheet to drain and let cool, pouring any excess water back into the pot once you have transferred all the blanched mustard greens.

3. In a medium saucepan, combine 2½ quarts (2½ L) water, salt and sugar. Place over high heat and stir occasionally until sugar and salt dissolve and brine is clear. It does not need to boil. Remove brine from heat and set aside and let cool.

4. When salty brine has cooled, place blanched mustard greens in glass jar. Add cooled brine to cover well. Cover and place in the refrigerator for 2 days. Open and serve as pickled greens or use in soups and stir-fried dishes. Keeps in the refrigerator for 1 week.

Cauliflower with Garlic and Pepper

Cook the cauliflower until it's tender and nicely seasoned but still in possession of a little crunch. You could add a splash of sesame oil just before that last toss for a delicious variation. This is usually served hot with rice, soup and other dishes, but I also like it at room temperature or cold if I have any left over.

◇◇

Serves 4

Variation

Use broccoli florets instead of cauliflower and cook the same way.

2 tbsp	vegetable oil	30 mL
1 tbsp	chopped garlic	15 mL
4 cups	small cauliflower florets (approx.)	1 L
2 tbsp	fish sauce	30 mL
2 tbsp	water	30 mL
1 tsp	granulated sugar	5 mL
½ tsp	freshly ground black pepper	2 mL
2	green onions, trimmed and cut into 1-inch (2.5 cm) lengths	2
2 tbsp	coarsely chopped fresh cilantro, dill or mint	30 mL

1. Heat oil in a large skillet over medium-high heat until a bit of garlic sizzles at once and then add rest of garlic. Toss well and add cauliflower. Cook for 1 minute and then toss well, exposing the other sides to the hot pan. Add fish sauce, water, sugar, pepper and green onions and cook, tossing often, until cauliflower is tender but still pleasantly crunchy, about 2 minutes. Stir in cilantro, toss once more and transfer to a serving plate deep enough to hold the sauce or to a shallow bowl. Serve hot or warm.

Cabbage Stir-Fried with Eggs

Everyday ingredients team up to make a most pleasing tangle of comfort food to go with rice or to accompany meat loaf, barbecued chicken or a stack of sausages with a side of grits. Add a splash of chile sauce if you want some fireworks or just enjoy the simple goodness of this anytime can-do dish.

2	eggs	2
1 tbsp	Asian fish sauce	15 mL
½ tsp	salt	2 mL
½ tsp	freshly ground black pepper	2 mL
½ tsp	granulated sugar	2 mL
2 tbsp	vegetable oil	30 mL
1 tbsp	chopped garlic	15 mL
5 cups	chopped cabbage, cut into ribbons, about 2 by ½ inch (5 by 1 cm) (see Tip, left)	1.25 L
2 tbsp	water	30 mL

Serves 4

Tip

Cabbage can mean the big, smooth, sturdy rounded cruciferous vegetable in shades of pale green; curly, bubbly surfaced savoy cabbage; or even the white-to-pale green loaf-shaped napa cabbage, which is more stem than leaves. Any of these would work just fine in this recipe, which is comfort food, frugal food and fast food all in one dear, old-school dish.

1. In a medium bowl, combine eggs and fish sauce and beat to mix well. In a small bowl, combine salt, pepper and sugar. Place both bowls by the stove.

2. In a wok or a large deep skillet, heat oil over medium-high heat until a bit of garlic sizzles at once. Add garlic and cook, tossing often, until fragrant, about 30 seconds.

3. Add cabbage and toss well. Cook, tossing occasionally, until cabbage is shiny and beginning to wilt, about 2 minutes. Add water around edges of pan and continue cooking, tossing occasionally, until cabbage has softened and turned a brighter green.

4. Move cabbage away from center of pan and pour in egg. Cover egg with shreds of cabbage and let cook, undisturbed, for 30 seconds. Add salt mixture, toss once more. Transfer to a serving platter and serve hot or warm.

Spinach Sautéed with Garlic and Pepper

Elsewhere in Southeast Asia, cooks tend to fortify stir-fried vegetables with a handful of meat. In the Vietnamese kitchen, vegetables often make a solo appearance, cooked simply to enhance their natural appeal. Such vegetable dishes are usually enjoyed with lots of rice and other dishes featuring meat or fish. Each dish has its own distinct flavor and they are delicious eaten together or separately.

Serves 4

Tip

In Vietnam this dish is typically made with spinach's sturdier cousins, including bok choy, napa cabbage and various members of the collard-like cruciferous vegetable family. Spinach works wonderfully and cooks extremely quickly. Add its gorgeous color and you have a winner of a go-to any-day vegetable dish.

2 tbsp	vegetable oil	30 mL
1 tbsp	coarsely chopped garlic	15 mL
8 to 10 cups	fresh spinach leaves (about 1¼ lbs/625 g)	2 to 2.5 L
2 tbsp	fish sauce	30 mL
½ tsp	freshly ground black pepper	2 mL
3 tbsp	water	45 mL

1. In a large, heavy skillet or a wok over medium-high heat, combine oil and garlic and cook until garlic sizzles and releases its aroma, about 30 seconds. Add spinach and cook for 1 minute. Gently turn pile of spinach to expose all the leaves to the heat. Add fish sauce, pepper and water, toss well and cook, turning often, until spinach is wilted and tender, 1 to 2 minutes. Transfer to a deep platter, sauce and all, and serve hot, warm or at room temperature.

Green Beans with Shiitake Mushrooms, Garlic and Pepper

This vibrant green pile of vegetable goodness comes out wonderfully whether you use Asian-style long beans or the various green beans available in farmer's markets and supermarkets. Some are round and some flat, but they're all green, good and good for us. Some sliced garlic, fish sauce and sugar are all that's needed for a worthy accompaniment to hearty main event dishes, from Five-Spice Roast Chicken (page 59) and Grilled Garlic-Pepper Pork Chops (page 82) to Lemongrass Chicken (page 52) or Speedy Shrimp in Caramel-Chile Sauce (page 108). I love this dish with rice and a fried egg: simple and good.

Serves 4

Tip

If you like green beans to be very tender, add 3 or 4 tbsp (45 to 60 mL) water or chicken stock and cook until they are the texture you love. If the liquid cooks away, add a little more, and cook until done to suit you.

2 tbsp	vegetable oil	30 mL
2 tbsp	thinly sliced garlic	30 mL
1 cup	sliced fresh shiitake mushroom caps or button mushrooms	250 mL
4 cups	chopped trimmed green beans, about 2-inch (5 cm) lengths (approx.)	1 L
2 tbsp	fish sauce	30 mL
2 tbsp	water or chicken stock	30 mL
2 tsp	granulated sugar	10 mL
½ tsp	salt	2 mL
½ tsp	freshly ground black pepper	2 mL
2 tbsp	coarsely chopped fresh cilantro	30 mL

1. Heat oil in a large skillet or a wok over medium-high heat until a bit of garlic sizzles at once. Scatter in slices of garlic and toss well.

2. Add mushrooms and toss well and cook until softened and a little wilted, 1 to 2 minutes.

3. Add green beans and toss well and cook, undisturbed, for 1 minute. Then toss again. Add fish sauce, water, sugar, salt and pepper and continue cooking, tossing occasionally, until green beans are pleasingly tender and cooked to your liking, 3 to 4 minutes more. Stir in cilantro, toss well, and transfer to a serving plate or to a shallow bowl. Serve hot or warm.

Water Spinach Stir-Fried with Garlic

Though it's no relation to spinach, this elegantly proportioned leafy green vegetable goes by that name in English, unless it's labeled "morning glory," another misnomer, albeit a lovely one. You may find it labeled *ong choy*, its Cantonese name. A sheaf of long spears with distinctive hollow stems and arrow-shaped leaves, this nutritious vegetable enjoys star status among Vietnamese greens, and is beloved throughout Asia. Blanching it before stir-frying means that it cooks quickly and evenly while maintaining its emerald green beauty and crunch.

Serves 4		

Tip

Blanching the chopped vegetables in advance of stir-frying them may seem like an extra step, but it serves a good purpose. The very sturdy stems of this vegetable need long or intense cooking to make them tender. Long cooking in the wok would make them dull, and firing up the wok to cook them fast would cause them to burn. Hence blanching, or dropping them into wildly boiling water for a brief time, works perfectly, with the final stir-fry adding flavor.

1	bunch water spinach, about 1½ lbs (750 g) untrimmed	1
1 tsp	salt	5 mL
2 tbsp	vegetable oil	30 mL
2 tbsp	coarsely chopped fresh garlic	30 mL
1 tbsp	Asian fish sauce	15 mL
1 tsp	granulated sugar	5 mL
½ tsp	freshly ground black pepper	2 mL

1. Bring a large pot of water to a rolling boil over high heat. Meanwhile, trim water spinach, cutting off and discarding the large, hollow stems at the base. Keep upper two thirds with leaves and more delicate stems. Remove any dried or tired leaves and chop remaining stalks into 2- to 3-inch (5 to 7.5 cm) lengths.

2. Add salt and chopped water spinach to boiling water. Using tongs, chopsticks or 2 long-handled heatproof spoons, pull, lift and rearrange water spinach as it blanches in boiling water for 30 seconds to 1 minute.

3. In a colander, drain water spinach well. Rinse greens with cool water to stop from cooking more. Shake well to release most of the water and place by the stove.

4. In a wok or a large deep skillet, heat vegetable oil over medium-high heat until a bit of garlic sizzles at once. Add garlic and toss well, keeping it moving as it releases its aroma and just barely begins to brown.

Variation

This recipe would work well with broccoli rabe, trimmed at the base and chopped into 2-inch (5 cm) lengths.

5. Add blanched water spinach and use tongs or chopsticks to pull it apart and spread out a little in the pan. Cook, turning and pulling apart, for 1 minute. Add fish sauce, sugar and pepper and toss well to mix with water spinach. Cook, turning and tossing water spinach, until tender but still bright green, about 2 minutes more.

6. Transfer to a serving platter and serve at once. Enjoy hot, warm or at room temperature.

◇ Vietnamese Tales

Vietnamese cooks prepare water spinach simply with garlic and fish sauce. Or in intensely flavored versions in which fermented bean sauce or pungent shrimp paste adds a powerful accent to the dish. Whatever the flavorings, this dish is always enjoyed with rice.

Corn with Dried Shrimp, Green Onions and Butter

This late-night street food snack in Vietnam makes a superb and simple side dish to include in a rice-centered meal. You can make it with summertime sweet corn for a plush version or stir it up on a busy winter night using frozen or canned corn for a pleasing everyday dish.

◇◇◇

Serves 4

Variation

If you don't have dried shrimp, you could use chopped ham, crumbled bacon or simple omit the protein and enjoy this as corny-corn goodness, plain and simple.

2 tbsp	salty dried shrimp	30 mL
2 tbsp	butter	30 mL
1 tbsp	vegetable oil	15 mL
3 cups	corn kernels	750 mL
1 tbsp	Asian fish sauce	15 mL
½ cup	chopped green onions	125 mL
½ tsp	salt	2 mL
2 tbsp	water, optional	30 mL
	Hot sauce	

1. In a small bowl, add warm water to cover shrimp and let soak for 5 to 10 minutes. Then scoop out shrimp and chop coarsely. Set by the stove.

2. Heat butter and vegetable oil in a large heavy skillet over medium-high heat. When a bit of green onion sizzles at once, add corn and toss well. Cook, stirring occasionally, until corn is tender, shiny and almost done, 2 to 3 minutes.

3. Add dried shrimp and toss well to mix evenly with corn. Add fish sauce, green onions and salt and toss well. If pan becomes dry, add water a spoonful at a time.

4. Cook until corn is tender (taste a kernel or two if you're unsure) and everything is evenly combined, 3 to 4 minutes. Transfer to a serving bowl or plate and add a small dish of hot sauce as an accompaniment. Serve hot, at room temperature or cold.

Simple Stewed Kabocha Pumpkin

Whether you use kabocha pumpkin, butternut squash or a hardy thick-fleshed member of the pumpkin family, you will love the luscious simplicity of this sweet-and-salty cool-weather dish. Braising the pumpkin in chicken stock, fish sauce and sugar produces a smidgen of sauce and a lovely texture in the vegetable. Serve this as a satisfying accompaniment to a simple rice meal of steamed fish or roast chicken and a plate of sautéed spinach or napa cabbage.

Serves 4

1½ lbs	kabocha pumpkin, butternut squash or another winter squash	750 g
2 tbsp	vegetable oil	30 mL
1 tbsp	chopped garlic	15 mL
¾ cup	chicken stock, vegetable stock or water	175 mL
2 tbsp	fish sauce	30 mL
2 tbsp	granulated sugar	30 mL
½ tsp	salt	2 mL
½ tsp	freshly ground pepper	2 mL

1. Chop pumpkin lengthwise into halves or quarters. Scoop out and discard seeds and fibers inside. Using a vegetable peeler or a sharp knife, remove outer skin. Chop peeled pumpkin into 1-inch (2.5 cm) chunks. You will have about 4 cups (1 L) of prepared pumpkin.

2. In a medium saucepan, heat vegetable oil over medium-high heat until a bit of garlic sizzles at once. Add garlic and toss well. Cook, tossing occasionally, until fragrant but just beginning to brown, about 1 minute.

3. Add pumpkin and toss well. Cook, tossing occasionally, until shiny with oil and beginning to soften and brown, about 1 minute more. Add stock, fish sauce, sugar, salt and pepper. Stir well and bring to a boil.

4. Reduce heat and cook at a lively simmer until pumpkin is very tender and has a small amount of creamy sauce, about 20 minutes. Remove from heat and serve hot, warm or at room temperature.

Rice

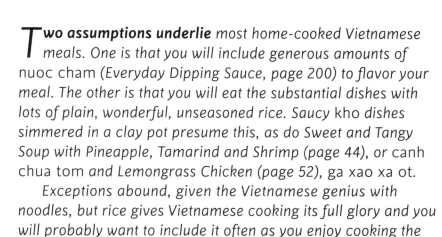

*T*wo assumptions underlie most home-cooked Vietnamese meals. One is that you will include generous amounts of nuoc cham (*Everyday Dipping Sauce, page 200*) to flavor your meal. The other is that you will eat the substantial dishes with lots of plain, wonderful, unseasoned rice. Saucy kho dishes simmered in a clay pot presume this, as do Sweet and Tangy Soup with Pineapple, Tamarind and Shrimp (page 44), or canh chua tom and Lemongrass Chicken (page 52), ga xao xa ot.

Exceptions abound, given the Vietnamese genius with noodles, but rice gives Vietnamese cooking its full glory and you will probably want to include it often as you enjoy cooking the recipes in this book.

On page 142, you will find a recipe for Everyday Rice, which you can cook first thing and then set on the back burner, literally, to finish cooking on its own while you put the rest of the meal together. If you eat rice often, as I do, you may want to consider an electric rice cooker, which makes the job quite simple and gives excellent results.

Fried rice is worth putting in your repertoire ASAP. It takes the place of a sandwich in the Asian home kitchen, a speedy, satisfying something to eat made with whatever happens to be in the fridge. Fried rice calls for a little more action than sandwich making (chopping, heat, timing and tossing), but not much, and it is well worth the time.

Often enjoyed with roasted and grilled meat, Sticky Rice (page 144) is a mainstay within Vietnamese cuisine, enjoyed in snacks both savory and sweet, and sometimes in place of everyday long-grain rice. I adore sticky rice and hope you will try it and enjoy it as well. Everyday Rice Porridge (page 150) serves many roles in Vietnamese cuisine. It's a pleasing food for small children and old folks; a breakfast favorite as well as a late night pleasure, especially after indulging in spirits far into the night. It's considered ideal for anyone who is ill, but it's also appreciated as comfort food with no reason required.

Everyday Rice

While I count on an electric rice cooker as a mainstay of my kitchen, I like knowing how to cook rice in a pot on top of the stove. That way I'm ready even if the power goes off (we have a gas stove) or if I'm on a camping trip or if I want to cook a Vietnamese feast at someone else's home. Get good at it and then keep doing it until you have the recipe in your head and hands.

◇◇

Serves 4

Makes 4 to 5 cups (1 to 1.25 L)

Variation

Brown rice is not traditional in Vietnamese cuisine, but it makes a fine, delicious accompaniment to all the dishes in this book. Keep in mind that it takes longer to cook and requires more water. To cook brown rice: In a medium saucepan, combine 1½ cups (375 mL) long-grain brown rice with 3 cups (750 mL) water and bring to an active boil. Reduce heat to maintain a gentle but visible simmer. Cover and cook for 40 minutes. Remove from heat and let stand for 10 minutes. Stir well and serve hot or warm.

1½ cups	long-grain white rice	375 mL
2 cups	water	500 mL

1. Measure rice into a medium saucepan and add cold water to cover grains. Swirl grains with your hand, drain well and then add water. Bring to a gentle boil, uncovered, over medium heat. Let rice continue to boil gently until water level drops below the level of rice so that it looks dry.

2. Stir well, cover and reduce heat to low and cook for 15 minutes. Remove from heat and let stand, covered, for 10 minutes. Fluff gently with a fork and serve hot or warm.

Red Rice

This modern recipe is enjoyed with Shaking Beef (page 72), one of the dishes in the signature banquet menu known as Seven Course Beef. It's made with cooked, cooled or even chilled rice, so make a big batch and set some aside for this delicious and handsome dish.

Shaking Beef (page 72)

Serves 4

Tip

Tomato paste comes in small cans, and what's left from one recipe tends to mold in the refrigerator before it's used. To keep tomato paste on hand, use a tablespoon (15 mL) to make small mounds of tomato paste and place them on a pie plate or 9-inch (23 cm) square baking pan, about 1 inch (2.5 cm) apart. Freeze solid, and then transfer the frozen tomato paste lumps to a resealable bag. Store in the freezer for 6 to 8 months. Use frozen, or after thawing on a plate at room temperature.

2 tbsp	vegetable oil	30 mL
1 tbsp	chopped garlic	15 mL
3 cups	cooked rice, chilled or at room temperature	750 mL
2 tbsp	tomato paste (see Tip, left)	30 mL
1 tbsp	fish sauce	15 mL
¼ tsp	salt	1 mL
¼ tsp	freshly ground black pepper	1 mL

1. In a wok or a large, deep heavy skillet, heat oil over medium-high heat. Add garlic and cook, tossing often, until fragrant, about 30 seconds.

2. Crumble in rice and cook, tossing often to break up grains, until shiny and heated through, 2 to 3 minutes.

3. Add tomato paste and continue cooking, tossing and pressing to mix into rice evenly, for 2 to 3 minutes. Add fish sauce and cook, tossing often, and adding 1 to 2 tbsp (15 to 30 mL) water occasionally as needed to avoid sticking, for 2 minutes more.

4. When rice is hot, tender and evenly colored, add salt and pepper. Toss well. Transfer to a serving platter and serve hot.

Sticky Rice

Look for long-grain sticky rice in Asian markets. Most packages label it "glutinous rice" or "sweet rice," even though it contains no gluten and is not sweet unless you add sugar to it. Plan ahead to make sticky rice because it needs to soak for at least 3 hours in order to steam properly. The ideal kitchen tool for steaming sticky rice is a Laotian-style cone-shaped woven basket, which nests in a deep metal pot containing boiling water (see Tip, below). The basket of soaked rice sits directly over the flow of steam, allowing the rice to cook evenly and quickly (see Tip, right, for more options to cook rice).

Serves 4 to 6

Makes about 4½ cups (1.125 L)

Tip

If you enjoy sticky rice as much as I do, consider getting a cone-shaped steaming set, designed for the job of steaming soaked sticky rice. It's an inexpensive, charming traditional country-cooking implement that is still viable in the kitchens of the third millennium. The simple way in which it does its job more than compensates for the need to find a spot for one more thing in your kitchen. You can buy this two-part steamer set in many Asian markets or see Resources (page 229).

1½ cups	long-grain sticky rice	375 mL
	Water for soaking and steaming	

1. Place raw sticky rice into a medium bowl and add enough water to cover by 2 inches (5 cm). Let soak for at least 3 hours or overnight. Set out your steaming vessel (see Tip, right).

2. To cook rice, bring 4 to 6 inches (10 to 15 cm) water to a vigorous boil over medium heat in base of your steamer. If you are using a Laotian-style steamer, drain rice well and transfer to cone-shaped steaming basket. Set basket of rice grains securely over boiling water, cover with a folded kitchen towel or a metal lid and let rice cook in a steady flow of steam until it plumps up, glistens and changes color from bright white to translucent ivory, 20 to 30 minutes. To use bamboo or metal trays, line tray with a kitchen towel, cheesecloth or a banana leaf and spread soaked and drained sticky rice over it in a fairly even layer. Or steam rice in a shallow, heatproof bowl placed directly on the tray. When the time is up, test rice by scooping up a small mouthful, rolling it into a ball and eating it. If it is tender and pleasantly chewy, the rice is ready.

3. Turn out cooked sticky rice onto a cutting board or tray and quickly spread out into a fairly even layer. Let cool and release steam for 5 to 10 minutes. Then gather warm rice into a large clump and transfer to a serving plate or a covered serving basket. To keep for more than 30 minutes before serving, cover with a kitchen towel or place in a tightly closed container to help keep moist. Serve hot, warm or at room temperature. To reheat cooked sticky rice, sprinkle with water and heat gently in steamer or in a microwave just until softened and warm.

Tip

You could also use large bamboo steamer trays designed to fit over 2 to 3 inches (5 to 7.5 cm) of water in a wok. A third option is a big metal steaming set, which has several trays through which steam can flow. It takes up some storage space, but it has multiple uses as a steaming vessel, unlike the cone-shaped basket setup, which works only for sticky rice.

◈ Vietnamese Tales

Sticky rice is an amazing ingredient. It requires a little extra attention, since it needs 3 hours or more of soaking in advance and a means of steaming it to bring it to its tender, nourishing and fun-to-eat state. In Laos and in the northern and northeastern regions of Thailand, plain long-grain sticky rice is the daily bread, but in Vietnam it is a much-loved option, often eaten as a breakfast on the run or a between-meals snack, topped with various simple, incredibly delicious toppings, including peanuts, toasted sesame seeds, coconut shreds, sugar and salt.

Black Sticky Rice

In Vietnam, black sticky rice is enjoyed at breakfast or lunch, as well as in Black Sticky Rice Pudding (page 185), a sweet treat. *Xoi nep* is a form of brown rice with a dense, chewy texture. It needs a little longer cooking time than polished white rice. High in amylopectin, the starch that causes rice grains to cling together, it can be soaked and steamed like white, milled sticky rice. Serve this with chopsticks or a fork as the centerpiece of a rice meal or season it with butter and salt and enjoy it as a side dish with grilled or roasted food. For breakfast we like it with a topping of brown sugar, toasted sweetened shredded coconut and chopped roasted and salted peanuts or walnuts.

Serves 4

♦ Medium saucepan with tight-fitting lid

1½ cups	black sticky rice	375 mL
3 cups	water	750 mL

1. In medium saucepan with tight-fitting lid, rinse rice and drain well. Add water and bring to a lively boil over medium-high heat. Stir well and cook for 10 minutes. Stir well again and reduce heat to medium, maintaining a lively simmer. Cook, stirring well occasionally, until rice is plump, shiny and tender with a soft, nutty crunch, about 25 minutes. It should be fairly dry. Reduce heat to low and cook for 3 minutes more, stirring and scraping once or twice. Remove from heat, transfer to a serving bowl and serve hot or warm.

Sticky Rice with Mung Beans, Northern-Style

Morning markets in Vietnam offer countless satisfying little breakfast options, of which this is one. It can be a standalone dish or part of a small round up of easy to eat options found while shopping for the day's meals. You can enjoy this as a snack any time of day or as a rice dish to enjoy along with grilled meats and fish.

Serves 4

Makes about 3 cups (750 mL)

Tip

To toast sesame seeds: Heat a medium saucepan over medium-high heat until hot. Add sesame seeds and reduce heat to medium. Toast sesame seeds, stirring and tossing often to help brown gently and evenly without burning, 1 to 2 minutes. When just golden and fragrant, transfer to a saucer and set aside and let cool.

Sticky Rice

¾ cup	long-grain sticky rice	175 mL
¼ cup	yellow mung bean centers (see Tip, right)	60 mL
	Water for soaking and steaming	
½ tsp	vegetable oil	2 mL
¼ tsp	salt	1 mL

Topping (optional)

3 tbsp	white sesame seeds, toasted (see Tip, left)	45 mL
⅓ cup	coarsely chopped dry-roasted salted peanuts	75 mL
2 tbsp	granulated sugar	30 mL

1. At least 3 hours before you plan to serve, combine raw sticky rice and mung bean centers in a medium bowl. Add water to cover, swirl with your hands and drain well. Repeat process, rinsing away most of the yellow color released by the beans. Add fresh water to cover by about 1 inch (2.5 cm) and set aside to soak for at least 3 hours or for up to 12 hours.

2. To cook rice and beans, drain well and then mix in oil and salt. Scrape mixture into basket or onto cloth-lined tray of your steaming vessel (see Tip, page 145) and place over a steamer base filled with 4 to 6 inches (10 to 15 cm) of water. Bring water to a rolling boil over high heat and then adjust heat to maintain an active flow of steam.

Tip

Look for yellow mung bean centers in Asian and South Asian markets. They are often labeled "peeled split mung beans," and offered in clear sacks showing off their petite golden size and shape. Transfer any unused portion to a jar and store airtight for up to 1 year. It's easy to confuse this ingredient with yellow split peas, which you may find with the lentils, pulses and beans sold loose or packaged in South Asian markets. Those are rounded and flattened out, while the ones you want are smaller and oval-shaped.

3. When steam is flowing through rice and beans, cover with a folded kitchen towel, a big square of banana leaf or a lid and let steam until the tiny yellow beans are tender and the rice plumps up, changing from bright white to a warm ivory shade, 20 to 35 minutes. The rice should be tender to the bite. It should stick to itself when rolled into a little ball, but not stick to your fingers.

4. While rice and beans steam, prepare topping, if using. You can chop toasted sesame seeds, pound lightly with a mortar and pestle or leave whole. In a small bowl, combine peanuts, sesame seeds and sugar, stirring to mix well. Place on the serving platter you will use for the rice and beans.

5. Turn out cooked sticky rice and beans onto a cutting board or tray and quickly spread out into a fairly even layer. Let cool and release steam for 5 to 10 minutes.

6. Gather warm rice and beans into a large clump and transfer to the serving platter with the bowl of topping, if using. Sprinkle topping over rice and serve hot, warm or at room temperature.

◇ Vietnamese Tales

The tiny, oval, yellow centers of mung beans are beloved in Vietnamese cuisine. Often used in sweets and in steamed foods wrapped in banana leaf packets, they are also cooked with sticky rice in various ways. In northern Vietnam, mung bean centers are soaked and steamed along with sticky rice, giving the rice a lovely golden color while increasing its nutritional value. Southern versions of sticky rice with mung beans usually include coconut milk and sugar, taking the dish in a sweeter direction. The topping is extraordinarily delicious — doubly crunchy and pleasingly salty and sweet.

Fried Rice with Sweet Chinese Sausage, Cilantro and Peas

Deep red in color and marbled with fat, lap cheong sausage is often sliced on the diagonal into ovals and stir-fried quickly to be served with rice and cucumbers for a speedy meal. A fried egg on the side makes this fried rice even more tasty.

<<<<<<<<<<<<<<<<<<<<<<<<<<<<<<<<<<<<<<<<<<<<<<<<<<<<<<<<<<<<<<<<<<<<<<<<>>

Serves 4

Tip

You'll find the rich sweet, very firm-textured sausage called lap cheong in Asian markets, usually in sealed packages in the refrigerated section.

Variation

In place of lap cheong sausage, you can use either ham or Char Shiu-Style Pork (page 88), diced into small cubes and cooked in the same way as the rich sausage.

4 cups	cold cooked rice (page 142)	1 L
2 tbsp	vegetable oil, divided	30 mL
¾ cup	chopped lap cheong Chinese sausage (see Tip, left)	175 mL
½ cup	shredded carrot	125 mL
½ cup	coarsely chopped onion	125 mL
1 tbsp	coarsely chopped garlic	15 mL
1 cup	frozen peas, preferably petite peas	250 mL
2 tbsp	fish sauce	30 mL
½ tsp	salt	2 mL
¼ tsp	freshly ground black pepper	1 mL
3 tbsp	coarsely chopped green onions	45 mL

1. Crumble rice with your fingers to break up any big lumps and place a serving platter by the stove. Heat a large, deep skillet or a wok over medium-high heat. Add about 2 tsp (10 mL) of the oil and swirl to coat pan lightly. Add sausage and toss well. Cook, undisturbed, for 1 minute. Then toss again.

2. Add carrot, onion and garlic and toss again. Cook, tossing occasionally, until garlic and onion are fragrant and carrot is brightly colored and shiny, for 1 minute more.

3. Add the remaining oil and toss everything well. Add peas and rice and cook, tossing occasionally, until everything is well combined, 3 to 4 minutes.

4. Add fish sauce, salt and pepper, toss well, and cook, tossing often, until rice is hot and tender and green peas are cooked, 1 minute more. Mound fried rice on serving platter, sprinkle with green onions and serve hot or warm.

Fried Rice with Shrimp, Egg and Green Onion

Throughout Asia, fried rice is a standard dish and the Vietnamese version is a delicious, endlessly variable ticket to quick and easy feasts. This recipe is a little bit fancy because it includes an egg pancake that is cooked ahead and shredded. You can leave out the egg or push the rice away from the center and scramble the egg right in the middle of the pan toward the end of the cooking time. I add frozen peas or edamame beans when I want fried rice to be a one-plate supper.

Serves 4

Tip

For a vegetarian version, omit fish sauce and shrimp, increase salt to 1½ tsp (7 mL) and add pineapple, cashews and frozen peas.

Variation

You can also use chopped cooked chicken or ham instead of the shrimp, adding either meat to the pan along with the rice since they are already cooked.

4 cups	cold cooked rice (page 142)	1 L
2 tbsp	vegetable oil, divided	30 mL
1	egg, well beaten	1
1 tbsp	coarsely chopped garlic	15 mL
½ cup	coarsely chopped onion	125 mL
12	medium shrimp, peeled and deveined	12
2 tbsp	fish sauce	30 mL
½ tsp	salt	2 mL
¼ tsp	freshly ground black pepper	1 mL
3 tbsp	coarsely chopped green onion	45 mL

1. Crumble rice with your fingers to break up any big lumps and place a serving platter and a table knife by the stove. Heat a large, deep skillet or a wok over medium-high heat. Add about 2 tsp (10 mL) of the oil and swirl to coat pan lightly. Add beaten egg and tilt pan to make a thin egg pancake. Cook until set, about 1 minute and then turn out onto serving platter.

2. Add remaining oil to pan, along with garlic and onion and cook until sizzling and fragrant, 1 to 2 minutes. Scatter in shrimp and cook, tossing once or twice, until pink, 1 to 2 minutes. Add rice and cook, tossing occasionally, until shiny and heated through, 3 to 5 minutes.

3. Meanwhile, roll up egg pancake into a cylinder and cut crosswise into thin ribbons with a table knife. Add fish sauce, salt, pepper and green onion to rice and toss. Add egg ribbons and cook, tossing well, for 1 minute more. Mound fried rice on a serving platter and serve hot or warm.

Everyday Rice Porridge

This simple comfort food is beloved throughout Asia as a satisfying breakfast, nourishment for wee ones, elders and anyone under the weather. It's also considered a late night sustenance that may even curb the effects of intoxication. Known as *chao* in Vietnamese, as *jook* in Cantonese and congee in many English-language sources, it's an elemental and ancient dish of raw rice cooked off to creaminess in an abundance of water. Diners flavor and enhance this porridge with salty preserved duck eggs, tidbits of pickled or salted fish or meat, Egg Pancake Strips (page 215), Everyday Sweet and Salty Ground Pork (page 93), chile sauce and an array of pickles and herbs.

◇◇

Serves 4

| ½ cup | raw long- or short-grain rice | 125 mL |
| 5 cups | water | 1.25 L |

Tip

If you make this porridge in advance, note that it thickens as it stands. Refrigerate until near serving time, add about ⅓ cup (75 mL) water and bring back to a gentle boil. Stir well and add more water, ⅓ cup (75 mL) at a time, until you reach the original texture or the texture you prefer.

Variations

To season your porridge, set out any of these ingredients or choose flavorful additions that suit your fancy. Consider fish sauce, soy sauce, salt and pepper, Asian sesame oil, salty egg, chopped thousand-year egg, strips of ham, smoked fish or chopped cilantro and green onions.

1. In a medium saucepan, combine rice and water. Place over medium-high heat and bring to a rolling boil. Adjust heat to maintain a visible simmer and cook, stirring occasionally, until rice loses its shape and softens into a thick, creamy porridge, 35 to 45 minutes. Serve hot or warm.

Hearty Chicken and Rice Porridge with Fresh Ginger

Comfort food isn't always this easy to make, nor this tasty. Chao ga is hearty enough for supper and simple enough to fix on the busiest day. Serve chao ga with a bowl of either Everyday Dipping Sauce (page 200) or Ginger-Lime Dipping Sauce (page 202) on the side.

<<<<<<<<<<<<<<<<<<<<<<<<<<<<<<<<<<<<<<<<<<<<<<<<<<<<<<<<<<<<<<<<<<<<<<<<<<<<<<<<<<<<<<<<<<<<<<<<<<<<<<<<<<<<<<<<<<<<<<<<<<

Serves 4 to 6

Tip

If you have time, add a little extra flavor by first frying the rice grains and a little chopped onion in 1 to 2 tbsp (15 to 30 mL) of oil, until the onion is fragrant and the rice grains turn bright white. Add them to the boiling stock and simmer until soft.

3 cups	Chicken Stock (page 216) or store-bought	750 mL
3 cups	water	750 mL
8 oz	boneless, skinless chicken breasts or thighs	250 g
½ cup	long-grain rice, rinsed and drained	125 mL
1 tbsp	finely chopped fresh gingerroot	15 mL
1 tbsp	fish sauce	15 mL
1 tsp	freshly ground black pepper	5 mL
2 tbsp	thinly sliced green onion	30 mL
1 tbsp	chopped fresh cilantro	15 mL

1. In a medium saucepan over high heat, combine stock and water and bring to a rolling boil. Add chicken, reduce heat to maintain a lively simmer and cook until chicken is no longer pink inside for breasts and juices run clear when pierced for thighs, about 10 minutes. Transfer to a plate and let cool and return stock to a boil.

2. Stir in rice and ginger and reduce heat to maintain a gentle simmer. Cook rice until soft, 25 minutes.

3. Meanwhile, pull apart or cut cooled chicken into shreds and set aside. When rice is tender, add shredded chicken, fish sauce, pepper, green onion and cilantro and stir well. Remove porridge from heat and serve hot.

Soothing Rice Porridge with Salmon and Fresh Dill

Serve this deluxe version of humble rice porridge with a saucer of sliced cucumbers and a bowl of steamed broccoli, seasoned with a splash of Asian sesame oil and a little salt. If you have *chao ca* left over, expect it to thicken up a good bit once it cools off. To reheat it you can add 1 to 2 cups (250 to 500 mL) chicken stock to return it to its original texture or simply enjoy it in its new substantial state, adding a little salt, a few herbs or a splash of lime as needed, to refresh the soup.

Serves 4 to 6		

Variation

You can also try *chao ca* with catfish, halibut, snapper or another firm-fleshed fish, but the salmon does add beautiful color.

3 cups	water	750 mL
3 cups	Chicken Stock (page 216) or store-bought	750 mL
½ cup	long-grain rice, rinsed and drained	125 mL
8 oz	salmon fillets	250 g
2 tbsp	fish sauce	30 mL
2 tbsp	thinly sliced green onion	30 mL
½ tsp	freshly ground black pepper	2 mL
2 tbsp	coarsely chopped fresh cilantro	30 mL
2 tbsp	coarsely chopped fresh dill	30 mL

1. In a medium saucepan over high heat, combine water and stock and bring to a rolling boil. Stir in rice and reduce heat to maintain a gentle simmer. Cook until rice is soft, 25 minutes.

2. Meanwhile, cut fish crosswise into 2-inch (5 cm) lengths and then cut each piece into generous chunks.

3. When rice is tender, add fish and let soup return to a gentle boil. Cook until fish is firm and opaque, 2 to 3 minutes. Add fish sauce, green onion and pepper and stir well. Remove from heat and stir in cilantro and dill. Serve hot or warm.

Plate Lunch, Vietnamese-Style

Known as *com dia*, this meal-on-a-plate can be found at cafés and casual restaurants in Vietnamese communities around the world, as well as in Vietnam. The constant is a generous scoop of rice, either long-grain Everyday Rice or "broken rice" grains from the milling process that are treasured for the somewhat creamy and unique texture they have when cooked. It's a flexible mix-and-match way to assemble a little of a lot of items to create a cohesive and satisfying lunch or supper. Cafés specializing in *com dia* plates draw plenty of customers. It's especially pleasing when one is eating alone but longs for the pleasures of a rice-centered meal with many components.

**Serves 1
(see Tip, below)**

Tip

You can double or triple this recipe to serve more.

1	generous scoop Everyday Rice (page 142)	1

A selection of any or all of the following components:

1	serving Grilled Garlic-Pepper Pork Chops (page 82)	1
1	serving Everyday Sweet and Salty Ground Pork (page 93)	1
1	serving Hearty Egg Pancake with Ground Pork, Bean Thread Noodles and Cloud Ear Mushrooms (page 64)	1
1	fried egg	1
1	serving Everyday Dipping Sauce (page 200)	1
1	serving Scallion Oil (page 214)	1
1	serving Everyday Pickled Carrots (page 128)	1
	Sliced ripe tomatoes or halved cherry tomatoes	
	Sliced cucumber	

1. Place a generous scoop of rice on a dinner plate.

2. Accompany rice with a selection of the other possible components listed above. Serve at room temperature.

Rice with Chicken, Sweet Chinese Sausage and Shiitake Mushrooms

Traditionally, this satisfying dish is cooked over charcoal in a clay pot (see Tip, below). Enjoyed throughout Asia, it can be a one-pot supper or the centerpiece of a rice meal with complementary dishes including soup, stir-fried greens and steamed fish. Lap cheong sausage adds a sweet, rich sheen and dried Chinese mushrooms echo the heartiness of chunks of chicken cooked in the flavorful rice. I love it with fresh shiitakes or button mushrooms, and enjoy it almost as much reheated the next day.

Serves 4

Tip

To use a clay pot or another Asian-style ceramic cooking pot, you will need to heat the chicken stock before adding it to the pot of rice that has been sautéed in oil. This is to avoid cracking the pot with the shock of temperature change when cold liquid is added to a hot clay pot.

Variation

In place of lap cheong sausage, you can use either ham or Char Shiu-Style Pork (page 88).

♦ 3-quart Dutch oven or large heavy saucepan with tight-fitting lid

Chicken

6 to 8	dried shiitake mushrooms	6 to 8
12 oz	boneless, skinless chicken thighs	375 g
1	link lap cheong Chinese sausage, about 4 oz (125 g)	1
3	green onions	3
1 tbsp	chopped garlic	15 mL
1 tbsp	chopped gingerroot	15 mL
1 tbsp	oyster sauce	15 mL
2 tsp	soy sauce	10 mL
1 tsp	Asian sesame oil	5 mL
1 tsp	granulated sugar	5 mL
1 tsp	salt	5 mL
$\frac{1}{2}$ tsp	freshly ground black pepper	2 mL

Rice

3 tbsp	vegetable oil	45 mL
2$\frac{1}{4}$ cups	long-grain rice	550 mL
4 cups	chicken stock (heated if using clay pot, see Tip, left)	1 L

1. *Chicken:* Soak dried shiitake mushrooms in warm water to cover until soft enough to slice, 20 minutes. Remove from water and quarter each cap. Place in a medium bowl.

2. Chop chicken into big bite-size chunks and add to bowl with mushrooms.

3. Halve sausage links lengthwise and then chop crosswise into $\frac{1}{4}$-inch (0.5 cm) pieces. (You should have about $\frac{3}{4}$ cup/175 mL.) Add to bowl with chicken and mushrooms.

Tip

You can make this recipe in a small Dutch oven or a heavy saucepan with a tight-fitting lid. Any crust that forms on the bottom of your pot is a bonus, to be scooped out and enjoyed along with the rice.

4. Trim green onions, thinly slicing green tops and chopping white bases. Add white portion to bowl with chicken, setting green portion aside to add to the finished dish.

5. Add garlic, ginger, oyster sauce, soy sauce, sesame oil, sugar, salt and pepper to bowl and stir to mix well. Cover and refrigerate for 30 minutes. (You can let the chicken marinate for up to 1 day.)

6. *Rice:* Heat vegetable oil in a 3-quart Dutch oven or large heavy saucepan with tight-fitting lid over medium-high heat for 1 minute. Add rice and spread into an even layer covering bottom of pot. Cook, undisturbed, for 30 seconds. Then toss well to heat rice evenly. Cook, stirring and turning often, until rice changes color, with many grains turning white and releasing a mild, toasty aroma, 3 to 5 minutes.

7. Add chicken stock and stir well. Let rice come to a lively boil over medium-high heat and stir again. Adjust heat to maintain an active simmer and cook, stirring occasionally, until chicken stock cooks down below surface of rice, 5 to 10 minutes.

8. Stir marinated chicken and sausage mixture well, then spread over rice in an even layer. Cover pot and cook, undisturbed, for 20 minutes.

9. Uncover and cook until rice is tender, 5 to 10 minutes more. Remove from heat and add sliced green onion tops. Stir rice gently to mix in meat and seasonings. Transfer to a serving platter and serve hot or warm.

Noodles

Asian noodle dishes have ancient roots in the cuisines of China, but nobody has cultivated, nourished and brought them to full flower like the people of Vietnam. Not only do they cook up spectacular renditions of the standard noodle repertoire (in soup, sautéed and in a bowl dressed with a few tasty condiments and herbs); they have also created a repertoire of superb noodle dishes unique to Vietnamese cuisine.

Many of these noodle feasts are beyond the scope of a quick-and-easy book, requiring multiple ingredients and extensive preparation methods. These dishes are seldom prepared at home, even in Vietnam, because of the effort involved. But many Vietnamese noodle dishes are far simpler and this chapter contains a dozen recipes you will love.

There are an array of soup noodle classics, including the signature Vietnamese favorites, Pho Noodles with Beef, Hanoi-Style (page 160), the legendary dish of northern Vietnam, and Pho Noodles with Chicken (page 162). Other big bowls of soup noodle goodness include Hu Tieu Noodles with Pork and Shrimp, Saigon-Style (page 164), and Coconut Curry Chicken Soup with Rice Noodles (page 166) These are dishes you can easily create at home, especially if you invite a few helpers to set out bowls, chop up herbs and keep you company as you put the dish together.

Rice noodles are easily stir-fried if you know a few guidelines. Once you have learned them, you can vary the components of the recipe for hu tieu xao or Rice Noodles Stir-Fried with Pork and Shrimp (page 176) to your liking. Bean thread noodles are the simplest noodles of all to work with. They are shelf stable, quick cooking, eager to absorb other flavors and inexplicably pleasing to eat. Two recipes showcase them: One is mien xao tom or Bean Thread Noodles Stir-Fried with Shrimp (page 173). The other is mien ga or Chicken Soup with Bean Thread Noodles, (page 174), a delicate, classic dish traditionally served with goi ga or Chicken and Cabbage Salad with Mint (page 124).

Big Cool Noodle Bowl with Roast Chicken, Cucumbers and Mint (page 178) illustrates Vietnam's culinary genius in devising new ways to put familiar ingredients together. It is a type of bun, a dish in which thin rice noodles are piled into a big bowl over a small bed of salad greens and then topped with hearty treats, such as grilled beef, pork meatballs, lemongrass shrimp or even Vietnam's crispy signature spring rolls, cha gio. It is finished with a carnival of toppings, from chopped peanuts and cilantro to cucumbers and Everyday Dipping Sauce (page 200).

Everyday Rice Noodles

With a few cellophane-wrapped rectangular packages of dried rice noodles in your pantry, you are never more than 15 minutes away from a satisfying, appealing and endlessly variable meal. Made from two simple ingredients, rice flour and water, dried rice noodles keep indefinitely at room temperature and can be the foundation for noodle soups, stir-fries, cool noodle bowls and even pasta dishes using your favorite pasta sauces. A bonus is that rice noodles are gluten-free, as well as inexpensive, speedily cooked, easily flavored in innumerable ways and delightful to eat. What's not to love about dried rice noodles, your pantry pal?

| Serves 4 | 1 | package (16 oz/500 g) dried rice noodles, any width | 1 |

Tips

To prepare noodles that will be cooked in a stir-fried dish or a soup, simply soak them as directed in Step 1. They will soften and become flexible, but will still be too tough to eat. Drain well and set aside until needed in the recipe.

For the thinnest rice noodles that are as slender as wire, you can drop them into boiling water, remove from heat, and let stand for 5 to 7 minutes. They will cook and soften in the water's residual heat. When tender enough to eat, drain, rinse with cold water, drain well, and serve.

1. Soften rice noodles by immersing in a medium bowl of warm water until flexible and bright white, 15 to 20 minutes. Drain well and set aside.

2. Bring a large saucepan of water to a rolling boil over high heat. Drop in softened noodles and cook, tossing and pulling noodles apart to help cook evenly. Cook for 5 minutes and then test for doneness. When noodles are cooked to the ideal tenderness, remove from heat and drain. Return cooked noodles to the hot, now-empty cooking pot. Rinse with cool water to keep from sticking and then toss and drain well. Transfer to a large bowl and set aside until needed for noodle soup or stir-fried noodles, for up to 2 hours.

3. To store cooked noodles, transfer to a covered container or a resealable plastic food storage bag and place in refrigerator until needed. Before using chilled noodles, dip in boiling water for about 1 minute, or heat in microwave oven briefly until tender, warm and a pleasing texture, 1 to 2 minutes. Use in curry noodle soup, stir-fried dishes, *pho* or other hearty dishes.

Bun Thang Noodles

Use leftover roast chicken and pork along with cold cuts from the deli for this fast feast. For a more traditional version, season the soup with 3 tbsp (45 mL) dried shrimp and 2 tsp (10 mL) Asian-style shrimp paste and top each serving with freshly squeezed lime juice.

◇◇

Serves 4

Tip

A noodle café in Vietnam would have all these ingredients, but you may find that too much. Don't worry about having every single type of meat and garnish listed here. Gather as many as you can and serve it up; you'll have a great, *bun thang*-inspired noodle bowl to enjoy.

8 oz	linguine-width dried rice noodles (*banh pho*)	250 g
2 tsp	vegetable oil	10 mL
2	eggs, well beaten with 1 tsp (5 mL) fish sauce	2
6 cups	Chicken Stock (page 216) or store-bought	1.5 L
2 tbsp	fish sauce	30 mL
2 tsp	granulated sugar	10 mL
1 tsp	salt	5 mL
1¼ cups	thinly sliced cooked chicken	300 mL
1¼ cups	thinly sliced Vietnamese pâté, such as *cha lua* or cold cuts, such as mortadella or baloney	300 mL
1¼ cups	thinly sliced roast pork or ham	300 mL
⅓ cup	thinly sliced green onions	75 mL
½ cup	coarsely chopped fresh cilantro	125 mL

1. Add rice noodles to a medium saucepan of boiling water. Remove from heat and let stand for 8 to 10 minutes, tossing and pulling apart occasionally to help them cook evenly. Drain, rinse with cold water, drain well and set aside.

2. For omelet shreds, heat oil in a large skillet for 1 minute over medium-high heat. Add eggs, swirl to coat pan evenly and cook until set and lightly browned, 1 to 2 minutes. Transfer to a cutting board, cool and cut into thin strips.

3. In a medium saucepan over medium-high heat, combine chicken stock, fish sauce, sugar and salt and bring to a rolling boil. Divide noodles among 4 large soup bowls. Top each noodle serving with 4 equal piles of egg, chicken, Vietnamese paté and pork. Pour 1½ cups (375 mL) hot soup into each bowl, top with chopped green onions and cilantro and serve at once with a big spoon for soup and chopsticks or forks for the noodles.

Pho Noodles with Beef, Hanoi-Style

Consider *pho*, a small word for a big bowl of noodles in soup. The soup is clear, delicate and redolent of cinnamon, star anise and ginger. The noodles swirl just below the surface of the steaming stock, barely visible beneath slices of beef, slivers of onion and a tumble of crisp bean sprouts. A minuscule mountain of aromatic herbs, big green slices of chile and a chunk of lime attend the bowl for seasoning everything just so. *Pho* takes a little more time than some dishes, but it gives you a memorable, delicious reward.

◇◇

Serves 4

Tip

You can prepare the stock for your *pho* in advance. Strain stock in Step 4 into a storage container. Let cool to room temperature, cover and refrigerate for up to 2 days.

Stock

8 cups	Chicken Stock (page 216) or store-bought	2 L
1 lb	round steak, sliced crosswise into 1-inch (2.5 cm) strips	500 g
3	pieces (each about 2 inches/5 cm) cinnamon sticks	3
3	whole cloves	3
3	star anise	3
1	unpeeled medium onion, quartered lengthwise	1
½ cup	peeled and very coarsely chopped fresh gingerroot	125 mL
8 oz	linguine-width dried rice noodles (*banh pho*)	250 g
2 tbsp	fish sauce	30 mL
1 tsp	granulated sugar	5 mL
½ tsp	salt	2 mL
3 cups	bean sprouts	750 mL
1 cup	very thinly sliced onion or shallots	250 mL
1 cup	coarsely chopped fresh Asian basil, cilantro or mint or a combination	250 mL
½ cup	thinly sliced green onion	125 mL
¼ cup	freshly squeezed lime juice	60 mL
2	fresh jalapeño chiles, cut diagonally into thin ovals	2
1¼ lbs	boneless rib-eye, strip or flank steak	625 g

1. *Stock:* In a stockpot or a very large saucepan, combine chicken stock, sliced round steak, cinnamon sticks, cloves and star anise. Bring to a gentle boil over medium-high heat.

Recipe continues on page 161...

Cha Ca Fish with Fresh Dill,
Hanoi-Style (page 104)

Chicken and Cabbage Salad with Mint (page 124)

Fried Rice with Shrimp,
Egg and Green Onion (page 149)

Big Cool Noodle Bowl with Roast Chicken, Cucumbers and Mint (page 178) and Everyday Pickled Carrots (page 128)

Pho Noodles with Beef, Hanoi-Style (page 160)

Vietnamese Iced Coffee (page 192), Almond Cookies (page 191)
and Sweet Coconut Ribbons (page 190)

Tip

You could prepare the noodles in advance, and then reheat them gently shortly before serving. Follow the instructions in Steps 3 and 7 until noodles are tender. Drain well and let cool to room temperature. Cover and refrigerate for up to 1 day. Shortly before serving time, bring a large saucepan of water to a rolling boil. Add cold noodles and remove from heat. Toss well and drain as soon as they are tender and hot, 1 to 2 minutes.

2. Meanwhile, heat a large skillet over medium-high heat until very hot, about 1 minute. Add quartered onion and ginger and cook on one side until handsomely browned but not burnt. Turn and sear other side and continue cooking until well browned and fragrant. Add charred onion and ginger to stockpot and let everything boil gently for 1 hour.

3. While stock is cooking, soften rice noodles by immersing in a medium bowl of warm water until flexible and bright white, 15 to 20 minutes. Drain well and set aside.

4. Remove stock from heat and stir in fish sauce, sugar and salt. Strain stock into a large saucepan, discarding the cooked meat along with the other solids (see Tip, left).

5. About 30 minutes before you plan to serve the dish, place bean sprouts, sliced onion, basil, green onion, lime juice and chiles near 4 big soup bowls in which you will serve the stock. Bring a large saucepan of water to a rolling boil over high heat for noodles.

6. Meanwhile, bring stock to a gentle boil over medium-high heat and adjust heat to maintain a lively simmer. Cut boneless steak in half crosswise. Place both pieces in the simmering stock and cook, until medium-rare, about 10 minutes. Transfer steak to a cutting board, slice into thin, bite-size strips and set aside.

7. Shortly before serving, cook noodles. Drop softened rice noodles into boiling water. Remove pot from heat and let stand, stirring once or twice to separate any noodle clumps into strands, for 10 minutes. Meanwhile, bring simmering stock to a rolling boil.

8. Drain noodles well and quickly divide among the 4 bowls (about 1 cup/250 mL per bowl). Top each noodle bowl with one-fourth of the sliced steak, bean sprouts, onion, basil, green onion, lime juice and chiles. Ladle hot stock (about $1\frac{1}{2}$ cups/375 mL) over noodles in each bowl and serve at once. Be sure to provide each guest with a fork or chopsticks and an Asian soupspoon or a large spoon.

Pho Noodles with Chicken

The quintessential incarnation of *pho* noodles is an enormous bowl of rice noodles floating in an aromatic and delicate beef broth, accented with beef in various forms and a crowning bouquet of fresh herbs. Chicken *pho* is a popular variation, served with the same aromatic herb bouquet and accents of sliced chiles and lime wedges. There's prep and lots of components, but the actual cooking tasks are simple, and the dish can wait until you have everything prepared. Having helpers come early to get the *pho* feast preparation up and running makes this spectacular Vietnamese meal in a bowl a pleasure to prepare at home.

◇◇◇

Serves 4

Tip

You can prepare the stock for your *pho* in advance. Strain stock in Step 5 into a storage container. Let cool to room temperature, cover and refrigerate for up to 2 days.

Stock

8 cups	Chicken Stock (page 216) or store-bought	2 L
3 lbs	bone-in, skin-on chicken breasts, legs and thighs	1.5 kg
3	pieces (each about 2 inches/5 cm) cinnamon sticks	3
3	whole cloves	3
3	star anise	3
1	unpeeled large onion, quartered lengthwise	1
½ cup	peeled and very coarsely chopped fresh gingerroot	125 mL
8 oz	linguine-width dried rice noodles (*banh pho*)	250 g
2 tbsp	fish sauce	30 mL
1 tsp	granulated sugar	5 mL
½ tsp	salt	2 mL
3 cups	bean sprouts	750 mL
1 cup	very thinly sliced onion or shallots	250 mL
1 cup	coarsely chopped fresh Asian basil, cilantro or mint or a combination	250 mL
½ cup	thinly sliced green onion	125 mL
¼ cup	freshly squeezed lime juice	60 mL
2	fresh jalapeño chiles, cut diagonally into thin ovals	2

1. *Stock:* In a stockpot or a very large saucepan, combine chicken stock, chicken breasts, cinnamon sticks, cloves and star anise. Bring to a lively boil over medium-high heat.

Tip

You could prepare the noodles in advance, and then reheat them gently shortly before serving. Follow the instructions in Steps 4 and 7 until noodles are tender. Drain well and let cool to room temperature. Cover and refrigerate for up to 1 day. Shortly before serving time, bring a large saucepan of water to a rolling boil. Add cold noodles and remove from heat. Toss well and drain as soon as they are tender and hot, 1 to 2 minutes.

2. Meanwhile, heat a large skillet over medium-high heat until very hot, about 1 minute. Add quartered onion and ginger and cook on one side until lightly browned, softened and fragrant. Turn and sear other side as well. Remove from heat.

3. Skim off and discard any foam in the boiling soup. Add onion and ginger to stockpot and adjust heat to maintain a gentle but visible simmer. Let cook until chicken is no longer pink inside for breasts and juices run clear when pierced for legs and thighs, 35 to 40 minutes.

4. While chicken and soup are cooking, soften rice noodles by immersing in a medium bowl of warm water until flexible and bright white, 15 to 20 minutes. Drain well and set aside.

5. When chicken is cooked, reduce heat to medium-low and transfer chicken breasts to a platter. Let stand until cool enough to handle. Pull off most of the meat and set aside, returning all the meaty bones and skin to the stockpot to continue cooking. Place cooked chicken in a bowl, cover and set aside. Continue cooking stock to develop its flavor, for 30 minutes more. Remove stock from heat and stir in fish sauce, sugar and salt. Strain stock into a large saucepan, discarding the solids.

6. About 30 minutes before you plan to serve the dish, place bean sprouts, sliced onion, basil, green onion, lime juice and chiles near 4 big soup bowls in which you will serve the stock. Bring a large saucepan of water to a rolling boil over high heat for the noodles. Meanwhile, bring stock to a gentle boil over medium-high heat and adjust heat to maintain a lively simmer.

7. Shortly before serving, cook noodles. Drop softened rice noodles into boiling water. Remove pot from heat and let stand, stirring once or twice to separate any noodle clumps into strands, for 10 minutes.

8. Drain noodles well and quickly divide among the 4 bowls (about 1 cup/250 mL per bowl). Top each noodle bowl with one-fourth of the chicken, bean sprouts, onion, basil, green onion, lime juice and chiles. Ladle hot stock (about $1\frac{1}{2}$ cups/375 mL) over noodles in each bowl and serve at once. Be sure to provide each guest with a fork or chopsticks and an Asian soupspoon or a large spoon.

Hu Tieu Noodles with Pork and Shrimp, Saigon-Style

Hu tieu starts with a stock of chicken and pork, often fortified with an infusion of dried squid and dried shrimp. Atop a mound of slender rice noodles, *hu tieu* vendors compose a colorful design: pink shrimp, thin slices of barbecued pork, thinly sliced celery, fresh bean sprouts, sprinklings of cilantro leaves, green onions and thinly sliced chiles, a shower of chopped peanuts and fried shallots and a squeeze of lime.

◇◇

Serves 4		

Tip

Hu tieu is sometimes served as a dry noodle bowl, with garnishes atop the hot rice noodles and a small steaming bowl of the stock presented on the side.

Noodles and Soup

8 oz	linguine-width dried rice noodles (*banh pho*)	250 g
5 cups	Chicken Stock (page 216) or store-bought	1.25 L
1 tbsp	fish sauce	15 mL
2	thick bone-in pork chops (about 1¼ lbs/625 g)	2
8 oz	medium shrimp, peeled and deveined	250 g

Accompaniments

2 cups	bean sprouts	500 g
3	stalks celery, trimmed and cut diagonally into thin slices (about 1 cup/250 mL)	3
½ cup	thinly sliced green onion	125 mL
½ cup	coarsely chopped fresh cilantro	125 mL
½ cup	coarsely chopped dry-roasted salted peanuts	125 mL
½ cup	Crispy Shallots (page 213), optional	125 mL
¼ cup	freshly squeezed lime juice	60 mL
2	fresh jalapeño chiles, cut diagonally into thin ovals	2

1. *Noodles and Soup:* Soften rice noodles in warm water to cover for about 15 minutes. Meanwhile, in a large saucepan over medium-high heat, bring stock and fish sauce to a gentle boil. Cut most of the meat off bones and then add both meaty bones and meat to stock. Reduce heat to maintain a lively simmer and cook, skimming off any foam that rises to the top, for 25 minutes.

Variation

Instead of pork chops, use 1 lb (500 g) boneless pork or 1 lb (500 g) barbecued or roast pork. If using boneless pork or barbecued or roast pork, slice thinly, add to stock in Step 1 and simmer until done, for 5 to 7 minutes. Barbecued or roast pork will need only to be heated through, 2 to 3 minutes.

2. Meanwhile, bring another large pot of water to a rolling boil over high heat. Drain softened noodles, add to pot and remove from heat at once. Let stand, stirring occasionally to pull apart any clumps, for 10 minutes. Drain well and set aside.

3. Strain the stock carefully through a colander or large strainer into another pot or a large bowl. Transfer the cooked pork to a platter to cool and discard the bones. Return the hot stock to the cooking pot and place on the stove over medium-high heat. Add shrimp to simmering stock and cook until bright pink, firm and opaque, 2 to 3 minutes. Remove at once and set aside with cooked meat. Cut meat into thin strips and cut shrimp in half lengthwise.

4. Place 4 big soup bowls near the stove, along with all the accompaniments. Bring stock to a rolling boil over high heat. Divide noodles among the bowls and then place one-fourth of remaining ingredients on top of noodles in each bowl: slices of pork, 3 shrimp halves, with the pink side up, bean sprouts, celery, green onion, cilantro, peanuts, Crispy Shallots, if using, lime juice and chiles. Ladle about $1\frac{1}{2}$ cups (375 mL) of hot stock over each bowl of noodles and serve at once, providing each diner with a fork or chopsticks and an Asian soup spoon or a large spoon.

◈ Vietnamese Tales

Hu tieu is a bright bowl of rice noodles in soup, enjoyed from dawn to midnight throughout the Mekong Delta. Noodle shops and itinerant noodle vendors do good business near fresh markets, schools, bus stations and ferry landings, wherever people congregate for commerce, company or en route from here to there.

Coconut Curry Chicken Soup with Rice Noodles

Get out your chopsticks and a great big spoon so you can devour this luscious and lovely meal in a bowl without missing a drop or a noodle strand. Made with flavorful chicken thighs, carrots and onions in a curry-kissed coconut milk stew, it's fine for company with guests assembling their bowls themselves. It's also great for times when you want a great dinner for one without too much effort. With the curry prepared in advance and the rice noodles needing only about 10 minutes to cook, this is good fast food.

Serves 4 to 6

Tip

To prepare lemongrass, trim away and discard any dried root portion (to make a smooth base), the top half of stalks and any dry, tired outer leaves. Cut remaining portion of each stalk diagonally into 2-inch (5 cm) lengths.

8 oz	wide or medium dried rice noodles (banh pho)	250 g
2 tbsp	vegetable oil	30 mL
1 tbsp	coarsely chopped garlic	15 mL
1 tbsp	chopped fresh gingerroot	15 mL
1 cup	thinly sliced onion	250 mL
2	stalks fresh lemongrass, chopped (see Tip, left)	2
3 tbsp	curry powder	45 mL
1 lb	boneless, skinless chicken thighs or breast	500 g
2 tbsp	fish sauce	30 mL
1 tsp	granulated sugar	5 mL
1 tsp	hot pepper flakes or chili-garlic sauce	5 mL
½ tsp	salt	2 mL
2 cups	Chicken Stock (page 216), store-bought or water	500 mL
1	can (14 oz/400 mL) unsweetened coconut milk (about 1½ cups/ 375 mL)	1
2 cups	big bite-size chunks carrots	500 mL
¼ cup	finely chopped green onions	60 mL
⅓ cup	chopped cilantro	75 mL
1	lime, quartered lengthwise	1

1. Place rice noodles in a large bowl and add warm water to cover by 1 inch (2.5 cm). Set aside to soften.

2. In a large deep saucepan or Dutch oven, heat oil over medium-high heat for 1 minute. Add garlic, ginger, onion and lemongrass and toss well. Add curry powder and cook, tossing often, until mixture is fragrant and onion is translucent, 1 to 2 minutes.

Tip

Like most stews, this curry's flavor blossoms as it stands. If you'd like to prepare it in advance, stop after Step 6. Leave the lemongrass in the pot and don't add the green onions until serving time. Let cool to room temperature and then cover and refrigerate for up to 1 day. Reheat gently while cooking the rice noodles and continue from Step 7.

3. Add chicken, spreading out in one layer if you can, and cook for 1 minute. Toss well and cook until chicken changes color and begins to brown. Add fish sauce, sugar, hot pepper flakes and salt and toss again. Add stock and bring to a boil. Reduce heat to maintain a lively simmer and cook, stirring occasionally, for 10 minutes. While curry simmers, set out individual serving bowls or one large serving bowl for the curry.

4. When curry has simmered for 10 minutes, add coconut milk and carrots to pot. Keep curry simmering actively until carrots are tender and chicken juices run clear when pierced for thighs or breasts are no longer pink inside, 10 to 15 minutes.

5. Meanwhile, bring a large pot of water to a rolling boil over high heat. Remove softened rice noodles from soaking water and add to pot of boiling water. Boil, lifting noodles up and out of the water to help cook evenly, until noodles are tender but still pleasingly chewy and just done, 2 to 3 minutes.

6. Remove from heat. Pour cooked rice noodles into a colander in the sink. Shake to release water, and then run cool water over noodles to discourage sticking. Return drained tender noodles to hot empty pot and set aside.

7. When curry is done, scoop out and discard lemongrass. Stir in green onions. Set curry next to rice noodles and serving bowls or one large serving bowl.

8. Divide noodles among serving bowls. Spoon a generous serving of coconut curry soup over noodles, adding chicken and carrots to bowl along with curry sauce. Sprinkle with cilantro. Set a chunk of lime on noodles for seasoning by each diner. Serve hot or warm.

Wonton Soup with Egg Noodles and Barbecued Pork

This delightful, bountiful and delicious dish wins fans around the world. A classic Chinese one-dish meal, it is popular all over Vietnam, and is often topped off with slices of barbecued pork and crispy shallots. Treat yourself to a set of large wide noodle soup bowls available at Asian markets so you can enjoy the sight of curly egg noodles, wontons, greens and gorgeous red-edged *char shiu* pork awaiting your chopsticks in a steaming tasty soup.

◇◇

Serves 6 to 8

Tip

This recipe takes time and attention to detail, but it produces an extraordinary and delightful result in exchange for the investment you make in preparing it. If you have helpers, the tasks pass by quickly and everyone enjoys the fruits of their labor. You could make the wontons in advance and freeze them for another day. Then it's only a matter of cooking them, cooking the noodles, heating up the broth and assembling the remaining components.

Wontons

8 oz	ground pork	250 g
8 oz	medium shrimp, peeled, deveined and finely chopped	250 g
2 tbsp	finely chopped green onion	30 mL
1 tsp	Asian sesame oil	5 mL
½ tsp	salt	2 mL
¼ tsp	freshly ground black pepper	1 mL
1 lb	wonton wrappers	500 g

Soup

1 lb	fresh Chinese-style egg noodles or thin spaghetti	500 g
12 cups	Chicken Stock (page 216) or store-bought	3 L
2 cups	fresh baby spinach leaves, or large spinach leaves, torn into 2-inch (5 cm) pieces	500 mL
16	slices Char Shiu-Style Pork (page 88), optional	16
½ cup	finely chopped green onions	125 mL
½ cup	chopped fresh cilantro leaves	125 mL
⅓ cup	Crispy Shallots (page 213), optional	75 mL
¼ cup	Asian sesame oil	60 mL

1. *Wontons:* In a medium bowl, combine pork, shrimp, green onion, sesame oil, salt and pepper and mix well.

2. Prepare to fold wontons by arranging the following on a table where you can sit and work: package of wonton wrappers, measuring spoons, a small bowl of water to use when sealing filled wontons, a cutting board on which to lay out wrappers as you fill them and a platter or cookie sheet on which to place filled wontons as you work.

Variation

A bowl of freshly cooked wontons makes its own simple and delightful little meal. Simply prepare the wontons, cook as directed, drain and place in an individual bowl along with cooked noodles. Top with a dash of sesame oil, sliced green onions, and for an extra treat, some crispy shallots.

3. Place a wrapper before you and place about 1 tsp (5 mL) of filling in center of wrapper. Moisten edges with a little water and fold into a triangle shape. Press edges together to seal well. Bring the two bottom corners together on top of filling and seal with a little water, making a plump little envelope with top point free. Set aside and continue filling wrappers. You will have around 40 wontons. (To freeze them, place on a platter that will fit in the freezer, at least 1 inch/2.5 cm apart. When completely frozen, place in a resealable plastic bag or airtight container and store for up to 1 month. You need not thaw but do allow an extra few minutes' cooking time.)

4. Bring a large stockpot of water to a rolling boil over high heat. Add fresh egg noodles and cook until just tender but still pleasingly chewy, 2 to 3 minutes. Remove from heat and scoop out noodles into a large bowl. If you use thin spaghetti instead of fresh egg noodles, allow more time for them to cook, 10 to 12 minutes.

5. To cook wontons, bring about 12 cups (3 L) water to a rolling boil in a large pot over high heat. Have about 3 cups (750 mL) cold water handy, along with a 1-cup (250 mL) measure. Drop wontons into boiling water one by one, stirring occasionally to keep separate. As soon as water returns to a boil, add 1 cup (250 mL) of the cold water to stop the boiling.

6. When water boils again, add another cup (250 mL) of cold water. When it boils a third time, add last cup (250 mL) of water. When it boils again, scoop wontons out gently and drain well. Transfer to a large serving bowl or tureen in which you will serve the soup. Cover to keep warm while you make the soup.

7. *Soup:* In a large saucepan over medium heat, bring chicken stock to a rolling boil. Prepare an individual bowl for each guest, dividing equally noodles, wontons, spinach, *char shiu* pork, if using, soup, green onions, cilantro, Crispy Shallots, if using, and sesame oil among the bowls, using enough to fill each bowl and reserving any extra for seconds or for another meal.

Mi Quang Noodles

Mi quang's signature accompaniments are many. Crunchy items lead the list. Chopped peanuts on top, and sides of thinly sliced banana flower and thick shards of delightful rice crackers studded with black sesame seeds keep things interesting as diners enjoy textural contrasts between bites of noodles and spoonfuls of soup. The rich broth is made from meaty bones of pork and shrimp with dried shrimp added for briny-salty depth. This spectacular dish is an investment of time and preparation, but it provides marvelous rewards in return.

◇◇

Serves 4 to 6

Tip

This particular noodle dish calls for even more attention to detail and steps, since it involves blanching meat and bones as a first step, and working with both meat and seafood in multiple steps. A good advance plan would be to prepare the stock, stopping after Step 4. Instead of keeping it hot as you finish the dish, cool the strained stock and refrigerate it for up to 1 day in advance. Close to serving time, bring it back to a boil, keep it hot, and continue with Step 5.

Noodles

1 lb	yellow wide flat dried rice noodles (*mi quang*) or regular fettuccine-width dried rice noodles	500 g

Stock

3 lbs	meaty pork bones	1.5 kg
1½ lbs	chicken legs and thighs	750 g
¼ cup	salty dried shrimp, optional	60 mL
1	medium onion, quartered	1
5	large slices fresh gingerroot	5
1 tsp	granulated sugar	5 mL
1 tsp	salt	5 mL

Toppings

2 tbsp	vegetable oil	30 mL
12 oz	boneless pork, cut into bite-size pieces (fatty pork is fine)	375 g
12 oz	medium shrimp, peeled and deveined	375 g
1 tbsp	chopped shallots	15 mL
1 tbsp	chopped garlic	15 mL
2 tbsp	fish sauce	30 mL
2 tsp	granulated sugar	10 mL
½ tsp	salt	2 mL
½ tsp	freshly ground black pepper	2 mL

Accompaniments

1 cup	thinly sliced green onions	250 mL
1 cup	coarsely chopped cilantro	250 mL
1½ cups	chopped dry-roasted salted peanuts	375 mL
2 cups	bean sprouts	500 mL
	Thinly sliced fresh banana flowers, sliced crosswise into curly strips, optional	
	Toasted black sesame seed rice crackers, optional	
2	limes, quartered lengthwise	2

1. *Noodles:* Soften rice noodles by immersing in a medium bowl of warm water until flexible and softened, 15 to 30 minutes. Drain well and set aside.

2. *Stock:* In a large pot, combine pork bones and chicken pieces. Cover with water and bring to a rolling boil and let cook, 3 to 5 minutes. Place a colander in the sink and dump out the water (yes, dump it out; you are cleaning the bones). Set meaty bones and chicken aside.

3. Clean pot and return bones and chicken. Add 12 cups (3 L) water and return to a boil over high heat. When boiling, adjust heat to maintain a lively simmer. Skim off and discard any foam that rises to the surface in the first few minutes. Add dried shrimp, onion, ginger, sugar and salt and stir well. Cook, stirring once, for 2 hours.

4. This time, you will save the broth, so take care! Carefully strain out pork bones, chicken and dried shrimp and discard, leaving only the wonderful, flavor-packed broth. Check seasonings and adjust with a little salt or sugar, if needed. Keep hot while you complete the other ingredients.

5. *Toppings:* Heat oil in a large skillet or wok over medium-high heat until hot. When a bit of garlic sizzles at once, scatter in pork and spread out into a single layer. Let cook, undisturbed, until it changes color along sides, about 1 minute. Toss well and cook 1 minute more. Add shrimp, shallots and garlic and toss well. Let cook, undisturbed, until shrimp change color and then toss well, 1 minute more. Add fish sauce, sugar, salt and pepper and cook just until pork is done and shrimp are pink, firm and opaque and there's a little sauce. Transfer to a bowl and place by stove.

6. Bring a large pot of water to a rolling boil over high heat. Drop in drained, softened rice noodles and cook, pulling apart using large tongs or chopsticks or two long-handled heatproof spoons. This helps them cook quickly and evenly. Cook, until still a bit chewy and not mushy, 2 to 5 minutes, depending on the noodles. Drain at once and then rinse with cool tap water to help prevent sticking. Return noodles to empty cooking pot and place by stove.

continued...

Mi Quang Noodles (continued)

7. Set out individual bowls for each guest. Give each guest a good handful of noodles, half-filling the bowl. Add a good serving of the pork-shrimp stir-fried topping to one side. Add broth, leaving noodles and meat showing at top of bowl. Sprinkle with green onions and cilantro and a flourish of chopped peanuts. Add a small amount of bean sprouts to one side, along with banana flower shreds and a chunk of sesame cracker, if using. Serve at once, inviting guests to squeeze lime juice over their portions and to tear off and add in herbs as they enjoy their noodles.

◇ Vietnamese Tales

This extraordinary bowl of rice noodles with shrimp and pork comes from Vietnam's central region, but is beloved and available throughout the country and in overseas Vietnamese communities around the world. Traditionally it's made with rice noodles rendered a lovely golden color by the addition of turmeric to the rice flour when they are made. Typically it's served in more modest-size bowls than those used for *pho* and other noodles, for which the broth is the star.

Bean Thread Noodles Stir-Fried with Shrimp

Bean thread noodles absorb seasonings exceptionally well: they deliver an abundance of flavor in a delicate way. Perfect with seafood and fresh herbs, they soften quickly and cook fast. Once softened, cut these noodles into 3-inch (7.5 cm) lengths; otherwise, they will be difficult to stir-fry and unwilling to mingle with their fellow ingredients. If you like, substitute fresh or canned crabmeat for the shrimp and you will have *mien xao cua*.

Serves 4

Tip

Look for small, 1- to 2-ounce (15 to 30 g) packets of dried bean thread noodles combined into a larger string sack and keep them on your pantry shelf.

4 oz	dried bean thread noodles (2 small packets), about 2 cups (500 mL)	125 g
2 tbsp	vegetable oil	30 mL
1 tbsp	coarsely chopped garlic	15 mL
2 tbsp	coarsely chopped shallots	30 mL
10 to 12	medium shrimp, peeled and deveined, or 8 oz (250 g) cooked crabmeat	10 to 12
¾ cup	Chicken Stock (page 216) or store-bought	175 mL
2 tbsp	fish sauce	30 mL
1 tbsp	soy sauce	15 mL
½ tsp	freshly ground black pepper	2 mL
2 tbsp	thinly sliced green onion	30 mL
2 tbsp	coarsely chopped fresh cilantro	30 mL

1. Soften bean thread noodles in warm water to cover until pliable, 10 to 15 minutes. Drain noodles, line them up on a cutting board in a long pile and cut crosswise into 3-inch (7.5 cm) lengths. Place all the ingredients by the stove: this stir-fry comes together fast.

2. In a large, heavy skillet or a wok, heat oil over medium-high heat until a bit of garlic sizzles at once. Add garlic and shallots and toss until fragrant and shiny. Add shrimp and cook until bright pink on one side, 1 minute. (If using crabmeat, add with green onions at the end of cooking.) Turn shrimp to cook other side and then add noodles. Cook for 1 minute and then toss again.

3. Add stock, fish sauce, soy sauce and pepper and cook, tossing often, until noodles are clear and tender and shrimp are firm, pink and opaque, 3 to 5 minutes. Add a little more stock or a little more oil if noodles stick.

4. Add green onion and cilantro, toss once more and transfer to a serving platter. Serve hot, warm or at room temperature.

Chicken Soup
with Bean Thread Noodles

This classic dish is very simple, very fast and very good. *Ga* means "chicken" and *mien* means "noodles." Traditionally it is served with *goi ga*, Chicken and Cabbage Salad with Mint (page 124). Poaching chicken for the salad creates a tasty stock, perfect for simmering bean thread noodles and a handful of fresh herbs to make this dish.

◇◇◇

Serves 4 to 6

Variation

If you serve this with Chicken and Cabbage Salad (page 124), your daily vegetable quota will be met. If you are not making the salad and want your daily greens here, toss in a double handful of shredded napa cabbage, spinach, edamame beans or frozen peas shortly before serving. Your *mien ga* will become a perfect little meal.

4 oz	dried bean thread noodles (2 small packets), about 2 cups (500 mL) (approx.)	125 g
4 cups	Chicken Stock (page 216) or store-bought	1 L
2 cups	water	500 mL
8 oz	boneless, skinless chicken breasts or thighs or 1 lb (500 g) bone-in, skin-on chicken thighs	250 g
2 tbsp	fish sauce	30 mL
½ tsp	salt	2 mL
½ tsp	freshly ground black pepper	2 mL
2 tbsp	thinly sliced green onion	30 mL
2 tbsp	coarsely chopped fresh cilantro	30 mL

1. Place tight, wiry bundles of bean thread noodles in a medium bowl and add warm water to cover. Let soften until pliable, 10 to 20 minutes.

2. Meanwhile, in a medium saucepan over medium-high heat, bring stock and water to a boil. Add chicken, return to a boil and then adjust heat to maintain a lively simmer. Cook until chicken is no longer pink inside for breasts or juices run clear for thighs, about 10 minutes. Add 15 minutes for bone-in chicken. Transfer chicken to a plate and let cool. Add fish sauce and salt to stock and set aside.

Tip

I like to cut the bean thread noodles down to a manageable size after softening and before cooking; otherwise they seem to stretch out beyond arm's length when it's time to eat. Use kitchen scissors or shears if you have them, or arrange the softened noodles on your cutting board in a rectangular pie and cut them crosswise into 2-inch (5 cm) lengths using a sharp knife.

3. When chicken is cool enough to handle, tear or chop into bite-size shreds and set aside. Drain noodles well, transfer to a cutting board and cut into 6-inch (15 cm) lengths.

4. To serve *mien ga*, bring stock to a boil, stir in noodles and cook until they swell and become shiny and clear, 1 to 2 minutes. Stir in chicken, pepper, green onion and cilantro. Transfer to a serving bowl and serve hot or warm in individual bowls with a fork or chopsticks and a spoon.

Rice Noodles Stir-Fried with Pork and Shrimp

You, too, can cook a fabulous platter of stir-fried rice noodles right in your own kitchen if you follow a few simple rules. First, prepare the dried rice noodles so that they will soften and season themselves with just a few turns in the hot pan. Second, set everything you'll need right by the stove, measured out and ready to cook. Third, have a serving platter and any guests handy because hot-out-of-the pan noodles are a true Asian treat. Once you've cooked this a time or two, you'll know how to create noodle feasts galore based on what you like and have handy (see Variation, right). It may never be quite as easy for you as making a sandwich, but it might be close.

◇◇

Serves 2 to 4

Tip

Wide rice noodles are the typical choice, but use any width of fresh or softened rice noodle, Chinese egg noodles or any cooked pasta.

4 oz	fettuccine- or linguine-width dried rice noodles (see Tip, left)	125 g
6	green onions, trimmed, white part coarsely chopped and green tops cut into 2-inch (5 cm) lengths	6
2 tbsp	fish sauce	30 mL
2 tbsp	water	30 mL
2 tbsp	soy sauce	30 mL
½ tsp	granulated sugar	2 mL
½ tsp	salt	2 mL
½ tsp	freshly ground black pepper	2 mL
2 tbsp	vegetable oil	30 mL
1 tbsp	chopped garlic	15 mL
4 oz	boneless pork, cut against the grain into thin 2-inch (5 cm) strips, or Chinese-style roast pork or roast duck	125 g
12	medium shrimp, peeled and deveined	12
2½ cups	fresh spinach leaves	625 mL
1 cup	mung bean sprouts, optional	250 mL

1. Soften rice noodles in warm water to cover until flexible and bright white, 15 to 20 minutes. Bring a large pot of water to a rolling boil over high heat. Drain softened noodles, add to pot and remove from heat. Let stand for 6 to 8 minutes. Drain well and place in a bowl by the stove. You will have about 2½ cups (625 mL) of noodles.

Variation

Leave out the pork or toss in mushrooms, zucchini or shredded carrots. Scramble an egg into the pan near the end of cooking, add a spoonful of chopped fresh chiles or hot sauce or finish the dish with cilantro, chopped peanuts and a squeeze of lime.

2. In a small bowl, combine green onion tops, fish sauce, water, soy sauce, sugar, salt and pepper and stir well to dissolve sugar and salt. Place by stove, along with tongs or a big spatula for moving the noodles around, and all the remaining ingredients.

3. In a large, deep skillet or a wok, heat oil over medium-high heat for 30 seconds. Add garlic and white portion of green onions and toss well. Add pork and cook just until it changes color, about 1 minute. Add fish sauce mixture, toss well and then add noodles. Cook, tossing and pushing noodles to season and heat evenly.

4. Push noodles to one side and add shrimp. Cook on one side until pink. Toss to cook other side. Add spinach and bean sprouts, if using. Gently scoop the mass of noodles to cover shrimp and vegetables and let cook for 30 seconds. Toss everything well, adding up to $\frac{1}{4}$ cup (60 mL) water if pan is dry. Check to see that pork has browned and is no longer pink and shrimp are firm, pink and opaque. Transfer noodles to a serving platter. Place a few shrimp on top and serve at once.

Big Cool Noodle Bowl with Roast Chicken, Cucumbers and Mint

This recipe is a pattern for innumerable delicious variations on the meal-in-a-bowl known in Vietnam as *bun*. You can compose a go-to version using ready-to-savor ingredients, such as chunks of rotisserie chicken, slices of Char Shiu-Style Pork (page 88), roast duck from an Asian market or tender slices of grilled flank steak from yesterday's grill-centered feast. Keep a couple of packages of dried rice noodles (or angel hair pasta) in your pantry, stay stocked up on fresh herbs and lettuces and mix up a jar of pickles (pages 128 to 131), and you'll be set for pantry meals of irresistible deliciousness on a moment's notice.

<><><><><><><><><><><><><><><><><><><><><><><><><><><><><><><>

Serves 4

Variations

Instead of the roast chicken, use 8 oz (250 g) grilled shrimp, Lemongrass Beef (page 68), Lemongrass Shrimp (page 20) or Pork Meatballs (page 24).

If thin dried rice noodles are difficult to find, you can substitute with angel hair pasta. Cook the same amount of dried angel hair pasta in a large pot of boiling water until tender but still firm, according to package directions. Drain, rinse with cool water, and drain well. You will need about 6 cups (1.5 L) cooked angel hair pasta.

1 lb	thin dried rice noodles	500 g
2 cups	shredded lettuce or spring salad mix	500 mL
3 cups	shredded roast chicken	750 mL
2 cups	sliced peeled cucumber	500 mL
1 cup	small sprigs fresh mint and fresh cilantro combined	250 mL
2 cups	mung bean sprouts, optional	500 mL
1 cup	Everyday Pickled Carrots (page 128) or shredded carrots, optional	250 mL
⅓ cup	thinly sliced green onions	75 mL
¾ cup	chopped dry-roasted salted peanuts	175 mL
	Double recipe Everyday Dipping Sauce (page 200), about 1 cup (250 mL)	
	Cool Shredded Cucumber Salad (page 126)	

1. Bring a large saucepan, Dutch oven or pasta pot of water to a rolling boil over high heat. Drop in noodles, remove from heat and let stand, using tongs or a slotted spoon and a fork to separate the noodles and let them cook evenly, for 10 minutes. When noodles are tender, drain, rinse in cold water and drain again. You'll have about 6 cups (1.5 L) of cooked noodles. Let stand while you prepare the remaining ingredients.

Tip

These delicious mix-and-match main course noodle salads make an ideal buffet where each guest can choose their favorite ingredients in quantities they like. Set out the ingredients in the order guests will add them, with noodles first, along with tongs or two forks for easy serving. Next come meat, cucumbers, mint and bean sprouts; followed by pickled carrots, green onions and peanuts. Have the sauce in a bowl with a ladle or big spoon or a small pretty glass pitcher if you have one, so they can add the seasoning at the end.

2. Set out 4 big Asian-style noodle or soup bowls. Divide ingredients evenly among the bowls: lettuce first, topped with 1½ cups (375 mL) noodles in each bowl.

3. Place roast chicken on one side and cucumber, fresh herbs and any optional ingredients you're using on the other.

4. Sprinkle green onions and peanuts over chicken, pour ¼ cup (60 mL) of Everyday Dipping Sauce over each portion of the noodles and serve at once, inviting your guests to toss everything together as they begin to eat. Serve with Cool Shredded Cucumber Salad.

◇ Vietnamese Tales

The menu category of *bun* at a Vietnamese café or restaurant guides you with a winning formula: a pile of soft rice noodles crowned with a generous portion of flavorful roasted or grilled meat; a refreshing array of crunchy-cool greens and vibrant fresh herbs; and a generous splash of Vietnam's incomparably delicious theme-condiment, Everyday Dipping Sauce, known in Vietnamese as *nuoc cham*.

Sweets and Drinks

*I*n **Vietnam, sweets,** *puddings and other confections delight
everyone: tiny children, stylish urban youth, civil servants
and white-haired elders. Sweets rule from dawn to bedtime.
Eaten with spoons, out of hand or sipped from straws, they are
relished at bus stops, in schoolyards and in chic sidewalk cafés.
Sweet foods are far too important to Vietnamese people to be
confined to a niche, like "desserts."*

*Coconut stars in Vietnamese desserts, as a creamy component
in puddings and as sparkling candied Sweet Coconut Ribbons
(page 190), which are a beloved New Year treat. European-inspired
desserts including cookies and Crème Caramel (page 188) share
the sweet state with classic Asian favorites such as Sticky Rice
Dumplings in Ginger Syrup (page 186). Popular beverages vary
as well, from Vietnamese Iced Coffee (page 192) and fruit-based
drinks to tea and gorgeously luxurious Avocado Shake (page 197).*

*Try some of the sweet offerings at Asian markets when you
go shopping for ingredients or cookware. Like the* cho *or fresh
markets in Hanoi, Hoi An, Cantho or Nha Trang, your local
Asian market probably sells a variety of sweet puddings, cakes,
candies and the unique Vietnamese pudding drink made with
pearl tapioca beans, corn and coconut milk. If you would like to
try your hand at the inviting and rewarding repertoire of sweet
things and beverages from coffee and tea to fruit drinks and
shakes made the Vietnamese way, here are an inviting array
of edible and sippable treats you can cook up at home.*

Luscious Banana Cake

This cake can be a dense street food sweet snack or a dessert suited to serving after a meal. This version has a delicate texture like a bread pudding, perfect for serving as a dessert or even breakfast treat. Small sweet Asian bananas are traditionally used, but you can make a great version using the bananas found in the West.

Serves 8 to 10

Tip

Instead of the round cake pan, you could also use 9- or 10-inch (23 or 25 cm) springform pan or 13- by 9-inch (33 by 23 cm) baking pan, generously greased.

◈ Vietnamese Tales

This sweet treat is enjoyed throughout Vietnam as a street food snack. You'll find versions made with a flour batter as well as ones like this one, in which soft white bread gives the dessert its substance and airy texture.

♦ Preheat oven to 375°F (190°C)
♦ 9-inch (23 cm) round cake pan, generously greased (see Tip, left)

3½ lbs	very ripe bananas (3 to 4 bananas)	1.75 kg
¾ cup	granulated sugar, divided	175 mL
9	slices soft white bread	9
1	can (14 oz/400 mL) unsweetened coconut milk (about 1½ cups/375 mL)	1
½ tsp	salt	2 mL
3 tbsp	melted butter	45 mL
	Ice cream or whipped cream, optional	

1. Chop bananas into 1-inch (2.5 cm) rounds. In a medium bowl, combine bananas and ⅓ cup (75 mL) of the sugar and stir gently to coat evenly. Set aside.

2. Trim away crusts from bread, reserving for bread crumbs or discarding. Gently cut or tear bread into small pieces or cubes.

3. In a large bowl, combine remaining sugar, coconut milk and salt and stir well. Add bread and mix well. Add melted butter and stir to combine well.

4. Arrange about one-third of the bananas on bottom of prepared pan, spacing out evenly. Add half the coconut milk mixture and spread to cover bottom of pan. Add another third of the banana slices, scattering over batter. Add remaining batter, smoothing out to make an even surface. Place remaining bananas evenly over top of cake.

5. Bake in center of preheated oven for 15 minutes. Reduce heat to 350°F (180°C) and bake until cake has puffed up, browned nicely and become firm, about 45 minutes.

6. Remove from oven and transfer to a cooling rack or folded kitchen towel and let cake come to room temperature. Slice and serve as is or with ice cream or whipped cream.

Warm Banana-Coconut Pudding with Tapioca Pearls

This is comfort food in any language, lovely for breakfast on a cold morning or anytime you crave something soothing and sweet. Traditionally *che chuoi* is served warm. Its texture is more like a sweet stew than a thick, Western-style pudding. In Vietnam, cooks use a petite, sturdy variety of banana, which simmers for a while in the sauce. I use big ripe bananas from the grocery store and add them right before the pudding is ready, since they are already quite tender and sweet. I like to serve all the bananas right away, even if I have pudding leftover. When I serve the leftover pudding the next day, I warm it gently and add a fresh batch of bananas.

Serves 8 to 10

Variation

If you love this pudding as I do, try it with chunks of cooked sweet potatoes or kabocha pumpkin or fresh or frozen corn. *Che chuoi* is often served with a sprinkling of chopped peanuts or toasted sesame seeds on top.

3 cups	water	750 mL
1/3 cup	very small tapioca pearls	75 mL
3 to 4	bananas	3 to 4
1	can (14 oz/400 mL) unsweetened coconut milk (about 1½ cups/375 mL)	1
½ cup	granulated sugar	125 mL
⅛ tsp	salt	0.5 mL

1. In a medium saucepan over high heat, bring water to a rolling boil. Sprinkle in tapioca, stirring water so it whirls around in the pan. Stir well for another minute or so to prevent tapioca from clumping. Adjust heat to maintain a lively simmer and cook, stirring often, until tapioca pearls are clear except for their tiny white centers, about 10 minutes.

2. Meanwhile, peel bananas, halve them lengthwise and then cut crosswise into 1-inch (2.5 cm) chunks. Set aside about 2 cups (500 mL) (and nibble the rest).

3. When tapioca has softened, add coconut milk, sugar and salt, stirring well to dissolve sugar. Add bananas, cook for another 1 to 2 minutes and remove from heat. Serve hot or warm.

Coconut Pudding with Sticky Rice and Black-Eyed Peas

I make this pudding with canned or frozen black-eyed peas, which I stir into the pudding in time to heat them up. This spares me the steps of soaking them and cooking them; too much trouble when all I want is a lovely little stirred and simmered pudding. This batch makes enough for a wintry afternoon snack, with plenty left over for breakfast later in the week.

Serves 10 to 12

Variation

Instead of the black-eyed peas, use corn or cubes of cooked butternut squash, kabocha pumpkin or sweet potato.

½ cup	long-grain sticky rice or long-grain rice	125 mL
3½ cups	water	875 mL
¾ cup	unsweetened coconut milk	175 mL
½ cup	canned or frozen black-eyed peas	125 mL
½ cup	granulated sugar	125 mL
	Generous pinch of salt	

1. Place rice in a medium saucepan, add water to cover, swirl to rinse well and then drain. Add 3½ cups (875 mL) water, place over medium heat and bring to a boil. Adjust heat to maintain a gentle simmer and cook until rice swells and softens, 10 to 15 minutes.

2. Add coconut milk, black-eyed peas, sugar and salt and stir well. Cook for 2 to 3 minutes to dissolve sugar and mix everything thoroughly. Remove from heat and let stand for 10 to 15 minutes. Serve warm or at room temperature. Or cover and refrigerate for up to 2 days and reheat gently just before serving time.

Black Sticky Rice Pudding

The velvety purple color of this sweet, satisfying dish is almost as delicious as the pudding itself. At my house we love it just like this, but if we have extra coconut milk or half-and-half cream handy, we crown each serving with a little splash, just to enjoy the contrast with that purple, before we dig in. The rice's plump black grains are dappled with white and brown, offering no hint of the purple waiting to emerge as it cooks. Like white sticky rice, it is high in amylopectin, the starch that causes rice grains to cling together when cooked. Because it is a brown or whole-grain rice, it needs a little more cooking time than polished white rice.

Serves 6 to 8

Tip

You will find *xoi nep* or black sticky rice in many Asian markets or through mail-order (see Resources, page 229).

1½ cups	black sticky rice (see Tip, left)	375 mL
3 cups	water	750 mL
½ cup	unsweetened coconut milk	125 mL
⅓ cup	granulated sugar	75 mL
½ tsp	salt	2 mL

1. Place rice in a medium bowl, add water to cover rice by at least 2 inches (5 cm) and soak for at least 3 hours or for up to 12 hours.

2. Drain rice well and transfer to a medium saucepan. Add water, stir well and bring to a lively boil over medium-high heat. Reduce heat to maintain a very gentle boil and let rice cook, stirring well occasionally, for 30 minutes.

3. Meanwhile, in a small saucepan over medium-high heat, combine coconut milk, sugar and salt and bring to a gentle boil. Stir well to dissolve sugar and salt and set aside.

4. When rice has cooked for 30 minutes, reduce heat to low and cook until shiny, tender, plump and a gorgeous purple hue, about 10 minutes. It will still have the pleasingly rustic texture of brown rice, rather than that of polished white rice.

5. Remove rice from heat, mix in the warm coconut sauce and stir well. Serve hot, warm or at room temperature in small bowls. Or cover and refrigerate the cooled pudding for up to 3 days, reheating gently just before serving time.

Sticky Rice Dumplings in Ginger Syrup with Coconut Crème and Toasted Sesame Seeds

These plump and chewy little pillows are a sweet sensation, as a comfort food snack or celebration dessert. Traditionally made by the expert hands of sweets vendors, this treat involves four steps: the ginger syrup, the coconut sauce, the toasted sesame seeds and making the dumplings. Your reward is a most pleasing bowl of sweetness with a side of good luck, as their round shape symbolizes harmony and unity.

Serves 4 to 6

Tips

To prepare in advance, make both the ginger syrup and the coconut sauce ahead of time. Let cool to room temperature and then refrigerate until you are ready to make the dumplings and serve the dish. Reheat both sauces gently while you make the dumplings.

Read the flour packages carefully, so that you buy "sticky rice flour," rather than "rice flour." The texture of sticky rice flour is needed for these dumplings. You may see it labeled "glutinous rice flour" or "sweet rice flour." It has no gluten and is not sweet, but these are common English names for the rice and its flour, so be aware.

Ginger Syrup

1 cup	dark or light brown sugar	250 mL
1 cup	water	250 mL
¼ cup	thinly sliced fresh gingerroot	60 mL

Coconut Sauce

¾ cup	canned unsweetened coconut milk, well-stirred	175 mL
¼ cup	water	60 mL
¼ cup	granulated sugar	60 mL
¼ tsp	salt	1 mL

Sesame Seeds

3 tbsp	white sesame seeds	45 mL

Sticky Rice Dumplings

¾ cup	sticky rice flour (see Tips, left)	175 mL
⅓ cup	boiling water	75 mL

1. *Ginger Syrup:* In a medium saucepan over high heat, combine brown sugar, water and ginger and bring to a lively boil. Reduce heat to maintain an active, visible simmer and cook, stirring occasionally, until a thickened golden syrup, about 10 minutes. Remove from heat and set aside.

2. *Coconut Sauce:* In a small saucepan over medium-high heat, combine coconut milk, water, sugar and salt and bring to a very gentle boil. Adjust heat to maintain a simmer and cook until sauce is smooth and thickened, 8 to 10 minutes. Remove from heat and set aside.

◈ Vietnamese Tales

This lovely and substantial confection is a Vietnamese rendition of the classic Chinese dish *tang yuan.* Plump, chewy little orbs made from sticky rice flour are simmered in syrup and served as a special occasion snack or dessert. Sometimes stuffed with sweet bean paste or black sesame seed purée, they are served in sweet syrup and considered lucky since their roundness symbolizes good luck in general and family harmony in particular. Ginger syrup is typical of the original, but the coconut milk sauce is a luscious Southeast Asian addition to the traditional dish.

3. *Toasted Sesame Seeds:* Heat a small skillet over medium-high heat until hot. Add sesame seeds and shake to spread out on pan. Cook, shaking pan and stirring occasionally, until a handsome golden brown but not burnt. Tip out onto a saucer and let cool.

4. *Sticky Rice Dumplings:* Bring a large pot of water to a rolling boil over high heat. Meanwhile, place sticky rice flour in a medium bowl. When water boils, reduce heat to maintain an active simmer and measure out $\frac{1}{3}$ cup (75 mL) boiling water. Add to rice flour and quickly stir with a fork to create a crumbly dough. Scrape and press to incorporate most of flour into dough. When cool enough to touch, turn dough and crumbs out onto a cutting board. Gather into a lump and knead and press to form a smooth dough, springy and losing its stickiness. Knead a few times until it is no longer sticky.

5. Divide dough into 2 equal portions. Roll each half into a log about $\frac{3}{4}$ inch (2 cm) thick. Cut each log into pieces about $\frac{1}{2}$ inch (1 cm) thick. Roll each piece into a little ball about the size of a marble. Place in a bowl. (You will have about 50 dumplings.)

6. To cook rice dumplings, bring the pot of water back to a rolling boil. Drop in about 10 dumplings at a time and stir well. Let cook, stirring occasionally, until plump and they float to the top, 2 to 3 minutes. Transfer dumplings to bowl of cool water. Continue cooking remaining dumplings in the same way.

7. Now you are ready to serve! Set out serving bowls and small spoons for enjoying the dumplings and sauces. Scoop out about 8 dumplings and place in one bowl. Continue with remaining dumplings. Ladle on a generous spoonful or two of ginger syrup. Sprinkle dumplings with toasted sesame seeds and then drizzle a nice dollop of coconut sauce over dumplings and syrup. Serve warm.

Crème Caramel

Sweet and luscious custard enjoyed favor in Vietnam and throughout Southeast Asia long before French cuisine arrived on the scene. Made with coconut milk, duck eggs and palm sugar, it was steamed rather than baked in a bain-marie or water bath. The classic French *crème renversée au caramel* quickly found favor when French rule came to Vietnam and was part of the country's culinary repertoire by the time the colonial era came to an end.

◇◇◇

Serves 8

Tip

Some versions of *banh ca ra men* are enriched by a combination of milk and coconut milk or several egg yolks in addition to whole eggs.

♦ Preheat oven to 350°F (180°C)
♦ 8 custard cups or ½-cup (125 mL) ramekins or small ovenproof glass bowls

Caramel

¾ cup	granulated sugar	175 mL
½ cup	water	125 mL

Custard

5	eggs	5
¾ cup	granulated sugar	175 mL
3 cups	milk	750 mL

1. *Caramel:* Place custard cups by the stove, ready to receive a dollop of hot caramel as soon as it's ready. In a heavy, medium saucepan over medium heat, combine sugar and water and cook, tilting pan to swirl liquid until sugar dissolves and combines with water to make a clear syrup, about 5 minutes. Increase heat to medium-high and gently boil syrup, lifting and tilting the pan now and then to cook it evenly, until syrup turns golden, then light brown and suddenly a whiskey or tea color. Quickly and carefully pour caramel into the custard cups, dividing evenly among them and tilting each cup to coax caramel to cover the bottom. Don't worry if it is uneven; it will all cook together into a beautiful crown. Set aside.

2. *Custard:* In a medium bowl, whisk or beat eggs until foamy and then add sugar. Beat well to dissolve sugar. Add milk and beat until well combined. Pour custard into custard cups over the caramel. Place in a baking or roasting pan and add enough water to come halfway up the sides of the cups. Bake in preheated oven until custard is firm around edges and fairly set in center and the tip of a knife stuck in the center comes out clean, 40 to 50 minutes.

Tip

Making the caramel for this dessert is a little tricky, so be sure you have everything you needed prepared and measured out and placed by the stove. The sugar can zoom from just browned enough to burnt in seconds. If this happens, simply start over. Let the pan cool down, and then fill it with water. If you need it to make the sauce again, bring it to a boil in order to loosen the burnt caramel. When it's clean, start over. If you don't need it right away, save this cleanup step for after your wonderful dessert is cooking.

3. Remove from oven. Carefully remove cups from pan of hot water and place on a cooling rack. Cover and chill if serving time is more than 1 hour away, for up to 2 days.

4. Serve at room temperature or chilled. Very gently, loosen edges of each custard with a table knife. Place a small serving plate upside down over custard cup and invert cup so that the custard drops onto the plate, displaying its dark, caramel-infused crown and releasing a small pool of thin, delicious sauce.

◇ Vietnamese Tales

Crème Caramel is a souvenir of the time when France ruled much of Indochine from its colonial beachhead in Vietnam. This can be made richer with coconut milk, half-and-half cream or extra egg yolks, depending on how luscious you like your custard. Vietnamese delis and takeout shops sell this delicious item unmolded into portable containers — a practical solution to the challenge of making something fragile available to go.

Sweet Coconut Ribbons

These beautiful curving strips of sugared coconut appear on platters of sweets, nuts and dried fruits that are traditionally offered to guests during Lunar New Year celebrations. Made with fresh coconut sliced into strips, or dried coconut flakes, it's a treat that keeps well and can be used as a garnish for cakes and other desserts, as well as a treat to eat out of hand. These are often tinted in pastel colors, but I love their snowy white sparkle as is.

¾ cup	granulated sugar	175 mL
½ tsp	salt	2 mL
¼ cup	water	60 mL
2 cups	large, freshly pared coconut chunks or wide strips or flakes of dried coconut (see Tip, left)	500 mL

Makes about 2 cups (500 mL)

Tip

You can use a fresh coconut or make it with wide strips or flakes of dried coconut, available in many health-food stores. I use a vegetable peeler to shred the coconut meat into thin ribbons, each about 2 inches (5 cm) long. To do this, hold a chunk of coconut firmly in one hand over a plate and shave strips off its curved edge. Stop when a chunk shrinks enough in size to bring the peeler close to your fingers. (You can save the small chunks in the refrigerator or freezer until you have enough to grate for a dessert.) Or shred the coconut meat with a food processor fitted with the slicing disk. This is faster, but the shreds come out thicker and less pliable than hand-shredded coconut. Either way, you should have about 2 cups (500 mL) of shredded coconut.

1. In a heavy-bottomed, medium saucepan over medium heat, combine sugar, salt and water and bring to a gentle boil. Add coconut ribbons, reduce heat to maintain a gentle simmer and cook, stirring often and coating ribbons with the gradually reducing and thickening syrup.

2. Once syrup forms large bubbles and begins to crystallize on the sides of the pot, stir constantly with a fork to keep the ribbons separate and moving around, until syrup dries up completely into dry, white grains. Turn out the ribbons onto a platter, pulling apart any clumps so they cool and dry evenly. Serve warm or at room temperature. Or cool completely and store in a tightly sealed glass jar.

◈ Vietnamese Tales

Sweet Coconut Ribbons or *mut dua* represent the candied fruits and nuts prepared at home or purchased in time to celebrate Tet, the lunar New Year festival, which occurs at the new moon between January and February. It is a celebration of Vietnamese family and culture, during which life slows down and families and friends gather to reflect, renew, rejoice and eat lots of good things, including sweets like these ribbons.

Almond Cookies

As long as there's soft butter handy and the energy to do a bit of vigorous stirring, these cookies can be on the table in less time than it takes to go to the store, park, stand in line and come home. Chinese bakery-style almond cookies are bigger and crispier, and elegant Vietnamese bakery tuiles are more elegant and serene; but these cookies are just right. Enjoy them with a small bowl of coconut ice cream, or a lovely glass of Vietnamese Iced Coffee (page 192).

Makes about 36 cookies

♦ Baking sheets, lined with parchment paper or waxed paper or greased well

3 cups	all-purpose flour	750 mL
1 tsp	baking soda	5 mL
1 tsp	salt	5 mL
1 cup	butter, softened	250 mL
1 cup	granulated sugar	250 mL
2	eggs	2
1 tbsp	almond extract	15 mL
¾ cup	thinly sliced almonds or whole almonds	175 mL

1. In a medium bowl, combine flour, baking soda and salt, using a fork to stir well.

2. In a large bowl, using a whisk or handheld electric mixer, beat or stir butter well, until fluffy and soft. Add sugar and beat well, stirring and mashing until well combined, about 2 minutes. Add eggs and almond extract and beat well until very smooth, creamy and soft, about 2 minutes.

3. Add flour mixture and, using a big wooden or metal spoon, mix well until a smooth, even-textured dough. Remove from bowl and form dough into a big ball. Press down into a thick disk and wrap in waxed paper or plastic wrap. Cover and let chill for 30 minutes to 1 hour or for up to 2 days.

4. Preheat oven to 350°F (180°C). Pinch dough into 1½-inch (4 cm) balls. Roll well and flatten in your palm to make a 2-inch (5 cm) cookie. Place on prepared baking sheet. Press sliced almond or whole almond in center of each cookie. Bake in preheated oven until cookies puff up, become dry and turn brown just at edges, 8 to 10 minutes. Let cool on the pan for 5 minutes. Continue to cool on a plate or wire rack. Serve at room temperature.

Vietnamese Coffee, Iced or Hot

Vietnamese coffee is a lingering souvenir of the French colonial presence in Vietnam. Along with delicious baguettes and the fabulous sandwiches they inspired, *ca-phé sua da* long ago made itself at home, embraced with such passion that it has become something very Vietnamese. You can make it at home with ease, with or without the signature top-hat contraption used to prepare *ca-phé* in Vietnamese establishments. If you lack the metal filter but long for the taste, pour 2 tbsp (30 mL) of sweetened condensed milk into a coffee cup or sturdy bistro glass. Brew some espresso, add it to the cup and stir like crazy. Voilà *ca-phé sua!* Pour over ice and it's *ca-phé sua da*.

◇◇

Serves 1

Tips

If you're buying ground coffee, look for espresso so that it will be strong and robustly flavored. If you're buying whole beans, look for French roast or Italian roast and grind the beans as finely as possible.

You'll find the top-hat contraption in many Asian markets and through mail-order sources (page 229).

2 tbsp	sweetened condensed milk	30 mL
2 tbsp	finely ground dark-roast coffee	30 mL
¾ cup	boiling water	175 mL

1. Spoon condensed milk into a coffee cup or a short drinking glass and place Vietnamese coffee filter on top. For iced coffee, fill a tall glass with ice cubes and set aside. Remove coffee filter's lid, unscrew inner press and set both aside. Add ground coffee and then screw the press lightly in place to pack coffee down a bit. Add boiling water, cover with lid and let water drip through coffee, 3 to 5 minutes.

2. Remove lid and rest upside down. Then place drained filter basket on inverted lid to catch any last drops of coffee. Stir well to mix coffee with milk. For iced coffee, pour coffee into ice-filled glass and serve. For hot coffee, skip the glass of ice or *da* and sip (carefully) your steaming *ca-phé sua*.

◈ Vietnamese Tales

Ca-phé sua and *ca-phé sua da* are the fabulous Vietnamese take on coffee with sweetened condensed milk, hot or iced. Glorious for those who love coffee, of whom I am one. If you, too, love coffee sweet and strong, indulge yourself in a *phin pha ca-phé*, the tiny, top-hat-shaped metal coffee filters of Vietnam. Make yourself a cup of *ca-phé sua da* and sip it while you browse your way through this book. It's a time-out for grownups, since the coffee drips on its own timetable rather than yours. Stare out the window, call your faraway friend or sibling or make a grocery list if you must multitask! Sweet, very sweet.

Preserved Plum Drink

Next time you're at an Asian market, keep an eye out for a jar of Asian-style preserved plums. About the size of a wrinkled cherry, they can be rusty red to autumnal brown, and while you can find them dried, the best kind for enjoying this classic Chinese-style beverage is a jar of plums preserved in brine.

◇◇

Makes 1 glass

Tip

Make up a small pitcher if you want to share this refreshing traditional beverage with guests on a warm afternoon. Simply multiply by the number of servings, stir it up, and serve over ice. Keep any extra in the refrigerator as you would lemonade.

2	soft Asian-style pickled plums	2
1 tbsp	granulated sugar	15 mL
	Ice cubes	
	Club soda or water	

1. Place plums in a tall glass. Add sugar and enough ice cubes to nearly fill glass. Add club soda almost to top and stir well. (You could use plain water instead of club soda if you wanted a milder taste.)

◇ Vietnamese Tales

In Vietnam, this old-school refreshment is enjoyed with plain water as well as with club soda, and people vary the amount of sugar added according to their own taste. Old-timers buy dried plums and let them soften up in the glass for half a day to release their flavor, but with pickled ones, this drink is ready when you are.

Fresh Soy Milk

I love the taste of freshly made soy milk and I enjoy making it as a treat. Do it when you are not in a hurry, as it involves advance preparation (soaking the soybeans for at least 6 hours) and a straightforward but messy middle step (puréeing the soaked beans and straining them well). The third and final step is short and sweet: simmering the soy milk briefly until its raw, beany aroma softens to a sweet, smooth scent and flavor. Then it is ready to sip, sweeten or infuse with lemongrass, fresh ginger or another flavor you like. A good supply of cheesecloth is a plus for making soy milk, but you can use kitchen towels instead.

Serves 2

Makes about 2 cups (500 mL)

Tip

You can buy dried whole soybeans in most Asian markets and in many health-food stores. They are hard, dry, a beautiful café au lait brown in color and about the size of green peas.

♦ Blender

| ⅔ cup | whole dried soybeans (see Tip, left) | 150 mL |
| 3 cups | water | 750 mL |

1. In a large bowl, combine soybeans and water and set aside to soak for 6 to 8 hours. The soybeans will triple in size and swell to an oval shape. When you're ready to make the soy milk, set out a medium saucepan, a large spoon and a fine-mesh strainer. (You could also use a medium bowl lined with 2 to 3 layers of cheesecloth or a clean kitchen towel.)

2. Place about half the soybeans and water in a blender and process to a fairly smooth purée, pulsing on and off as needed. Place strainer over saucepan and pour in purée. Use spoon to press soybean purée against strainer to extract as much liquid as possible. Repeat with remaining soybeans and water. Or pour purée into the bowl lined with cheesecloth or a kitchen towel in small batches, gathering the cheesecloth and squeezing gently but diligently to extract as much liquid as possible. Transfer to saucepan. Place saucepan over medium-high heat and bring soy milk to a gentle boil. Reduce heat to low and simmer, stirring often, until the aroma changes from "beany" to a fresh, sweet scent, about 10 minutes.

3. Remove from heat and serve hot or warm, or cool to room temperature, chill and serve cold. The soy milk will keep for 1 or 2 days in the refrigerator.

Fresh Lemongrass Tea

Cooking Vietnamese food puts you "up close and personal" with the ethereal herb known in English as lemongrass and in Vietnamese as *xa*. If you love its aroma and flavor as I do, you will enjoy this simple and beautiful tea, made with fresh lemongrass stalks.

◇◇

Serves 5

Makes about 1 quart (1 L) tea

4 cups	water	1 L
6	stalks fresh lemongrass	6
¼ to ⅓ cup	granulated sugar	60 to 75 mL

1. In a medium saucepan over medium-high heat, bring water to a lively boil.

2. Meanwhile, prepare lemongrass. Trim 1 inch (2.5 cm) off the grassy top and pare away any dried root portion at the base, leaving a smooth end below the bulb. Remove any dried, sad-looking outer leaves as well. Cut each stalk diagonally into 1-inch (2.5 cm) pieces to expose its purple-tinged, aromatic core. You should have about 2 cups (500 mL).

3. When water boils, add lemongrass and sugar to taste and stir well. Adjust heat to maintain a gentle boil and simmer for 5 minutes. Remove from heat, cover and let tea steep for at least 10 minutes.

4. To serve hot, strain tea into cups or a teapot. To serve cold, leave lemongrass chunks steeping in the tea as it cools to room temperature. Strain cooled tea, transfer to a pitcher and serve over ice. The tea will keep in the refrigerator for up to 2 days.

Limeade

Bright sharp flavors turn serenely sweet in this swiftly made, leisurely enjoyed drink. Make up a small pitcher and keep it handy for summertime sipping or year-round thirst-quenching pleasure.

Variation

Use lemons instead of limes with great results. The particular lime that thrives in Vietnam is a vibrant thin-skinned citrus fruit, green-yellow in color and between lime and lemon in flavor.

1½ cups	water	375 mL
1½ cups	granulated sugar	375 mL
⅔ cup	freshly squeezed lime juice	150 mL
1½ cups	club soda or water	375 mL
	Ice cubes	
	Thin slices of lime for garnish, optional	

1. In a medium saucepan over high heat, combine water and sugar. Stir and swirl to heat water and dissolve sugar until water and sugar have turned a clear syrup. Remove from heat and transfer to a pitcher and let cool.

2. When syrup is cool, add lime juice and club soda or additional water and stir well. Serve or chill for later use.

3. To serve, fill 4 tall glasses with ice cubes. Add a few lime slices, if using, and fill with limeade. Serve at once.

Avocado Shake

Known in Vietnam as "butter fruit" in recognition of its rich and luscious properties, the avocado stars in a wildly popular and incredibly simple to prepare beverage known as an Avocado Shake. No milkshake machine involved here, though there is milk in two different forms. Since it's blender-based, "smoothie" would be a better name, but since it has the delightful power to shake up what many who are new to it believe about what is sweet and what is savory, let's stick with that lovely name.

◇◇◇

Makes 2 to 4 servings

Tip

You can serve this with the oversize straws popularly offered with frozen coffee drinks and bubble tea. Or treat it like soft-serve ice cream and present it in small bowls with big spoons.

◆ Blender

1	ripe avocado, such as Hass (about 8 oz/250 g)	1
10 to 12	ice cubes or 1½ cups (375 mL) crushed ice	10 to 12
¼ cup	sweetened condensed milk	60 mL
⅓ cup	milk	75 mL

1. In blender, combine chunks of ripe avocado, ice, sweetened condensed milk and milk. Cover tightly and blend until smooth, about 1 minute.

2. Stop and scrape down sides to make sure everything is evenly combined. Taste and check texture. If you want more sweetness, add more sweetened condensed milk. If too thick, add milk, 1 tbsp (15 mL) at a time, until desired thickness.

3. Pour into glasses and serve at once with spoons for enjoying every bit. Or cover and chill for up to 3 hours and serve cold.

Sauces and Other Basic Recipes

Here are your paints and brushes — an array of simple, flavorful condiments, components and finishing touches with which to complete your Vietnamese dishes. Everyday Dipping Sauce (page 200) is just that, an incomparable, delicate sauce that appears throughout the repertoire of Vietnamese dishes, from spring rolls and fritters to grilled meatballs, enormous bowls of rice noodles, table-top fondue feasts and simple country meals of rice and fish. You can make it in a traditional mortar, in a mini food processor or a blender or with a knife and a spoon. It is marvelous. Made with surprisingly simple ingredients, it complements and brings harmony to the cuisine of Vietnam.

You'll also find numerous other dipping sauces, each with a particular traditional use, but tasty on its own. These include Ginger-Lime Dipping Sauce (page 202), Lime Pepper–Salt Dipping Sauce (page 203) and Sweet and Tangy Tamarind Sauce (page 208). Only Everyday Dipping Sauce or Vegetarian Everyday Dipping Sauce (page 201) is essential; the other sauce recipes are rewarding extras, a part of the big picture of cooking quick and easy Vietnamese food.

This chapter also includes recipes for dishes that are used as ingredients in cooking or as accompaniments for various dishes. These include Crispy Garlic (page 212), Scallion Oil (page 214) and Chicken Stock (page 216), recipes that you may find yourself using in your everyday cooking.

Everyday Dipping Sauce

This traditional sauce appears on the table at most Vietnamese meals. Add a small handful of shredded carrots and you have a vegetable relish. For the ultimate *nuoc cham*, grind the garlic, chile and sugar with a mortar and pestle. Or smash the garlic through a garlic press or mince it finely and mash it with the sugar and chiles on the side of the bowl with the back of your spoon. Or simply stir it all together. As long as you dissolve the sugar, you will have a delicious sauce.

Makes about ½ cup (125 mL)

Tip

If you love this sauce as much as I do, you will want to make a double batch or more to have some on hand in the refrigerator for spooning over scrambled eggs, adding to a salad dressing or serving with a quick rice-centered lunch. I make a fresh batch for any special dish, but love having a go-to amount for spur of the moment goodness.

◆ Mortar and pestle, optional

1 tbsp	chopped garlic	15 mL
2 tbsp	granulated sugar	30 mL
½ tsp	chile-garlic sauce, finely chopped fresh hot red chiles or 1 tsp (5 mL) hot pepper flakes	2 mL
3 tbsp	fish sauce	45 mL
3 tbsp	water	45 mL
2 tbsp	freshly squeezed lime juice	30 mL

1. In the bowl of a mortar, if using, combine garlic, sugar and chile-garlic sauce and mash with a pestle to a paste. (Or combine them on your cutting board and mash to a coarse paste with a fork and the back of a spoon.)

2. Scrape paste into a small bowl and stir in fish sauce, water and lime juice. Stir well to dissolve sugar. Transfer to small serving bowls for dipping. Or cover and refrigerate for up to 1 week.

Vegetarian Everyday Dipping Sauce

Many Vietnamese dishes are seasoned in expectation that they will be served with *nuoc cham* or another flavorful table sauce. This sauce doesn't re-create *nuoc cham*, but it does provide a delicious vegetarian accompaniment to vegetarian versions of Summer Rolls (page 16), grilled vegetables, tofu, noodle dishes and rice. It tastes great to non-vegetarians as well.

Makes about 2/3 cup (150 mL)

Tip

I love this vibrant sauce on veggie burgers, lentils or pasta salads. If you like it, make a double batch to have on hand for snacks and quick suppers. Keep it in a jar so you can shake it up just before using.

◆ Mini food processor or blender

¼ cup	soy sauce	60 mL
¼ cup	freshly squeezed lime juice or white vinegar	60 mL
¼ cup	pineapple juice	60 mL
¼ cup	fresh or canned pineapple chunks	60 mL
3 tbsp	granulated sugar	45 mL
2 tsp	Asian sesame oil	10 mL
2 tsp	salt	10 mL
2 tbsp	coarsely chopped fresh cilantro	30 mL
1 tbsp	coarsely chopped garlic	15 mL
¼ tsp	chile-garlic sauce, chopped fresh hot chiles, hot pepper flakes or other hot sauce	1 mL

1. In mini food processor or blender, combine soy sauce, lime juice, pineapple juice, pineapple chunks, sugar, sesame oil, salt, cilantro, garlic and chile-garlic sauce and blend until smooth. Serve in small bowls at room temperature or cover and refrigerate for up to 5 days.

Ginger-Lime Dipping Sauce

The fabulous flavor of this classic sauce lights up simple poached and grilled foods, such as Hainan Chicken and Rice (page 56), grilled or boiled shrimp or grilled salmon or tuna. It's also terrific with a simple platter of grilled or oven-roasted vegetables.

Makes about ½ cup (125 mL)

♦ Mini food processor or blender

2 tbsp	chopped fresh gingerroot	30 mL
2 tsp	chopped garlic	10 mL
3 tbsp	granulated sugar	45 mL
½ tsp	salt	2 mL
3 tbsp	fish sauce	45 mL
3 tbsp	freshly squeezed lime juice	45 mL
2 tbsp	water	30 mL
½ tsp	chile-garlic sauce, hot pepper flakes or chopped fresh hot chiles	2 mL

1. In mini food processor or blender, combine ginger, garlic, sugar, salt, fish sauce, lime juice, water and chile-garlic sauce and blend until a fairly smooth sauce. Transfer to a small bowl, stirring until sugar is dissolved. Set aside until serving time. Or combine ginger, garlic, sugar and salt in the bowl of a mortar and grind to a grainy paste. Transfer to a medium bowl and add fish sauce, lime juice, water and chile-garlic sauce, stirring until sugar is dissolved and sauce is fairly smooth. Pour sauce into small serving bowls. Or cover tightly and refrigerate for up to 1 week.

Lime Pepper–Salt Dipping Sauce

This little condiment displays the Vietnamese genius with seasonings. Three bold ingredients, arranged in a small bowl, are kept apart until show time, then stirred together by the diner for a wonderful condiment. The lime pepper–salt mixture shows up in Chicken Curry with Sweet Potatoes (page 54) and Shaking Beef with Purple Onions and Watercress (page 72) and is also delicious with steamed clams or mussels, grilled or boiled shrimp and fried rice. Traditionally it's presented as a single diner's condiment, but since you may be serving a crowd of hungry folks floating around the buffet table, I've given a variation for a shared portion.

½ tsp	salt	2 mL
½ tsp	freshly ground black pepper	2 mL
1	wedge of lime (about ⅙ of a whole lime)	1

Makes ½ cup (125 mL)

1. Mound salt on one side of a saucer and pepper on the other, leaving the center free for the wedge of lime. Let each guest squeeze the lime juice into the center and then stir, coaxing the three flavors into a thick little spot of sauce. Enjoy with grilled, roasted or fried food.

Tip

This signature Vietnamese sauce is somewhere between a dip and a sauce and is stirred together at the moment of serving with any remaining sauce discarded. Its intense flavors mean that a little goes a long way. If you like this as much as I do, look for small shallow bowls for individual servings of dipping sauces and condiments, available in Asian markets and online. Or serve sauces in bowls for passing around as the meal begins.

Variation

A Bowl for Sharing: In a small bowl, combine 2 tbsp (30 mL) salt, 2 tbsp (30 mL) black pepper and ½ cup (125 mL) freshly squeezed lime juice (2 or 3 limes) and stir well to dissolve seasonings into lime juice. Transfer to a small serving bowl. Guests can spoon the sauce onto their food or onto their plates or use it for dipping.

Tangy Brown Bean Dipping Sauce

This pungent sauce traditionally accompanies Summer Rolls with Shrimp and Mint (page 16) and Sugarcane Shrimp (page 14). It happens to be vegetarian and goes nicely with grilled or roasted food.

◇◇

Makes about ¾ cup (175 mL)

Tip

We love this rich, sweet-and-tangy sauce over noodles. Try it as a quick noodle dish tossed with spaghetti or linguine for a speedy cold noodle salad. Adding cooked chicken makes it hearty, and adding shredded lettuce and diced cucumbers makes it bright and fresh.

Sauce

½ cup	unsweetened coconut milk	125 mL
⅔ cup	water	150 mL
⅓ cup	brown bean sauce, also called ground bean sauce	75 mL
1 tbsp	white vinegar	15 mL
2 tbsp	peanut butter or finely ground roasted salted peanuts	30 mL
2 tbsp	granulated sugar	30 mL
1 tbsp	minced shallot or onion	15 mL

Garnishes

1 to 2 tbsp	chile-garlic sauce or any hot sauce	15 to 30 mL
2 tbsp	chopped roasted salted peanuts	30 mL

1. *Sauce:* In a small saucepan over medium-high heat, combine coconut milk, water, bean sauce, vinegar, peanut butter, sugar and shallot and bring to a boil. Adjust heat to maintain a gentle simmer and cook, stirring now and then, until sugar and peanut butter dissolve and sauce is fairly smooth, 3 to 5 minutes. Let cool to room temperature.

2. *Garnishes:* Serve in small bowls, each garnished with a dollop of chile-garlic sauce and a sprinkling of peanuts. Or cover and refrigerate for up to 5 days.

Chile-Lime Sauce

Add a sparkling accent to grilled or sautéed seafood with this vibrant yet simple accompaniment. Perfect with Grilled Salmon (page 100), it enhances the delicate taste of steamed fish and pairs well with the richness of fried snacks and entrées.

**Makes about
1/2 cup (125 mL)**

Tip

If you like a little chile heat, double or quadruple the amount of chile-garlic sauce in this recipe. This is a basic, just-a-tiny-hint-of-hot sauce, so taste and then adjust to suit yourself and your guests.

¼ cup	fish sauce	60 mL
3 tbsp	freshly squeezed lime juice or white vinegar	45 mL
2 tbsp	water	30 mL
2 tbsp	granulated sugar	30 mL
¼ tsp	chile-garlic sauce or other hot sauce	1 mL
1 tbsp	thinly sliced green onion	15 mL

1. In a small bowl, combine fish sauce, lime juice, water, sugar, chile-garlic sauce and green onion. Stir to dissolve sugar and mix well. Cover and refrigerate for up to 2 days.

Hoisin-Peanut Dipping Sauce

This plush sauce pairs sweetness with a tangy kick and is simple to make and easy to love. Traditionally, it accompanies Summer Rolls with Shrimp and Mint (page 16), the fresh soft spring rolls wrapped in rice paper and filled with lettuce, herbs and shrimp.

Makes about ³⁄₄ cup (175 mL)

Tip

Hoisin sauce is a sweeter, darker first cousin of brown bean sauce. Available in many supermarkets as well as Asian groceries, it is a shiny, chocolate-dark paste made from fermented soybeans. Some versions are thinned to a liquid consistency and bottled. Either works well in this recipe. Hoisin sauce combines well with peanut butter, and can enhance dressings, marinades and barbecue sauces, creating delicious dips or condiments.

½ cup	unsweetened coconut milk	125 mL
⅔ cup	water	150 mL
⅓ cup	hoisin sauce (see Tip, left)	75 mL
3 tbsp	smooth peanut butter	45 mL
1 tbsp	light or dark brown sugar	15 mL
1 tsp	salt	5 mL
2 tbsp	freshly squeezed lime juice or lemon juice	30 mL

1. In a small saucepan, combine coconut milk, water, hoisin sauce, peanut butter, brown sugar and salt and bring to a boil over medium-high heat. Adjust heat to maintain a gentle simmer and cook, stirring occasionally, until sugar and peanut butter dissolve and everything blends into a smooth sauce, 3 to 5 minutes. Remove from heat. Add lime juice and stir to mix in evenly and well. Let cool to room temperature and serve in small bowls. Cover and refrigerate for up to 5 days.

Pineapple-Chile Sauce

Sweet and sharp, tangy and alluring, this unique condiment lights up anything hot off the grill or fresh from the roasting oven. It enhances Grilled Tuna Steaks (page 98) and would make a fine companion to Fried Spring Rolls (page 28), fried seafood or boiled shrimp.

(page 98)

◇◇◇

Makes about ½ cup (125 mL)

Tip

Whisk a generous dollop of this bright-flavored sauce with a splash of olive oil and then toss with tender lettuces and watercress for a cool salad.

♦ Mini food processor or blender

⅓ cup	fresh or canned pineapple chunks or drained crushed pineapple	75 mL
3 tbsp	freshly squeezed lime juice	45 mL
2 tbsp	chopped green onion	30 mL
2 tbsp	chopped fresh cilantro	30 mL
2 tbsp	granulated sugar	30 mL
1 tbsp	anchovy paste, chopped anchovies or fish sauce	15 mL
2 tsp	minced garlic	10 mL
½ tsp	chile-garlic sauce or chopped fresh hot chiles	2 mL

1. In mini food processor or blender, combine pineapple, lime juice, green onion, cilantro, sugar, anchovy paste, garlic and chile-garlic sauce and blend until fairly smooth. Transfer to a small bowl and set aside until serving time. Cover and refrigerate for up to 2 days.

Sweet and Tangy Tamarind Sauce

This luscious sauce brings out the briny goodness in seafood and can enhance the pleasures of eating almost anything hot off the grill. Enjoy it with Grilled Shrimp (page 106) and Pork-Stuffed Squid (page 112), and consider it as an accompaniment to Hearty Crab Cakes (page 110) and Sugarcane Shrimp (page 14).

<<<<<<<<<<<<<<<<<<<<<<<<<<<<<<<<<<<<<<<<<<<<<<<<<<<<<

Makes about ½ cup (125 mL)

Tip

For the tamarind liquid, you could also use Indian-style tamarind chutney.

1 tsp	vegetable oil	5 mL
1 tsp	minced garlic	5 mL
⅓ cup	prepared tamarind liquid or freshly made Tamarind Liquid (page 209)	75 mL
2 tbsp	fish sauce or 1 tsp (5 mL) salt	30 mL
2 tbsp	water	30 mL
2 tbsp	granulated sugar	30 mL
1 tbsp	brown sugar	15 mL
½ tsp	freshly ground black pepper	2 mL
¼ tsp	hot pepper flakes or chile-garlic sauce	1 mL

1. In a small saucepan or skillet, heat oil and garlic over medium heat until garlic is fragrant and sizzles, about 1 minute. Add tamarind liquid, fish sauce, water, granulated sugar, brown sugar, pepper and hot pepper flakes and stir well. Cook, stirring often, until sugars dissolve and sauce is smooth and thickened a bit, 3 to 5 minutes. Serve warm or at room temperature or cover and refrigerate for up to 2 days.

Tamarind Liquid

You can transform the ebony-colored soft bricks of processed tamarind pulp into a luscious, velvety and utterly delicious sweet-sharp purée. Simply soak a portion of the gooey tamarind in warm water and then squeeze, press and mash it through a fine sieve to subtract the seeds, fibers and husks that remain in the block before soaking. Use this tart purée in making dressings, marinades and sauces, such as Sweet and Tangy Tamarind Sauce (page 208). For more on tamarind, see page 226.

Makes about ¾ cup (175 mL)

Tip

If you have tamarind liquid on hand in the fridge and want a tangy beverage, stir a spoonful or two into a glass of water, along with a spoonful of sugar, honey or another sweetener you enjoy. Add ice and you've got a tamarind drink popular in Southeast Asia.

♦ Fine-mesh strainer
♦ 1 glass jar with tight-fitting lid

½ cup	wet tamarind	125 mL
1 cup	warm water	250 mL

1. In a medium bowl, combine tamarind with warm water. Soak, occasionally using your hands to press, squeeze and mash dark, rich pulp as it softens in water, 20 to 30 minutes. Mix and mash to separate seeds and husks from tamarind fruit, which turns to a handsome rusty brown goo as it softens and mixes with the water.

2. Strain mixture through fine-mesh strainer into another bowl. Press and scrape to coax as much tamarind pulp as possible through the mesh and into the bowl of processed tamarind liquid. It will be very thick, like apple butter. Scrape rounded outside of strainer to get every speck of this powerful seasoning. Discard contents of strainer and transfer tamarind liquid to a glass jar. Cover and refrigerate for up to 5 days.

Everyday Caramel Sauce

Making caramel is the kitchen paradox — it can be very easy, but also very easily botched. The sugar seems to be caramelizing as slowly as molasses in January and then, just when you lose patience and step over to the sink for a tiny sip of water, it starts smoking and changing color very fast. Making this sauce is a lesson in patience and focus (areas in which I can always find room to improve). Caramel sauce is used in a number of Vietnamese dishes because of its handsome color and rich flavor note, but it is not essential to creating a wonderful dish.

Makes about 1 cup (250 mL)

Variation

If you don't want to make this sauce, you can substitute an equal amount of brown sugar for the Caramel Sauce in any recipe or make the Speedy Caramel Sauce (page 211).

¼ cup	cold water	60 mL
¾ cup	granulated sugar	175 mL
¼ cup	hot water	60 mL

1. In a sturdy medium saucepan over medium-high heat, combine cold water and sugar and stir well. Cook, tilting pan to swirl sauce occasionally until liquid becomes syrupy and color begins to change, 5 to 7 minutes. Have the hot water handy by the stove.

2. Watch carefully as soon as syrup turns from clear to soft gold to color of honey. Swirl syrup gently occasionally and be vigilant; this is the point at which things start to happen fast. When syrup is as dark as maple syrup, but not as dark as molasses, carefully pour hot water down the side of the saucepan and expect a small eruption of bubbling, steamy chaos. Once syrup settles down, continue cooking, stirring, until syrup is smooth, thin and caramel colored.

3. Set aside and let cool and then transfer to a jar and close tightly. The syrup will keep at room temperature for up to 1 month.

Speedy Caramel Sauce

When you need the traditional Vietnamese condiment caramel sauce in a hurry, you can use this shortcut version made with brown sugar. This works well, but does not hold up over time, tending to crystallize rather than remain liquid. Make a small amount and use it the day you make it.

◇◇

Makes about 1/2 cup (125 mL)

Tip

Leftover sauce can be poured over oatmeal at breakfast time, drizzled onto ice cream or a piece of cake, or stirred into a smoothie or cup of coffee or tea in lieu of sugar.

¾ cup	dark or light brown sugar	175 mL
¾ cup	water	175 mL

1. In a medium saucepan, combine brown sugar and water and stir well. Bring to a lively boil over medium-high heat. Cook, stirring occasionally to melt sugar and until you have a thin syrup, about texture of maple syrup but not as thick as honey, 5 to 10 minutes.

2. Remove from heat and transfer to a small bowl and let cool. Use within 1 to 2 days.

Crispy Garlic

This handsome golden garnish adds a bit of crunch and toasty flavor to noodles, rice and porridge. You can save the oil for frying eggs or stir-frying vegetables, adding a subtle garlicky goodness to an already tasty dish.

Makes ½ cup (125 mL)

Tip

Remove the garlic just before it is the shade of golden brown you want. It will continue cooking at first, so taking it out a bit early improves your chances of getting a warm, handsome golden brown color, without burning the garlic.

♦ Plate, lined with paper towels
♦ 1 glass jar with tight-fitting lid

¾ cup	vegetable oil	175 mL
½ cup	finely chopped garlic	125 mL

1. Heat oil in a small skillet over medium-high heat until a bit of garlic sizzles at once.

2. Add garlic and stir to fry evenly and quickly. As soon as it is mostly golden, scoop out swiftly and tip out onto prepared plate.

3. Let cool to room temperature. Transfer to a small jar, seal and store at room temperature for 2 to 3 days.

Crispy Shallots

Use on noodle dishes, over rice, or anytime a little color, texture and roasty-toasty flavor boost seems like a good plan. Once shallots drain and cool down, you can keep them in a sealed jar at room temperature for 2 or 3 days.

<><><><><><><><><><><><><><><><><><><><><><><><><><><><><><><><><><><><><><>

Makes ¾ cup (175 mL)

Tips

For extra crisp shallots, spread raw, sliced shallots out on a plate in a single layer and let dry for about 1 hour. This removes some of their natural moisture and can increase their crispness.

Remove the shallots just before they are the shade of golden brown you want. They continue cooking at first, so taking them out a bit early improves your chances of getting a warm, handsome golden brown color, without burning the shallots.

♦ Plate, lined with paper towels
♦ 1 glass jar with tight-fitting lid

| 1 cup | vegetable oil | 250 mL |
| ¾ cup | thinly sliced shallots | 175 mL |

1. Heat oil in a small heavy skillet over medium-high heat until a bit of shallot sizzles at once.

2. Scatter in sliced shallots and stir with a slotted spoon to separate and spread out. Cook, stirring occasionally, until golden brown (see Tips, left).

3. Scoop out shallots quickly and spread out on prepared plate. Let cool to room temperature. Transfer to a small bowl and use within 2 hours or transfer cooled shallots to a jar and seal tightly. Keep at room temperature for 2 to 3 days.

Scallion Oil

This savory accompaniment to noodles, grilled meat and seafood, soups and snacks can be made quickly and kept covered in the refrigerator for 3 to 5 days. You can use green tops only or whole scallions (also known as green onions), slicing them thinly and cooking them briefly in hot oil to release and enhance their flavor. If you need a large amount, simply increase the recipe proportions. For daily use, it's best to make modest amounts rather than keep it for long periods, as the flavor fades over time.

**Makes about
2/3 cup (150 mL)**

♦ 1 glass jar with tight-fitting lid

1/3 cup	vegetable oil	75 mL
3/4 cup	thinly sliced scallions, green part only or green and white	175 mL

1. Heat oil in a small saucepan over medium heat until hot enough that a bit of scallion sizzles gently at once. Add scallions, stir well, and cook for about 15 seconds.

2. Pour oil and scallions into a heatproof bowl and let cool to room temperature. Transfer to glass jar, cover, and keep refrigerated for up to 3 days. Remove from refrigerator in enough time to allow scallion oil to warm up to room temperature before using.

Egg Pancake Strips

These golden threads make an appealing and tasty addition to an array of dishes, including Fried Rice with Shrimp, Egg and Green Onion (page 149) to Bun Thang Noodles (page 159). You could also scatter them over a comforting bowl of Everyday Rice Porridge (page 150).

◇◇

**Makes about
½ cup (125 mL)
egg threads**

| 2 | large eggs | 2 |
| 2 tbsp | vegetable oil, divided | 30 mL |

1. In a small bowl, beat eggs with a fork or a whisk until bright yellow and thoroughly combined.

2. In a small skillet, heat 1 tbsp (15 mL) of the oil over medium-high heat until hot enough to make a bit of egg bloom at once. Add about one-quarter of the egg mixture and quickly swirl and tip pan to spread out into a thin even layer. Let flat pancake cook until set, dry and starting to curl at edges. Repeat to make 3 more pancakes, stacking them up as they are done.

3. Transfer stack of sunny yellow egg pancakes to a cutting board. Cut through stack with a sharp knife to make thin strips or threads. Fluff with your fingers to separate and use as directed in a recipe. To store, transfer to a container and seal airtight. Keep refrigerated for 3 days.

Chicken Stock

When you have time to pay occasional attention to a pot on the stove, make chicken stock and enjoy its satisfying flavor while storing some in the fridge or freezer for another day's cooking. Store-bought chicken stock works fine, but if you have time and storage space, this simple process gives you ample reward for taking the time to make it.

◇◇

Makes about 8 cups (2 L)

Tip

If you'd like to use the meat from the chicken, carefully remove chicken pieces and transfer them to a platter after 40 to 50 minutes of cooking time. Timing will vary depending on their size and weight. Let rest until cool enough to handle. Pull off the easily removed meat, leaving lots of meaty chunks on the bone. Return the meaty chunks and skin to the pot and cook for another 1½ to 2 hours. Use the meat for Chicken and Cabbage Salad with Mint (page 124), toss with noodles or serve with Pineapple-Chile Sauce (page 207) and rice.

◆ Stockpot with 16-cup (4 L) capacity

3½ lbs	chicken legs and thighs, or breasts, bone-in and skin on	1.75 kg
2	unpeeled medium onions, halved lengthwise	2
8	thick unpeeled diagonal slices fresh gingerroot	8
2 tsp	salt	10 mL
1 tsp	granulated sugar	5 mL

1. Place chicken pieces in a large stockpot and add enough cold water to cover by at least 1 inch (2.5 cm). Bring to a rolling boil over medium high-heat and let boil for 5 minutes.

2. Drain stock through a colander and discard. Transfer chicken to a platter and wash out pot. Return chicken to clean pot and add enough cold water to cover by 1 inch (2.5 cm), about 12 cups (3 L).

3. Return pot to stove and add onions and sliced ginger. Bring to a rolling boil over medium-high heat and cook, skimming off and discarding any foam that rises to the top, for 5 minutes. Reduce heat to maintain a gentle but visible simmer and cook for 2 hours.

4. Set out a large bowl and carefully strain stock into bowl, leaving behind chicken and solids that may have settled at bottom of pot. Discard chicken, which has released its flavor into the stock.

5. Let cool to room temperature and then transfer to storage containers in useful quantities such as 2-cup (500 mL) or 4-cup (1 L) portions. Keep covered and refrigerated for up to 3 days or frozen for 2 to 3 months.

Toasted Rice Powder

Used to enliven the texture and enhance the flavor of noodles, dumplings and salads, this aromatic condiment is a standard item in Vietnamese home kitchens. Traditionally it's made with sticky rice, but any raw long-grain rice will work fine.

◇◇

Makes about 1/2 cup (125 mL)

Tip

To keep on hand, store the toasted rice whole and grind as you need to use it. Once ground, the powder quickly loses its fragrance and flavor, so the less time between grinding and using, the better it is. Store airtight at room temperature for 1 month.

♦ Mortar and pestle or electric grinder or blender

| 1/2 cup | raw sticky rice, jasmine rice or any long-grain rice | 125 mL |

1. In a small dry skillet over high heat, fry raw rice grains, shaking pan often to prevent burning until darkened to a handsome golden brown, 3 to 5 minutes.

2. When rice is cool, transfer to a mortar, an electric coffee grinder or spice grinder or blender. Pound or blend until grains break down into an aromatic powder with only a few small visible grain bits remaining. You want a fine, sandy powder with a bit of crunch, not completely powdered.

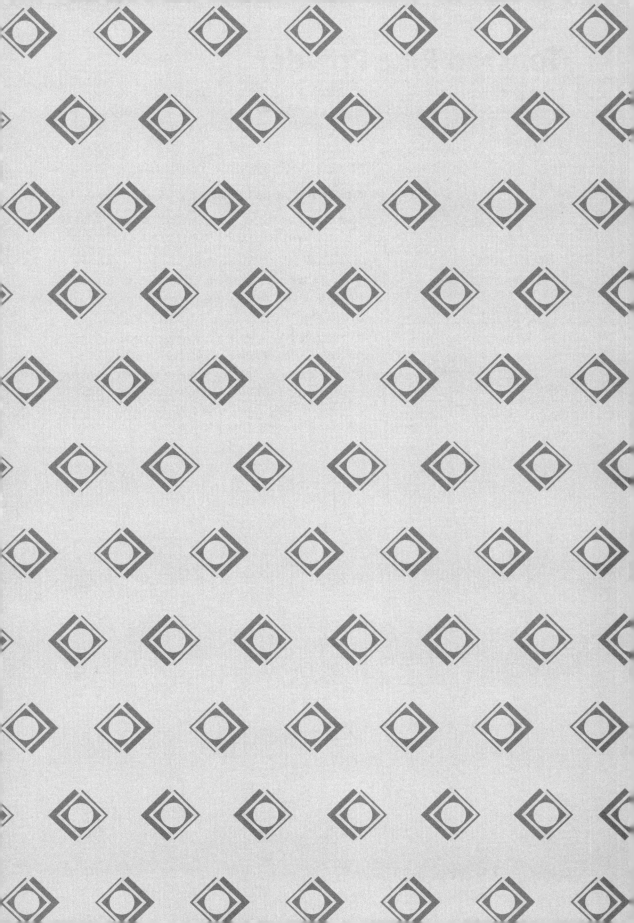

Glossary of Vietnamese Ingredients

Fresh Herbs for the Vietnamese Kitchen

No cuisine holds fragrant, flavorful herbs in higher esteem than that of Vietnam. The ubiquitous leafy platters of lettuce and herbs that adorn Vietnamese tables at mealtime are a silent affirmation of this truth. Nowhere else is there comparable devotion to sparkling flavors and aromas, nor such dedication to enhancing the pleasure of every bite. Many of the components of these platters, called *dia rau song*, are herbs well-known and easily found in the West: cilantro, mint, basil and dill, along with green onions, bean sprouts, sliced fresh hot chiles and chunks of lime. Here is a little herb primer, a field guide to the culinary herbs you are most likely to find in Vietnamese restaurants, grocery stores and farmers' markets in the West.

Asian basil (*rau que*)

Asian basil *(Ocimum basilicum)* has a familiar scent to basil-loving cooks in the West, but it looks a bit different from its European cousins. Look for sharp, pointy leaves on purple stems, often adorned with tiny white flowers and purple buds. This herb is also known as Thai basil and its Thai name is *bai horapah*.

Cilantro (*rau ngo*)

A staple of kitchens around the world, cilantro *(Coriandrum sativum)* is also known as fresh coriander and Chinese parsley. Keep cilantro on hand, as you will use it often when cooking Vietnamese food.

Crab claw herb (*rau cang cua*)

Named for its shape, this less common herb is appreciated for its peppery taste.

Dill (*rau thi la*)

Used in Laos and northern Vietnam, the feathery fronds of dill *(Anethum graveolens)* make a delicious and aromatic companion to fish. Its signature use in the cuisine of Vietnam is in Cha Ca Fish with Fresh Dill, Hanoi-Style (page 104), the famed northern dish made with catfish, turmeric and handfuls of dill.

Fish mint (*rau diep ca*)

Enjoyed as a piquant accompaniment to grilled meats and fish soups, the flavor of this soft heart-shaped leaf is widely described as "fishy" by both fans and detractors. This herb *(Houttuynia cordata)* has little fragrance. It is popular in southwestern China and northeastern India. The shape of *rau diep ca*'s leaves earns it an additional common name of fish-scale mint.

Mint (*rau hung lui*)

Spearmint (*Mentha arvensis*) is the type of mint most often used in Vietnamese cooking, but any type of mint you can find will work nicely. Also called *rau bac ha* and *rau thom*, mint is used often, so try to keep it on hand along with cilantro.

Piper leaf (*la lot*)

Also known as wild betel leaf, this beautiful, heart-shaped leaf (*Piper sarmentosum*) is used throughout Southeast Asia as a delicately flavored edible wrapper for savory tidbits. Known in Thailand as *bai cha plu*, it is the namesake ingredient for Grilled Leaf-Wrapped Beef Kebabs (page 22) or *bo la lot*. Piper leaves are not common in the West, but you can use perilla leaves, large basil leaves, spinach leaves or grape leaves as a wrapper in their place.

Rau ram

Also known as Vietnamese coriander. With its bright, pungent flavor and aroma, *rau ram* (*Polygonum odoratum*) is earning a place for itself among the herbs appreciated in the West. Pale green and smooth, but not shiny, *rau ram* leaves resemble those of Asian basil in overall shape. But unlike basil, a *rau ram* leaf usually sports a dark, handsome mark at its widest point, on both sides of its spine. In Malaysia, Singapore and Indonesia, it is known as *laksa* leaf because of its role in the pungent seafood noodle soup *laksa*.

Red perilla (*rau tia to*)

Red perilla leaves (*Perilla frutescens*) are large, matte and beautifully two-toned; deep green on top and rich purple on the underside. Known in Japan as shiso and in English as beefsteak plant, they are often served with sushi. Beloved with Sizzling Savory Pancake with Shrimp and Pork (page 90), they work well in place of *la lot* leaves for Grilled Leaf-Wrapped Beef Kebabs (page 22) or *bo la lot*.

Rice paddy herb (*rau ngo om*)

This little herb sprouts tiny leaves widely spaced over its long, plump little stems. *Rau ngo om* (*Limnophila aromatica*) is chopped or torn up whole, stems as well as leaves, and then added to soups and curries at serving time. With its petite oval leaves attached to the stem at intervals, from base to tip, *rau ngo om* looks like a sprig of thyme that has been magically inflated. But the resemblance ends there; don't try to replace it with thyme.

Saw-leaf herb (*rau ngo gai*)

Long, straight, smooth leaves set this aromatic and pungent herb (*Eryngium foetidum*) apart from the crowd. Picture a flat green ribbon as long as your finger and with a delicately serrated edge. Look for *rau ngo gai*, also known in English as saw-tooth herb, on the herb plate whenever you order a bowl of *pho* (pages 160 and 162).

Vietnamese balm (*rau kinh gioi*)

Also known as green perilla, this flavorful light-green leaf (*Elsholtzia ciliata*), bears a visual resemblance to perilla and hence its common name. It is actually a cousin to lemon balm. In Vietnam, it shows up among the abundant leafy herbs presented with soups.

Rice Noodles and Rice Paper Wrappers

Within the bounty of Asian ingredients widely available to the home cook, none have greater potential for the quick and easy kitchen than dried rice noodles and rice paper wrappers. Many supermarkets stock them nowadays and so do Asian groceries and mail-order sources (page 229). Their virtues are many: Rice noodles are a foundation for substantial meals at a minuscule cost. They come in many sizes, from wire-thin threads to big, fat, fettuccine-like ribbons. Rice paper wrappers range from small, medium and large translucent rounds to small triangles, perfect for wrapping up tiny spring rolls. They weigh very little and keep well for ages. Since they are shelf stable, stock up when you come across a supply and keep them on your pantry shelf next to the boxes of spaghetti and macaroni.

Rice noodles offer wonderful options for vegetarians, vegans and people allergic to wheat. They satisfy, accept flavors beautifully and cook very fast. Nobody makes better, more creative use of rice noodles and rice paper wrappers than the cooks of Vietnam, so it's time you became better acquainted with them.

Dried Rice Noodles

The major kinds of dried rice noodles differ mostly in their width. You'll find much variation in English-language nomenclature among various packages, but you needn't rely on linguistic markers. Your eyes will tell you all you need to know. For example, the words "rice sticks" and "rice vermicelli" appear on noodles of many different widths. Since you can interchange one width for another in most of these recipes, you can't really go wrong here. Just look through the cellophane wrapping and select the size you want. Here are the three basic sizes in which you will find dried rice noodles:

Banh pho

These are the linguine-sized noodles used in the signature Vietnamese noodle dish *pho* (pages 160 and 162). They are also perfect for other soupy noodle dishes, such as Hu Tieu Noodles with Pork and Shrimp, Saigon-Style (page 164). Thais use *banh pho*, also known as *Chantaboon* rice noodles, to make their eponymous noodle dish, *paht Thai*.

Thin dried rice noodles

Known as *bun*, *mai fun* and rice vermicelli, these very slender noodles are thinner than pho noodles, ranging from wire thin to about the width of thin spaghetti and angel hair pasta. Check out the noodles in a bowl of *bun* at your favorite Vietnamese restaurant and then hunt for that size. Or better yet, ask the restaurant people if they might show you the noodles they use for their noodle dishes in their uncooked state.

Wide rice noodles

These will probably be labeled "rice sticks," but even if they aren't, they will look like dried fettuccine: big wide ribbons all folded up in a rectangular bundle. They are my personal favorite, especially for stir-frying.

There are a few other kinds around, but these will get you started. Stay curious and ask for help. Fellow shoppers, grocery store proprietors, waiters and restaurant owners can be fabulous resources. You never know when it will be your lucky day; culinary advice and wisdom can find you right there in the middle of the grocery aisle.

Working with Noodles

For the wider forms of dried rice noodles, such as pho or linguine- or fettuccine-width noodles, your cook's drill will be the same: soak 'em, drain 'em and cook 'em. (For very thin dried rice noodles, just drop them into boiling water, remove from heat, and let stand 5 to 7 minutes until tender.) Soaking wider noodles is the traditional way to prep them and it takes only a few minutes. You can soak noodles in advance, drain them well and then cover and chill for 1 or 2 days. Using cold soaking water, it takes 20 to 30 minutes. Using warm to hot water speeds the process to 5 to 10 minutes. Softened noodles can be stir-fried or boiled until tender.

Vietnamese Rice Paper Wrappers (banh trang)

Brittle round rice paper wrappers and small triangular ones, embossed with a basket-weave design, are the key to *goi cuon* (page 16) or summer rolls, one of the many brilliant culinary inspirations from the kitchens of Vietnam. Think of them as a kind of big, flat, chewy and salty noodle — one that doesn't even need cooking to be ready to eat. They also enclose crispy *cha gio* spring rolls (page 28) and appear alongside salad platters for making wraps at the table.

Working with Rice Paper Wrappers

Your task is to soften and transfer them from their brittle state, which barely resembles food, into a handy, appealing little wrapper for all kinds of tasty fillings. Some recipes suggest that you brush them with water with a pastry brush or spritz them with water or beer. I, for one, have gotten nowhere with either of these delicate methods. I prefer a quick soak in a skillet filled with very warm water. My 10-inch (25 cm) skillet is just the right size for one wrapper at a time and I can easily add hot water from the kettle if the water cools too much before I'm finished rolling. Though many cooks can manage an assembly-line method, I like working with one wrapper at a time. I dunk it and set it out to soften for a minute or two. Then I fill and roll it, set it aside and start the next one.

More Ingredients for the Vietnamese Kitchen
Bean thread noodles (bun tau)

Also called glass noodles and cellophane noodles, these little wiry skeins are made from mung beans, the same little green pea-size legume that brings us cool, crunchy bean sprouts. They cook quickly and absorb flavorings beautifully. Vietnamese cooks use them in clear soups, stir-fried dishes (especially those featuring seafood), meat loaf, omelets and as a major ingredient in the magnificent crisp little spring roll *cha gio* (page 28).

Asian markets carry *bun tau* in big string bags full of 1- to 2-oz (30 to 60 g) packages, which are very handy for the pantry shelf. In dried form they look a lot like thin rice noodles, so check the ingredient list for words like "green bean starch," a reference to mung beans in their little green hulls.

Brown bean sauce (*tuong*)

Brown bean sauce is an ancient Asian seasoning of soybeans preserved with salt. It comes in various forms: ground bean sauce, fermented soybeans, bean paste, yellow beans and yellow bean sauce. They differ a bit in color and texture. Check the ingredient list; you want mostly soybeans and salt. Some versions, including hoisin sauce, have sugar, chiles and other seasonings. Any of these will work as long as you taste as you go. Avoid Chinese-style black beans, however, as they are too salty and dry to work in place of *tuong*.

Chile-garlic sauce (*tuong ot toi*)

This thick, red purée of fresh hot chiles makes an outstanding pantry staple. It provides much of what you get by grinding fresh hot chiles in a mortar and keeps well in the refrigerator. Many grocery stores carry it in plastic jars with a parrot-green lid. The words "*tuong ot toi*" often appear on the label, identifying the product, not a brand name. Though they differ slightly, most other thick hot red chile purées can substitute for chile-garlic sauce. Chinese chile paste is not ideal, as it is made with oil and dried red chiles (not fresh). It will do if you use the chile purée and avoid the oil.

Coconut milk, unsweetened (*nuoc dua*)

Canned coconut milk is really coconut cream, the luxurious essence extracted from the first pressing of grated coconut soaked in water. If you crack open a hairy brown coconut, extract the white, sturdy sweet meat attached to the hard brown shell, grate it finely, soak it in water and squeeze out several pressings in the standard Southeast Asian way, you will get about 4 cups (1 L) of coconut milk, about one-fourth of which will be rich cream. For the purpose of this book, "coconut milk" means the lovely rich liquid stirred well and poured straight from the can. Vietnamese cooks use coconut milk in curries, a few soups and many sweets and snacks. Canned is great, frozen coconut milk works wonderfully as well and I've seen cans and packets of dried powder lately that do the job.

Dried Chinese mushrooms (*nam huong kho*)

These are actually dried shiitake mushrooms. They look like they've seen better days, but they revive quickly, becoming a delicious, flavor-absorbing vegetable that adds color and texture to soups, noodle dishes and ground meat dishes such as Vietnamese Meat Loaf (page 78). A 15- to 20-minute immersion in warm water brings them back to their former glory. You'll need to trim away and discard their woody stems. They keep for ages; I transfer them to a jar and have them within easy reach in the pantry.

Fish sauce (*nuoc mam*)

Fish sauce is the quintessential Vietnamese ingredient, used in almost every dish, except sweets. Made from salt-cured anchovies, it provides a rustic flavor and salty, satisfying substance to food. Sometimes it shows its colors proudly, as in Salmon Steaks in Caramel Fish Sauce (page 102). Other times, it harmonizes with other flavors, acting as a subtle source of delicious depth. For people in need of maximum nutrition at minimal expense, fish sauce provides protein and vitamin B. Vietnam is the mother lode for fish sauce aficionados; the island of Phu Quoc is world renowned for the fine quality of its *nuoc mam*. Fish sauce from Thailand is what you will find most often in Asian markets and it works perfectly in all the recipes in this book.

Five-spice powder (*ngu vi huong*)

This fragrant ground seasoning mix is a classic from the Chinese tradition beloved throughout Asia for the sweet, deep flavor it brings to braised and roasted food, particularly pork, duck and hard-boiled eggs. Five is a handy number, expressing the presence of an array of aromatic spices rather than an exact count. No matter how many end up in a given version, you can expect that star anise, cinnamon, cloves and Szechuan peppercorns will be included.

Galanga (*rieng*)

This pungent member of the ginger family adds a citrusy tang to Vietnamese dishes and is often used with fish. Like its first cousins, turmeric, ginger and krachai, galanga is thought to provide medicinal value along with its extraordinary aroma and flavor. Fresh galanga resembles ginger, but it is rounded and shiny, with thin, dark concentric rings. Frozen galanga is widely available, whole or sliced, while dried galanga comes sliced or ground. Frozen and dried galanga work well, but the powdered form is merely dust. You can replace galanga with fresh ginger in recipes for a different but harmonious flavor and scent.

Ginger (*gung*)

Fresh ginger is a basic ingredient in Vietnamese cooking, beloved for its intense, sweet-and-sharp seasoning powers. It's often cooked with chicken and fish. Fresh ginger can be found in most supermarkets as well as in Asian markets. To chop it, cut off a good chunk, set it, cut side down, on the cutting board and shave off the peeling. Then cut it crosswise into coins. Stack these up, cut across the stack, making thin strips and you've got shreds. If you need chopped, go back across the shreds, cutting in the other direction.

Green papaya (*du du xanh*)

Papaya trees thrive in Vietnam. Their young, green fruit is appreciated as a cool, crunchy salad component, while the luscious, mature orange-colored flesh is eaten as fruit. Look for ready-to-eat, peeled and shredded fresh green papaya in Asian markets. It makes Green Papaya Salad (page 118) an almost instant dish. To prepare and shred a green papaya, peel half of it lengthwise (the white goo under the green skin is papain, a natural enzyme used in Asia for tenderizing meat). Cut it in half lengthwise, scoop out the seeds and shred the peeled half on a box grater or in the food processor. Refrigerate the other half for another time. I use shredded cabbage, thinly sliced cucumber or cooked spaghetti squash strands in place of green papaya when I don't have the real thing.

Hoisin sauce (sot hoisin)

Hoisin is the cousin from the salted preserved soybean family who went to Hollywood and came back a star. Hoisin sauce starts out as *tuong* (see Brown bean sauce, page 223) and is seasoned with five-spice powder, garlic, vinegar, sesame oil and lots of sugar. The result is a thick, intense sauce that is easy to like. Vietnamese cooks use hoisin as a component in dipping sauces and as a source of deep, rich, sweet flavor and color in marinades and braised dishes.

Lemongrass (xa)

Fresh lemongrass pervades Vietnamese cooking in a lovely, lyrical way. Used lavishly in marinades, stews and grilled foods, it provides a warm, tropical breeze entwining cool-climate dishes from the northern region and refined royal fare from Hue and the lush, ripe cooking of southern Vietnam. Fresh lemongrass stalks have joined fresh ginger in many supermarkets the past few years and are standard in Asian markets. If your source is unreliable, buy a supply when you find some and freeze it. Chop off and discard the top half, pull off any dried outer leaves, wrap the bottom tightly and use it straight from the freezer. It keeps well for 2 to 3 months. Recently, I've found wonderful frozen, finely ground lemongrass imported from Vietnam in clear plastic containers. Don't bother with dried lemongrass and lemongrass

powder, as *xa*'s remarkable flavor and aroma fade quickly once it is dried.

Mung bean centers, yellow (dau xanh)

Vietnam loves *dau xanh* — as a source of protein, steamed with both sweet and savory versions of sticky rice, in the parade of sweet coconut milk puddings and drinks enjoyed between meals and as a component for *banh chung*, the banana leaf–wrapped rice cakes essential to a New Year feast. *Dau* means "bean" and *xanh* means "green," the color of the little yellow bean's hull.

Peanuts (dau phong)

You know what peanuts are, but you may not always have them handy and you should. Adored especially in the south, they are sprinkled over sticky rice, grilled meats, Hu Tieu Noodles with Pork and Shrimp, Saigon-Style (page 164), Chicken and Cabbage Salad with Mint (page 124) and more. I buy a good-sized jar of roasted and salted peanuts and transfer half the peanuts into two medium-sized jars. One jar is mine for cooking. Since my husband devours peanuts for snacks, he gets his own jar. I store the remaining half in the freezer, since roasted peanuts go stale fast.

Sesame oil (hot me)

Made from toasted white sesame seeds (see 226), Asian sesame oil is dark brown, a ringer for maple syrup until you catch its divine, nutty aroma and taste its rich, alluring flavor. Vietnamese cooks use *hot me* in sauces, stir-fries and marinades.

Sesame seeds, white (*dau me*)

Stock up on white sesame seeds; they are a delightful finishing touch to many Vietnamese dishes, from snacks and sweets to grilled food. You can buy them in the spice section of the supermarket, but if you adore them as I do, you may want to buy them at the Asian market in cellophane bags, which are less expensive and will hold you for a while. They can be dry-fried in a hot pan to heighten their flavor, but I like to toast them in the oven, so that they brown evenly without burning. To do this, scatter about 1/4 cup (60 mL) white sesame seeds in a pie pan and place in a 400°F (200°C) oven until the sesame seeds are nicely browned, 10 to 12 minutes. Turn them out onto a plate and let cool completely, transfer to a jar and keep at room temperature for up to 1 month. Toasted sesame seeds chopped with peanuts and then mixed with sugar make a spectacularly delicious traditional topping for Sticky Rice (page 144).

Tamarind and tamarind liquid (*me; nuoc me chua*)

Tamarind fruit dangles from huge hardwood trees throughout Southeast Asia in big, fat, C-shaped pods. They ripen to a rich, soft, dark pulp, filled with seeds and enclosed in a brittle, light brown shell. Tamarind liquid is made by soaking ripe tamarind pulp and pressing it through a strainer to create a thick, luscious purée that is earthy brown, smoky, sour and sweet. You can buy blocks of tamarind pulp, processed enough to remove most of the seeds and stringy stuff between you and the lovely smoky-sweet-sour flavor it provides. You still need to soak, mash and strain out the essence, a messy bit of work for a quick and easy cook. To make tamarind liquid, place about 1/2 cup (125 mL) tamarind pulp in a bowl with 1 cup (250 mL) warm water. Soak for 15 to 20 minutes, pressing and mashing now and then to soften the pulp and mix it with the water. Strain through a fine-mesh strainer into another bowl, pressing and scraping with a large spoon to extract as much liquid and purée as you can. You will have about 3/4 cup (175 mL). I am happy with ready-to-use tamarind liquid imported from Thailand. It looks a lot like apple butter, dark and thick and it is delicious. It's sometimes called "concentrate cooking tamarind" on English-language labels. You'll also see the Vietnamese words for tamarind liquid, *nuoc me chua*, on the label. In a pinch, I also use Indian-style tamarind chutney in place of tamarind liquid, with tasty results.

Turmeric (*bot nghe*)

This knobby cousin of ginger and galanga is beloved not for its flavor (quite mild, even when it is fresh), but for its outrageous, gloriously gaudy yellow-orange hue, which it transmits to food and everything else it touches. The source of curry powder's trademark color, turmeric has been prized for centuries as a dye for cloth, including the traditional robes of Theravada Buddhist monks. Whole rhizomes of turmeric can sometimes be found fresh or frozen in Asian markets nowadays, but ground turmeric powder works fine in these recipes. It's widely used in Vietnam, transmitting its gorgeous golden color to such dishes as Cha Ca Fish with Fresh Dill, Hanoi-Style (page 104).

Suggested Menus

Here are ideas to get you started on putting Thai dishes together into menus you will enjoy. An asterisk (*) means the recipe is not included in this book.

Breakfast Special

Omelet with Crabmeat and Green
    Onions (page 60)
Warm baguette with butter and jam*
Vietnamese Coffee, Hot (page 192)

A Northern Feast

Grilled Pork Patties with Lettuce,
    Noodles and Fresh Herbs,
    Hanoi-Style (page 80)
Cha Ca Fish with Fresh Dill,
    Hanoi-Style (page 104)
Sticky Rice with Mung Beans,
    Northern-Style (page 146)
Chinese tea* with Almond Cookies
    (page 191)

A Southern Feast

Hu Tieu Noodles with Pork and
    Shrimp, Saigon-Style (page 164)
Pork in Caramel Sauce (page 83)
Everyday Rice (page 142)
Everyday Herb and Salad Plate
    (page 116)
Fresh pineapple, ripe melon
    or grapes*

Beach Weekend

Crab and Asparagus Soup (page 48)
Lemongrass Shrimp (page 20)
Grilled Tuna Steaks with
    Pineapple-Chile Sauce (page 98)
Lime sorbet and wonderful
    chocolates*

Meat-Lover's Menu

Shaking Beef with Purple Onions and
    Watercress (page 72)
Grilled Leaf-Wrapped Beef Kebabs
    (page 22)
Vietnamese Meat Loaf (page 78)
Delicious Lemongrass Burgers with
    Beef (page 70)
Big Cool Noodle Bowl with Pork
    Meatballs (Variations, page 178)
Everyday Dipping Sauce (page 200)

Classic Chicken Combo

Chicken and Cabbage Salad with Mint
    (page 124)
Chicken Soup with Bean Thread
    Noodles (page 174)
Spinach Sautéed with Garlic and Pepper
    (page 134)
Bread Sticks*
Limeade (page 196)

Fish and Seafood Feast

Salmon Steaks in Caramel Fish Sauce
    (page 102)
Sweet and Tangy Soup with Pineapple,
    Tamarind and Shrimp (page 44)
Everyday Rice (page 142)
Lemon and lime sorbet*

Too Hot to Cook

Big Cool Noodle Bowl with Roast
    Chicken, Cucumbers and Mint
    (page 178)
Thickly sliced ripe tomato sprinkled
    with salt and pepper*
Pomelo Salad with Shrimp and Cilantro
    (page 120)
Fresh Lemongrass Tea (page 195) over ice
Ice cream with summer berries*

Too Cold to Go Out

Meatball Soup (page 36), with spinach
  leaves
Rice with Chicken, Sweet Chinese
  Sausage and Shiitake Mushrooms
  (page 154)
Crusty bread with Cheddar or
  Jack cheese*
Black Sticky Rice Pudding (page 185)
  with cream

Tailgate Picnic or Campout Supper with a Twist

Summer Rolls with Shrimp and Mint
  (page 16)
Banh Mi (page 26)
Apples and grapes*
Trail mix*
Vietnamese Coffee, Iced (page 192)
Blondies and brownies*

Picnic Time!

Summer Rolls with Shrimp and Mint
  (page 16)
Banh Mi (page 26)
Deviled eggs*
Chicken and Cabbage Salad with Fresh
  Mint (page 124)
Corn with Dried Shrimp, Green Onions
  and Butter (page 138)
Slices of watermelon and pineapple*
Almond Cookies (page 191)

Campfire Cookout

Chicken and Pork Pâté (page 31) with
  French bread*
Shaking Beef with Purple Onion sand
  Watercress (page 72)
Fried Rice with Sweet Chinese Sausage,
  Cilantro and Peas (page 148)
Sliced Cucumber Salad (page 127)
S'mores*

Resources

Here is information to put you in touch with vendors who carry everything you need to cook Vietnamese food at home including resources for seeds and plants.

Evergreen Seeds

P.O. Box 17538
Anaheim, CA 92817
USA
(714) 637-5769

www.evergreenseeds.com
(Ships worldwide)

Superb source of seeds for Asian herbs and vegetables. You'll find holy basil and other Asian basil types, edamame beans, long beans, winged beans, Thai and other eggplant varieties, bok choy and other cabbage varieties, garlic chives, cilantro and many types of chile peppers.

Golda's Kitchen

2885 Argentia Road, Unit 6
Mississauga, ON L5N 8G6
Canada
(866) 465-3299 or (905) 816-9995

www.goldaskitchen.com
(Ships worldwide)

Thai granite mortars and pestles and woks.

Gold Mine Natural Food Company

13200 Danielson Street, Suite A-1
Poway, CA 92064
USA
(800) 475-3663 (U.S. only)
or (858) 537-9830

shop.goldminenaturalfoods.com
(Ships worldwide)

A good source for rice, noodles and soy sauce.

ImportFood.com

P.O. Box 2054
Issaquah, WA 98027
USA
(888) 618-8424 (U.S. only)
or (425) 687-1708

www.importfood.com
(Ships worldwide)

One of my favorite sources for Southeast Asian ingredients and equipment. Import Food stocks fresh herbs, as well as dried ones, curry pastes and sauces, and traditional equipment from granite mortars and pestles to sticky rice baskets.

Penzeys Spices

12001 West Capital Drive
Wauwatosa, WI 53222
USA
(800) 741-7787 or (414) 760-7337

www.penzeys.com
(Ships to U.S. and Canada)

Penzeys offers a superb selection of whole spices and ground spices, along with glass jars in many sizes for storing spices purchased in Asian markets.

Qualifirst Foods Ltd.

4-40 Ronson Drive
Toronto, ON M9W 1B3
Canada
(800) 206-1177

www.qualifirst.com
(Ships to U.S. and Canada)

Extensive selection of whole and ground spices and spice mixtures, curry pastes, and aromatic rice.

Richters Herbs

357 Highway 47
Goodwood, ON L0C 1A0
Canada
(905) 640-6677

www.richters.com

(Ships worldwide)

Excellent selection of both seeds and plants for your home garden. Asian treasures include lemongrass, garlic chives, Asian basil, holy basil, cilantro, various types of mint and an array of chile peppers.

Temple of Thai

(877) 811-8773

www.templeofthai.com

(Ships worldwide)

Extensive selection of essentials and specialty items for cooking Vietnamese and Southeast Asian cuisines, including spices, seasonings, sauces, rice noodles and fresh herbs, along with cooking equipment including mortars and pestles and sticky rice steaming sets.

Thai Kitchen

P.O. Box 13242
Berkeley, CA 94712-4242
USA
(800) 967-8424

www.thaikitchen.com

(Ships to U.S. only)

Curry pastes, coconut milk, rice noodles, seasoning pastes and sauces.

The Spice House

1941 Central Street
Evanston, IL 60201
USA
847-328-3711

www.thespicehouse.com

(Ships to U.S., Canada and Mexico. Canadian orders please email spices@thespicehouse.com)

Wide selection of whole and ground spices for soups, stews, and curry pastes, as well as an array of chile peppers.

The Spice Trader

877 Queen Street West
Toronto, ON M6J 1G3
Canada
(647) 430-7085

www.thespicetrader.ca

(Ships throughout Canada)

Fine quality whole and ground spices, and a selection of salts.

Library and Archives Canada Cataloguing in Publication

McDermott, Nancie, author
   Simply Vietnamese cooking : 135 delicious recipes / Nancie McDermott.

Includes index.
Previous title: Quick & easy Vietnamese.
ISBN 978-0-7788-0521-2 (pbk.)

   1. Cooking, Vietnamese. 2. Cookbooks. I. Title. II. Title: Quick & easy Vietnamese.

TX724.5.V53M34 2015   641.59597   C2015-902574-5

Index

(v) = variation